MznLnx

Missing Links Exam Preps

Exam Prep for

Calculus

Anton, Bivens & Davis, 7th Edition

The MznLnx Exam Prep is your link from the texbook and lecture to your exams.
The MznLnx Exam Preps are unauthorized and comprehensive reviews of your textbooks.

All material provided by MznLnx and Rico Publications (c) 2010
Textbook publishers and textbook authors do not particpate in or contribute to these reviews.

MznLnx

Rico
Publications

Exam Prep for Calculus
7th Edition
Anton, Bivens & Davis

Publisher: Raymond Houge
Assistant Editor: Michael Rouger
Text and Cover Designer: Lisa Buckner
Marketing Manager: Sara Swagger
Project Manager, Editorial Production: Jerry Emerson
Art Director: Vernon Lowerui

Product Manager: Dave Mason
Editorial Assitant: Rachel Guzmanji
Pedagogy: Debra Long
Cover Image: Jim Reed/Getty Images
Text and Cover Printer: City Printing, Inc.
Compositor: Media Mix, Inc.

(c) 2010 Rico Publications
ALL RIGHTS RESERVED. No part of this work
covered by the copyright may be reproduced or
used in any form or by an means--graphic, electronic,
or mechanical, including photocopying, recording,
taping, Web distribution, information storage, and
retrieval systems, or in any other manner--without the
written permission of the publisher.

Printed in the United States
ISBN:

For more information about our products, contact us at:
Dave.Mason@RicoPublications.com

For permission to use material from this text or
product, submit a request online to:
Dave.Mason@RicoPublications.com

Contents

CHAPTER 1
FUNCTIONS — 1

CHAPTER 2
LIMITS AND CONTINUITY — 31

CHAPTER 3
THE DERIVATIVE — 45

CHAPTER 4
THE DERIVATIVE IN GRAPHING AND APPLICATIONS — 64

CHAPTER 5
INTEGRATION — 89

CHAPTER 6
APPLICATIONS OF THE DEFINITE INTEGRAL IN GEOMETRY, SCIENCE, AND ENGINEERING — 108

CHAPTER 7
EXPONENTIAL, LOGARITHMIC, AND INVERSE TRIGONOMETRIC FUNCTIONS — 121

CHAPTER 8
PRINCIPLES OF INTEGRAL EVALUATION — 142

CHAPTER 9
MATHEMATICAL MODELING WITH DIFFERENTIAL EQUATIONS — 157

CHAPTER 10
INFINITE SERIES — 170

CHAPTER 11
ANALYTIC GEOMETRY IN CALCULUS — 172

CHAPTER 12
THREE-DIMENSIONAL SPACE; VECTORS — 174

CHAPTER 13
VECTOR-VALUED FUNCTIONS — 176

CHAPTER 14
PARTIAL DERIVATIVES — 178

CHAPTER 15
MULTIPLE INTEGRALS — 181

CHAPTER 16
TOPICS IN VECTOR CALCULUS — 183

ANSWER KEY — 186

TO THE STUDENT

COMPREHENSIVE

The *MznLnx* Exam Prep series is designed to help you pass your exams. Editors at MznLnx review your textbooks and then prepare these practice exams to help you master the textbook material. Unlike study guides, workbooks, and practice tests provided by the texbook publisher and textbook authors, *MznLnx* gives you **all** of the material in each chapter in exam form, not just samples, so you can be sure to nail your exam.

MECHANICAL

The MznLnx Exam Prep series creates exams that will help you learn the subject matter as well as test you on your understanding. Each question is designed to help you master the concept. Just working through the exams, you gain an understanding of the subject--its a simple mechanical process that produces success.

INTEGRATED STUDY GUIDE AND REVIEW

MznLnx is not just a set of exams designed to test you, its also a comprehensive review of the subject content. Each exam question is also a review of the concept, making sure that you will get the answer correct without having to go to other sources of material. You learn as you go! Its the easiest way to pass an exam.

HUMOR

Studying can be tedious and dry. MznLnx's instructional design includes moderate humor within the exam questions on occassion, to break the tedium and revitalize the brain

Chapter 1. FUNCTIONS

1. A _____ is a symbolic representation denoting a quantity or expression. It often represents an "unknown" quantity that has the potential to change.
   - a. Thing
   - b. Variable0
   - c. Undefined
   - d. Undefined

2. _____ is an adjective usually refering to being in the centre.
   - a. Central0
   - b. Thing
   - c. Undefined
   - d. Undefined

3. _____ is a mathematical subject that includes the study of limits, derivatives, integrals, and power series and constitutes a major part of modern university curriculum.
   - a. Thing
   - b. Calculus0
   - c. Undefined
   - d. Undefined

4. The mathematical concept of a _____ expresses the intuitive idea of deterministic dependence between two quantities, one of which is viewed as primary and the other as secondary. A _____ then is a way to associate a unique output for each input of a specified type, for example, a real number or an element of a given set.
   - a. Function0
   - b. Thing
   - c. Undefined
   - d. Undefined

5. _____ is a synonym for information.
   - a. Data0
   - b. Thing
   - c. Undefined
   - d. Undefined

6. _____ are the basic objects of study in graph theory. Informally speaking, a graph is a set of objects called points, nodes, or vertices connected by links called lines or edges.
   - a. Thing
   - b. Graphs0
   - c. Undefined
   - d. Undefined

7. _____ is the difference between the monetary value of exports and imports in an economy over a certain period of time.
   - a. Trade balance0
   - b. Thing
   - c. Undefined
   - d. Undefined

8. In business, particularly accounting, a _____ is the time intervals that the accounts, statement, payments, or other calculations cover.
   - a. Period0
   - b. Thing
   - c. Undefined
   - d. Undefined

9. _____ is the study of terms and their use — of words and compound words that are used in specific contexts.
   - a. Thing
   - b. Terminology0
   - c. Undefined
   - d. Undefined

10. In banking and accountancy, the outstanding _____ is the amount of money owned, or due, that remains in a deposit account or a loan account at a given date, after all past remittances, payments and withdrawal have been accounted for.

a. Balance0
b. Thing
c. Undefined
d. Undefined

11. The _____ of measurement are a globally standardized and modernized form of the metric system.
   a. Thing
   b. Units0
   c. Undefined
   d. Undefined

12. _____ is the level of functional and/or metabolic efficiency of an organism at both the micro level.
   a. Thing
   b. Health0
   c. Undefined
   d. Undefined

13. In astronomy, geography, geometry and related sciences and contexts, a plane is said to be _____ at a given point if it is locally perpendicular to the gradient of the gravity field, i.e., with the direction of the gravitational force at that point.
   a. Horizontal0
   b. Thing
   c. Undefined
   d. Undefined

14. In Euclidean geometry, a uniform _____ is a linear transformation that enlargers or diminishes objects, and whose _____ factor is the same in all directions. This is also called homothethy.
   a. Scale0
   b. Thing
   c. Undefined
   d. Undefined

15. In elementary algebra, an _____ is a set that contains every real number between two indicated numbers and may contain the two numbers themselves.
   a. Thing
   b. Interval0
   c. Undefined
   d. Undefined

16. _____ was a German mathematician and philosopher. He invented calculus independently of Newton, and his notation is the one in general use since.
   a. Person
   b. Leibniz0
   c. Undefined
   d. Undefined

17. Leonhard _____ was a pioneering Swiss mathematician and physicist, who spent most of his life in Russia and Germany.
   a. Euler0
   b. Person
   c. Undefined
   d. Undefined

18. The _____, the average in everyday English, which is also called the arithmetic _____ (and is distinguished from the geometric _____ or harmonic _____). The average is also called the sample _____. The expected value of a random variable, which is also called the population _____.
   a. Mean0
   b. Thing
   c. Undefined
   d. Undefined

19. _____ (Basel, July 27, 1667 - January 1, 1748) was a Swiss mathematician.
   a. Person
   b. Johann Bernoulli0
   c. Undefined
   d. Undefined

Chapter 1. FUNCTIONS

20. _____ is the ability to hold, receive or absorb, or a measure thereof, similar to the concept of volume.
    a. Capacity0
    b. Concept
    c. Undefined
    d. Undefined

21. The _____ of a solid object is the three-dimensional concept of how much space it occupies, often quantified numerically.
    a. Thing
    b. Volume0
    c. Undefined
    d. Undefined

22. Sir Isaac _____, was an English physicist, mathematician, astronomer, natural philosopher, and alchemist, regarded by many as the greatest figure in the history of science
    a. Newton0
    b. Person
    c. Undefined
    d. Undefined

23. In mathematics, a _____ is a countable collection of open covers of a topological space that satisfies certain separation axioms.
    a. Thing
    b. Development0
    c. Undefined
    d. Undefined

24. _____ is a kind of property which exists as magnitude or multitude. It is among the basic classes of things along with quality, substance, change, and relation.
    a. Thing
    b. Amount0
    c. Undefined
    d. Undefined

25. An _____ is the result from the sudden release of stored energy in the Earth's crust that creates seismic waves.
    a. Thing
    b. Earthquake0
    c. Undefined
    d. Undefined

26. _____ are a measure of time.
    a. Minutes0
    b. Thing
    c. Undefined
    d. Undefined

27. In mathematics, the concept of a _____ tries to capture the intuitive idea of a geometrical one-dimensional and continuous object. A simple example is the circle.
    a. Thing
    b. Curve0
    c. Undefined
    d. Undefined

28. _____ is finding a curve which matches a series of data points and possibly other constraints.
    a. Curve fitting0
    b. Thing
    c. Undefined
    d. Undefined

29. Mathematical _____ are the wide variety of ways to capture an abstract mathematical concept or relationship.
    a. Thing
    b. Representations0
    c. Undefined
    d. Undefined

Chapter 1. FUNCTIONS

30. A _____ function is a function for which, intuitively, small changes in the input result in small changes in the output.
    a. Event
    b. Continuous0
    c. Undefined
    d. Undefined

31. The word _____ comes from the 15th Century Latin word discretus which means separate.
    a. Thing
    b. Discrete0
    c. Undefined
    d. Undefined

32. In mathematics, _____ are the intuitive idea of a geometrical one-dimensional and continuous object.
    a. Thing
    b. Curves0
    c. Undefined
    d. Undefined

33. A _____, scatter diagram or scatter graph is a chart that uses Cartesian coordinates to display values for two variables.
    a. Thing
    b. Scatter plot0
    c. Undefined
    d. Undefined

34. _____ is a graph of the points representing a collection of data.
    a. Scatter plots0
    b. Thing
    c. Undefined
    d. Undefined

35. In common philosophical language, a proposition or _____, is the content of an assertion, that is, it is true-or-false and defined by the meaning of a particular piece of language.
    a. Statement0
    b. Concept
    c. Undefined
    d. Undefined

36. A _____ is a function that assigns a number to subsets of a given set.
    a. Thing
    b. Measure0
    c. Undefined
    d. Undefined

37. In plane geometry, a _____ is a polygon with four equal sides, four right angles, and parallel opposite sides. In algebra, the _____ of a number is that number multiplied by itself.
    a. Thing
    b. Square0
    c. Undefined
    d. Undefined

38. In mathematics, a _____ is a quadric surface, with the following equation in Cartesian coordinates: $(x/a)^2 + (y/b)^2 = 1$.
    a. Thing
    b. Cylinder0
    c. Undefined
    d. Undefined

39. In classical geometry, a _____ of a circle or sphere is any line segment from its center to its boundary. By extension, the _____ of a circle or sphere is the length of any such segment. The _____ is half the diameter. In science and engineering the term _____ of curvature is commonly used as a synonym for _____.

Chapter 1. FUNCTIONS

a. Radius0
b. Thing
c. Undefined
d. Undefined

40. In mathematics, a _____ is a mathematical statement which appears likely to be true, but has not been formally proven to be true under the rules of mathematical logic.
   a. Conjecture0
   b. Concept
   c. Undefined
   d. Undefined

41. _____ are activities that are governed by a set of rules or customs and often engaged in competitively.
   a. Sports0
   b. Thing
   c. Undefined
   d. Undefined

42. The _____ is the distance around a closed curve. _____ is a kind of perimeter.
   a. Circumference0
   b. Thing
   c. Undefined
   d. Undefined

43. In mathematics, an inequality is a statement about the relative size or order of two objects. For example 14 > 10, or 14 is _____ 10.
   a. Greater than0
   b. Thing
   c. Undefined
   d. Undefined

44. In mathematics, the _____ of a function is the set of all "output" values produced by that function. Given a function $f : A \to B$, the _____ of f, is defined to be the set $\{x \in B : x = f(a)$ for some $a \in A\}$.
   a. Range0
   b. Thing
   c. Undefined
   d. Undefined

45. In mathematics, an _____ is a statement about the relative size or order of two objects.
   a. Thing
   b. Inequality0
   c. Undefined
   d. Undefined

46. In mathematics, a _____ of a k-place relation $L \subseteq X_1 \times \ldots \times X_k$ is one of the sets X_j, $1 \le j \le k$. In the special case where k = 2 and $L \subseteq X_1 \times X_2$ is a function $L : X_1 \to X_2$, it is conventional to refer to X_1 as the _____ of the function and to refer to X_2 as the codomain of the function.
   a. Domain0
   b. Thing
   c. Undefined
   d. Undefined

47. _____ is a test to determine if a relation or its graph is a function or not
   a. Vertical line test0
   b. Thing
   c. Undefined
   d. Undefined

48. Acid _____ ratio measures the ability of a company to use its near cash or quick assets to immediately extinguish its current liabilities.
   a. Test0
   b. Thing
   c. Undefined
   d. Undefined

49. The _____ integers are all the integers from zero on upwards.

a. Nonnegative0
b. Thing
c. Undefined
d. Undefined

50. In mathematics, a _____ may be described informally as a number that can be given by an infinite decimal representation.
   a. Thing
   b. Real number0
   c. Undefined
   d. Undefined

51. The _____ of a mathematical object is its size: a property by which it can be larger or smaller than other objects of the same kind; in technical terms, an ordering of the class of objects to which it belongs.
   a. Magnitude0
   b. Thing
   c. Undefined
   d. Undefined

52. In mathematics, the _____ (or modulus) of a real number is its numerical value without regard to its sign.
   a. Absolute value0
   b. Thing
   c. Undefined
   d. Undefined

53. The plus and _____ signs are mathematical symbols used to represent the notions of positive and negative as well as the operations of addition and subtraction.
   a. Thing
   b. Minus0
   c. Undefined
   d. Undefined

54. In mathematics, a _____ is the result of multiplying, or an expression that identifies factors to be multiplied.
   a. Thing
   b. Product0
   c. Undefined
   d. Undefined

55. A _____ is a quantity that denotes the proportional amount or magnitude of one quantity relative to another.
   a. Thing
   b. Ratio0
   c. Undefined
   d. Undefined

56. A _____ is one of the basic shapes of geometry: a polygon with three vertices and three sides which are straight line segments.
   a. Thing
   b. Triangle0
   c. Undefined
   d. Undefined

57. _____ is the theorem stating that for any triangle, the measure of a given side must be less than the sum of the other two sides but greater than the difference between the two sides.
   a. Thing
   b. Triangle inequality0
   c. Undefined
   d. Undefined

58. _____ are objects, characters, or other concrete representations of ideas, concepts, or other abstractions.
   a. Symbols0
   b. Thing
   c. Undefined
   d. Undefined

59. In mathematics, a _____ of a number x is a number r such that $r^2 = x$, or in words, a number r whose square (the result of multiplying the number by itself) is x.

a. Thing
b. Square root0
c. Undefined
d. Undefined

60. In mathematics, a _____ of a complex-valued function f is a member x of the domain of f such that f(x) vanishes at x, that is, x : f (x) = 0.
   a. Root0
   b. Thing
   c. Undefined
   d. Undefined

61. _____ is a branch of mathematics concerning the study of structure, relation and quantity.
   a. Concept
   b. Algebra0
   c. Undefined
   d. Undefined

62. A _____ defined function $f(x)$ of a real variable x is a function whose definition is given differently on disjoint subsets of its domain.
   a. Piecewise0
   b. Thing
   c. Undefined
   d. Undefined

63. In Euclidean geometry, a _____ is the set of all points in a plane at a fixed distance, called the radius, from a given point, the center.
   a. Thing
   b. Circle0
   c. Undefined
   d. Undefined

64. A _____ given two distinct points A and B on the _____, is the set of points C on the line containing points A and B such that A is not strictly between C and B.
   a. Ray0
   b. Thing
   c. Undefined
   d. Undefined

65. In mathematics, _____ geometry was the traditional name for the geometry of three-dimensional Euclidean space — for practical purposes the kind of space we live in.
   a. Thing
   b. Solid0
   c. Undefined
   d. Undefined

66. A _____ is a special kind of ratio, indicating a relationship between two measurements with different units, such as miles to gallons or cents to pounds.
   a. Rate0
   b. Thing
   c. Undefined
   d. Undefined

67. _____ is a term applied when talking about the movement of air from one place to the next.
   a. Wind speed0
   b. Thing
   c. Undefined
   d. Undefined

68. In combinatorial mathematics, a _____ is an un-ordered collection of unique elements.
   a. Combination0
   b. Concept
   c. Undefined
   d. Undefined

69. The word _____ is used in a variety of ways in mathematics.

Chapter 1. FUNCTIONS

    a. Index0
    c. Undefined
    b. Thing
    d. Undefined

70. _____ is a physical property of a system that underlies the common notions of hot and cold; something that is hotter has the greater _____.
    a. Thing
    b. Temperature0
    c. Undefined
    d. Undefined

71. A central concept in science and the scientific method is that all evidence must be _____, or empirically based, that is, dependent on evidence or consequences that are observable by the senses.
    a. Thing
    b. Empirical0
    c. Undefined
    d. Undefined

72. In mathematics, an _____ is any of the arguments, i.e. "inputs", to a function. Thus if we have a function f(x), then x is a _____.
    a. Independent variable0
    b. Thing
    c. Undefined
    d. Undefined

73. A _____ is a numeral used to indicate a count. The most common use of the word today is to name the part of a fraction that tells the number or count of equal parts.
    a. Thing
    b. Numerator0
    c. Undefined
    d. Undefined

74. _____ is the largest positive integer that divides both numbers without remainder.
    a. Common Factor0
    b. Thing
    c. Undefined
    d. Undefined

75. A _____ is the part of a fraction that tells how many equal parts make up a whole, and which is used in the name of the fraction: "halves", "thirds", "fourths" or "quarters", "fifths" and so on.
    a. Concept
    b. Denominator0
    c. Undefined
    d. Undefined

76. In mathematics, defined and _____ are used to explain whether or not expressions have meaningful, sensible, and unambiguous values.
    a. Thing
    b. Undefined0
    c. Undefined
    d. Undefined

77. _____ is often used to describe the measurement of the steepness, incline, gradient, or grade of a straight line. The _____ is defined as the ratio of the "rise" divided by the "run" between two points on a line, or in other words, the ratio of the altitude change to the horizontal distance between any two points on the line.
    a. Slope0
    b. Thing
    c. Undefined
    d. Undefined

78. In mathematics, the notion of _____ is a generalization of the notion of invertible.

Chapter 1. FUNCTIONS

a. Thing
b. Cancellation0
c. Undefined
d. Undefined

79. In linear algebra, a _____ of a matrix A is the determinant of some smaller square matrix, cut down from A.
a. Minor0
b. Thing
c. Undefined
d. Undefined

80. In a function the _____, is the variable which is the value, i.e. the "output", of the function.
a. Dependent variable0
b. Thing
c. Undefined
d. Undefined

81. In mathematics and the mathematical sciences, a _____ is a fixed, but possibly unspecified, value. This is in contrast to a variable, which is not fixed.
a. Thing
b. Constant0
c. Undefined
d. Undefined

82. In mathematics, the _____ functions are functions of an angle; they are important when studying triangles and modeling periodic phenomena, among many other applications.
a. Thing
b. Trigonometric0
c. Undefined
d. Undefined

83. The _____ are functions of an angle; they are important when studying triangles and modeling periodic phenomena, among many other applications.
a. Trigonometric functions0
b. Thing
c. Undefined
d. Undefined

84. The _____ is a unit of plane angle. It is represented by the symbol "rad" or, more rarely, by the superscript c (for "circular measure"). For example, an angle of 1.2 radians would be written "1.2 rad" or "1.2c" (second symbol can produce confusion with centigrads).
a. Thing
b. Radian0
c. Undefined
d. Undefined

85. In statistics, _____ means the most frequent value assumed by a random variable, or occurring in a sampling of a random variable.
a. Concept
b. Mode0
c. Undefined
d. Undefined

86. The _____ of a geographic location is its height above a fixed reference point, often the mean sea level.
a. Elevation0
b. Thing
c. Undefined
d. Undefined

87. A _____ is a vehicle, missile or aircraft which obtains thrust by the reaction to the ejection of fast moving fluid from within a _____ engine.
a. Thing
b. Rocket0
c. Undefined
d. Undefined

Chapter 1. FUNCTIONS

88. In linear algebra, the _____ of an n-by-n square matrix A is defined to be the sum of the elements on the main diagonal of A,
   a. Thing
   b. Trace0
   c. Undefined
   d. Undefined

89. In geographic information systems, a _____ comprises an entity with a geographic location, typically determined by points, arcs, or polygons. Carriageways and cadastres exemplify _____ data.
   a. Thing
   b. Feature0
   c. Undefined
   d. Undefined

90. Equivalence is the condition of being _____ or essentially equal.
   a. Equivalent0
   b. Thing
   c. Undefined
   d. Undefined

91. In mathematics, there are several meanings of _____ depending on the subject.
   a. Degree0
   b. Thing
   c. Undefined
   d. Undefined

92. In geometry, an _____ of a triangle is a straight line through a vertex and perpendicular to (i.e. forming a right angle with) the opposite side or an extension of the opposite side.
   a. Concept
   b. Altitude0
   c. Undefined
   d. Undefined

93. A _____ is a unit of length, usually used to measure distance, in a number of different systems, including Imperial units, United States customary units and Norwegian/Swedish mil. Its size can vary from system to system, but in each is between 1 and 10 kilometers. In contemporary English contexts _____ refers to either:
   a. Mile0
   b. Thing
   c. Undefined
   d. Undefined

94. _____ forms part of thinking. Considered the most complex of all intellectual functions, _____ has been defined as higher-order cognitive process that requires the modulation and control of more routine or fundamental skills.
   a. Problem solving0
   b. Thing
   c. Undefined
   d. Undefined

95. In mathematics, a subset of Euclidean space R^n is called _____ if it is closed and bounded.
   a. Compact0
   b. Thing
   c. Undefined
   d. Undefined

96. A _____ is a set of numbers that designate location in a given reference system, such as x,y in a planar _____ system or an x,y,z in a three-dimensional _____ system.
   a. Thing
   b. Coordinate0
   c. Undefined
   d. Undefined

97. An _____ is when two lines intersect somewhere on a plane creating a right angle at intersection

Chapter 1. FUNCTIONS 11

    a. Thing   b. Axes0
    c. Undefined   d. Undefined

98. In mathematics, factorization (British English: factorisation) or factoring is the decomposition of an object (for example, a number, a polynomial, or a matrix) into a product of other objects, or _____, which when multiplied together give the original.
    a. Factors0   b. Thing
    c. Undefined   d. Undefined

99. A _____ is a negotiable instrument instructing a financial institution to pay a specific amount of a specific currency from a specific demand account held in the maker/depositor's name with that institution. Both the maker and payee may be natural persons or legal entities.
    a. Thing   b. Check0
    c. Undefined   d. Undefined

100. In mathematics, the _____ f is the collection of all ordered pairs . In particular, graph means the graphical representation of this collection, in the form of a curve or surface, together with axes, etc. Graphing on a Cartesian plane is sometimes referred to as curve sketching.
    a. Graph of a function0   b. Thing
    c. Undefined   d. Undefined

101. In geometry, a line _____ is a part of a line that is bounded by two end points, and contains every point on the line between its end points.
    a. Segment0   b. Concept
    c. Undefined   d. Undefined

102. In mathematics, the _____ of two sets A and B is the set that contains all elements of A that also belong to B (or equivalently, all elements of B that also belong to A), but no other elements.
    a. Intersection0   b. Thing
    c. Undefined   d. Undefined

103. In mathematics, a _____ is an expression that is constructed from one or more variables and constants, using only the operations of addition, subtraction, multiplication, and constant positive whole number exponents. is a _____. Note in particular that division by an expression containing a variable is not in general allowed in polynomials. [1]
    a. Thing   b. Polynomial0
    c. Undefined   d. Undefined

104. _____ is a set, with some particular properties and usually some additional structure, such as the operations of addition or multiplication, for instance.
    a. Thing   b. Space0
    c. Undefined   d. Undefined

105. A _____ is the result of the addition of a set of numbers. The numbers may be natural numbers, complex numbers, matrices, or still more complicated objects. An infinite _____ is a subtle procedure known as a series.

a. Thing
b. Sum0
c. Undefined
d. Undefined

106. The _____ is a nonnegative scalar measure of a wave's magnitude of oscillation, that is, the magnitude of the maximum disturbance in the medium during one wave cycle.
   a. Amplitude0
   b. Thing
   c. Undefined
   d. Undefined

107. A _____ is a part of a line that is bounded by two end points, and contains every point on the line between its end points.
   a. Thing
   b. Line segment0
   c. Undefined
   d. Undefined

108. In geometry, two lines or planes if one falls on the other in such a way as to create congruent adjacent angles. The term may be used as a noun or adjective. Thus, referring to Figure 1, the line AB is the _____ to CD through the point B.
   a. Perpendicular0
   b. Thing
   c. Undefined
   d. Undefined

109. _____ (Groups, Algorithms and Programming) is a computer algebra system for computational discrete algebra with particular emphasis on, but not restricted to, computational group theory.
   a. Gap0
   b. Thing
   c. Undefined
   d. Undefined

110. In mathematics, the additive inverse, or _____ of a number n is the number that, when added to n, yields zero. The additive inverse of n is denoted −n. For example, 7 is −7, because 7 + (−7) = 0, and the additive inverse of −0.3 is 0.3, because −0.3 + 0.3 = 0.
   a. Thing
   b. Opposite0
   c. Undefined
   d. Undefined

111. In mathematics, the _____ of a number n is the number that, when added to n, yields zero. The _____ of n is denoted −n. For example, 7 is −7, because 7 + (−7) = 0, and the _____ of −0.3 is 0.3, because −0.3 + 0.3 = 0.
   a. Thing
   b. Additive inverse0
   c. Undefined
   d. Undefined

112. _____ is a mathematical operation, written a^n, involving two numbers, the base a and the exponent n.
   a. Exponentiating0
   b. Thing
   c. Undefined
   d. Undefined

113. _____ is a mathematical operation, written a^n, involving two numbers, the base a and the exponent n.
   a. Exponentiation0
   b. Thing
   c. Undefined
   d. Undefined

114. In mathematics, a _____ of a number x is the exponent y of the power by such that $x = b^y$. The value used for the base b must be neither 0 nor 1, nor a root of 1 in the case of the extension to complex numbers, and is typically 10, e, or 2.

Chapter 1. FUNCTIONS

13

    a. Thing
    c. Undefined
    b. Logarithm0
    d. Undefined

115. _____ is the part of statistical practice concerned with the selection of individual observations intended to yield some knowledge about a population of concern, especially for the purposes of statistical inference.
    a. Thing
    c. Undefined
    b. Sampling0
    d. Undefined

116. In mathematics, the _____ of a coordinate system is the point where the axes of the system intersect.
    a. Thing
    c. Undefined
    b. Origin0
    d. Undefined

117. A _____ consists of one quarter of the coordinate plane.
    a. Quadrant0
    c. Undefined
    b. Thing
    d. Undefined

118. _____ or arithmetics is the oldest and most elementary branch of mathematics, used by almost everyone, for tasks ranging from simple daily counting to advanced science and business calculations.
    a. Thing
    c. Undefined
    b. Arithmetic0
    d. Undefined

119. The traditional _____ are addition, subtraction, multiplication and division, although more advanced operations (such as manipulations of percentages, square root, exponentiation, and logarithmic functions) are also sometimes included in this subject.
    a. Concept
    c. Undefined
    b. Arithmetic operations0
    d. Undefined

120. In mathematics, a _____ of a positive integer n is a way of writing n as a sum of positive integers.
    a. Thing
    c. Undefined
    b. Composition0
    d. Undefined

121. _____ refers to the reduction of the body of a formerly living organism into simpler forms of matter.
    a. Thing
    c. Undefined
    b. Decomposing0
    d. Undefined

122. An _____ is a combination of numbers, operators, grouping symbols and/or free variables and bound variables arranged in a meaningful way which can be evaluated..
    a. Expression0
    c. Undefined
    b. Thing
    d. Undefined

123. The _____ functions is determined by the nesting of two or more functions to form a single new function.
    a. Thing
    c. Undefined
    b. Composition of two0
    d. Undefined

124. _____ means "constancy", i.e. if something retains a certain feature even after we change a way of looking at it, then it is symmetric.

a. Thing
b. Symmetry0
c. Undefined
d. Undefined

125. _____ has many meanings, most of which simply .
   a. Thing
   b. Power0
   c. Undefined
   d. Undefined

126. _____ is a trigonemtric function that is important when studying triangles and modeling periodic phenomena, among other applications.
   a. Sine0
   b. Thing
   c. Undefined
   d. Undefined

127. In botany, _____ are above-ground plant organs specialized for photosynthesis. Their characteristics are typically analyzed by using Fiobonacci's sequences.
   a. Leaves0
   b. Thing
   c. Undefined
   d. Undefined

128. In mathematics, a _____ is a two-dimensional manifold or surface that is perfectly flat.
   a. Thing
   b. Plane0
   c. Undefined
   d. Undefined

129. In mathematics, a _____ is a curve in a Euclidian plane. The most frequently studied types are the smooth _____, and the algebraic _____.
   a. Plane curve0
   b. Thing
   c. Undefined
   d. Undefined

130. In mathematics, the _____ is a conic section generated by the intersection of a right circular conical surface and a plane parallel to a generating straight line of that surface. It can also be defined as locus of points in a plane which are equidistant from a given point.
   a. Thing
   b. Parabola0
   c. Undefined
   d. Undefined

131. In Euclidean geometry, a _____ is moving every point a constant distance in a specified direction.
   a. Concept
   b. Translation0
   c. Undefined
   d. Undefined

132. In mathematics, a _____ (also spelled reflexion) is a map that transforms an object into its mirror image.
   a. Reflection0
   b. Concept
   c. Undefined
   d. Undefined

133. In mathematics, a _____ is a statement that can be proved on the basis of explicitly stated or previously agreed assumptions.
   a. Theorem0
   b. Thing
   c. Undefined
   d. Undefined

Chapter 1. FUNCTIONS

134. A _____ is the curve defined by the path of a point on the edge of circular wheel as the wheel rolls along a straight line.
    a. Thing
    b. Cycloid0
    c. Undefined
    d. Undefined

135. Any point where a graph makes contact with an coordinate axis is called an _____ of the graph
    a. Intercept0
    b. Thing
    c. Undefined
    d. Undefined

136. In mathematics, a _____ is a constant multiplicative factor of a certain object. The object can be such things as a variable, a vector, a function, etc. For example, the _____ of $9x^2$ is 9.
    a. Thing
    b. Coefficient0
    c. Undefined
    d. Undefined

137. _____ is a fixed, but possibly unspecified, value. This is in contrast to a variable, which is not fixed.
    a. Constant term0
    b. Thing
    c. Undefined
    d. Undefined

138. The word _____ comes from the Latin word linearis, which means created by lines.
    a. Thing
    b. Linear0
    c. Undefined
    d. Undefined

139. A _____ is a first degree polynomial mathematical function of the form: $f(x) = mx + b$ where m and b are real constants and x is a real variable.
    a. Thing
    b. Linear function0
    c. Undefined
    d. Undefined

140. _____ is the technique and science of accurately determining the terrestrial or three-dimensional space position of points and the distances and angles between them.
    a. Thing
    b. Surveying0
    c. Undefined
    d. Undefined

141. Initial objects are also called _____, and terminal objects are also called final.
    a. Coterminal0
    b. Thing
    c. Undefined
    d. Undefined

142. An _____ is an increase, either of some fixed amount, for example added regularly, or of a variable amount.
    a. Increment0
    b. Thing
    c. Undefined
    d. Undefined

143. Any angle larger than 90 degrees and less than 180 degrees, is called an _____ angle.
    a. Obtuse0
    b. Concept
    c. Undefined
    d. Undefined

144. _____ is a unit of plane angle, equal to $180/\delta$ degrees, or about 57.2958 degrees

a. Thing
b. Radian measure0
c. Undefined
d. Undefined

145. Angles smaller than a right angle are called _____ angles (less than 90 degrees).
a. Acute0
b. Concept
c. Undefined
d. Undefined

146. _____ is the estimation of a physical quantity such as distance, energy, temperature, or time.
a. Thing
b. Measurement0
c. Undefined
d. Undefined

147. The metre (or _____, see spelling differences) is a measure of length. It is the basic unit of length in the metric system and in the International System of Units (SI), used around the world for general and scientific purposes.
a. Concept
b. Meter0
c. Undefined
d. Undefined

148. _____ of an object is its speed in a particular direction.
a. Thing
b. Velocity0
c. Undefined
d. Undefined

149. _____ is a trigonometric function that is the reciprocal of cosine.
a. Secant0
b. Thing
c. Undefined
d. Undefined

150. _____ of a curve is a line that intersects two or more points on the curve.
a. Thing
b. Secant line0
c. Undefined
d. Undefined

151. In mathematics, an _____, mean, or central tendency of a data set refers to a measure of the "middle" or "expected" value of the data set.
a. Concept
b. Average0
c. Undefined
d. Undefined

152. _____ is defined as the rate of change or derivative with respect to time of velocity.
a. Thing
b. Acceleration0
c. Undefined
d. Undefined

153. _____ is a special mathematical relationship between two quantities. Two quantities are called proportional if they vary in such a way that one of the quantities is a constant multiple of the other, or equivalently if they have a constant ratio.
a. Proportionality0
b. Thing
c. Undefined
d. Undefined

154. _____, Greek for "knowledge of nature," is the branch of science concerned with the discovery and characterization of universal laws which govern matter, energy, space, and time.

a. Thing
b. Physics0
c. Undefined
d. Undefined

155. In mathematics and logic, a _____ proof is a way of showing the truth or falsehood of a given statement by a straightforward combination of established facts, usually existing lemmas and theorems, without making any further assumptions.
   a. Direct0
   b. Thing
   c. Undefined
   d. Undefined

156. A _____ is an equation in which each term is either a constant or the product of a constant times the first power of a variable.
   a. Thing
   b. Linear equation0
   c. Undefined
   d. Undefined

157. _____ is the transport of people on a trip/journey or the process or time involved in a person or object moving from one location to another.
   a. Travel0
   b. Thing
   c. Undefined
   d. Undefined

158. _____, in economics and political economy, are the distributions or payments awarded to the various suppliers of the factors of production.
   a. Returns0
   b. Thing
   c. Undefined
   d. Undefined

159. _____ is electromagnetic radiation with a wavelength that is visible to the eye (visible _____) or, in a technical or scientific context, electromagnetic radiation of any wavelength.
   a. Light0
   b. Thing
   c. Undefined
   d. Undefined

160. _____ is a temperature scale named after the German physicist Daniel Gabriel _____, who proposed it in 1724.
   a. Fahrenheit0
   b. Thing
   c. Undefined
   d. Undefined

161. _____ is, or relates to, the _____ temperature scale .
   a. Celsius0
   b. Thing
   c. Undefined
   d. Undefined

162. Celsius is, or relates to, the Celsius temperature scale (previously known as the centigrade scale). The degree Celsius (symbol: °C) can refer to a specific temperature on the _____ as well as serve as unit increment to indicate a temperature interval (a difference between two temperatures or an uncertainty).
   a. Concept
   b. Celsius Scale0
   c. Undefined
   d. Undefined

163. In mathematics, a _____ is an n-tuple with n being 3.

a. Thing
b. Triple0
c. Undefined
d. Undefined

164. The _____ is a thermodynamic (absolute) temperature scale where absolute zero—the coldest possible temperature—is defined as being equivalent to zero kelvin (0 K).
a. Thing
b. Kelvin scale0
c. Undefined
d. Undefined

165. In mathematics, a _____ is the set of all points in three-dimensional space (R^3) which are at distance r from a fixed point of that space, where r is a positive real number called the radius of the _____. The fixed point is called the center or centre, and is not part of the _____ itself.
a. Sphere0
b. Thing
c. Undefined
d. Undefined

166. _____ is the property of a physical object that quantifies the amount of matter and energy it is equivalent to.
a. Thing
b. Mass0
c. Undefined
d. Undefined

167. U.S. liquid _____ is legally defined as 231 cubic inches, and is equal to 3.785411784 litres or abotu 0.13368 cubic feet. This is the most common definition of a _____. The U.S. fluid ounce is defined as 1/128 of a U.S. _____.
a. Gallon0
b. Thing
c. Undefined
d. Undefined

168. The _____ of a ring R is defined to be the smallest positive integer n such that n a = 0, for all a in R.
a. Thing
b. Characteristic0
c. Undefined
d. Undefined

169. _____ is a function whose values do not vary and thus are constant.
a. Constant function0
b. Thing
c. Undefined
d. Undefined

170. An _____ is an equality that remains true regardless of the values of any variables that appear within it, to distinguish it from an equality which is true under more particular conditions.
a. Thing
b. Identity0
c. Undefined
d. Undefined

171. A _____ is the quantity that defines certain relatively constant characteristics of systems or functions..
a. Parameter0
b. Thing
c. Undefined
d. Undefined

172. The existence and properties of _____ are the basis of Euclid's parallel postulate. _____ are two lines on the same plane that do not intersect even assuming that lines extend to infinity in either direction.
a. Parallel lines0
b. Thing
c. Undefined
d. Undefined

Chapter 1. FUNCTIONS

173. In mathematics, the multiplicative inverse of a number x, denoted 1/x or x^{-1}, is the number which, when multiplied by x, yields 1. The multiplicative inverse of x is also called the _____ of x.
   a. Reciprocal0
   b. Thing
   c. Undefined
   d. Undefined

174. In mathematics, an _____ number is any real number that is not a rational number- that is, it is a number which cannot be expressed as a fraction m/n, where m and n are integers.
   a. Irrational0
   b. Thing
   c. Undefined
   d. Undefined

175. In mathematics, two quantities are called _____ if they vary in such a way that one of the quantities is a constant multiple of the other, or equivalently if they have a constant ratio.
   a. Proportional0
   b. Thing
   c. Undefined
   d. Undefined

176. _____ element of an element x with respect to a binary operation * with identity element e is an element y such that x * y = y * x = e. In particular,
   a. Inverse0
   b. Thing
   c. Undefined
   d. Undefined

177. In mathematics and elsewhere, the adjective _____ means fourth order, such as the function x4. A _____ number is a number which equals the fourth power of an integer.
   a. Thing
   b. Quartic0
   c. Undefined
   d. Undefined

178. In mathematics, a _____ number is a number which can be expressed as a ratio of two integers. Non-integer _____ numbers (commonly called fractions) are usually written as the vulgar fraction a / b, where b is not zero.
   a. Rational0
   b. Thing
   c. Undefined
   d. Undefined

179. In mathematics, a _____ is any function which can be written as the ratio of two polynomial functions.
   a. Rational function0
   b. Thing
   c. Undefined
   d. Undefined

180. _____ is informally a function which satisfies a polynomial equation whose coefficients are themselves polynomials.
   a. Thing
   b. Algebraic function0
   c. Undefined
   d. Undefined

181. _____ is a straight line or curve A to which another curve B the one being studied approaches closer and closer as one moves along it.
   a. Thing
   b. Vertical asymptote0
   c. Undefined
   d. Undefined

Chapter 1. FUNCTIONS

182. An _____ is a straight line or curve A to which another curve B approaches closer and closer as one moves along it. As one moves along B, the space between it and the _____ A becomes smaller and smaller, and can in fact be made as small as one could wish by going far enough along. A curve may or may not touch or cross its _____. In fact, the curve may intersect the _____ an infinite number of times.
- a. Asymptote0
- b. Thing
- c. Undefined
- d. Undefined

183. A _____ is a movement of an object in a circular motion. A two-dimensional object rotates around a center (or point) of _____. A three-dimensional object rotates around a line called an axis. If the axis of _____ is within the body, the body is said to rotate upon itself, or spin—which implies relative speed and perhaps free-movement with angular momentum. A circular motion about an external point, e.g. the Earth about the Sun, is called an orbit or more properly an orbital revolution.
- a. Thing
- b. Rotation0
- c. Undefined
- d. Undefined

184. _____ is the design, analysis, and/or construction of works for practical purposes.
- a. Thing
- b. Engineering0
- c. Undefined
- d. Undefined

185. In Euclidean geometry, an _____ is a closed segment of a differentiable curve in the two-dimensional plane; for example, a circular _____ is a segment of a circle.
- a. Concept
- b. Arc0
- c. Undefined
- d. Undefined

186. A circular _____ or circle _____ also known as a pie piece is the portion of a circle enclosed by two radii and an arc.
- a. Thing
- b. Sector0
- c. Undefined
- d. Undefined

187. _____ is a branch of mathematics which deals with triangles, particularly triangles in a plane where one angle of the triangle is 90 degrees, and a variety of other topological relations such as spheres, in other branches, such as spherical _____.
- a. Thing
- b. Trigonometry0
- c. Undefined
- d. Undefined

188. A _____ fraction is a fraction in which the absolute value of the numerator is less than the denominator--hence, the absolute value of the fraction is less than 1.
- a. Proper0
- b. Thing
- c. Undefined
- d. Undefined

189. _____ also called rectification of a curve—was historically difficult.
- a. Arc length0
- b. Thing
- c. Undefined
- d. Undefined

190. In physics, the _____ momentum of an object rotating about some reference point is the measure of the extent to which the object will continue to rotate about that point unless acted upon by an external torque.

a. Thing
b. Angular0
c. Undefined
d. Undefined

191. The _____ of an angle is the ratio of the length of the adjacent side to the length of the hypotenuse.
   a. Cosine0
   b. Concept
   c. Undefined
   d. Undefined

192. In geometry, the _____ of an object is a point in some sense in the middle of the object.
   a. Thing
   b. Center0
   c. Undefined
   d. Undefined

193. In trigonometry, the _____ is a function defined as $\tan x = \sin x / \cos x$. The function is so-named because it can be defined as the length of a certain segment of a _____ (in the geometric sense) to the unit circle. In plane geometry, a line is _____ to a curve, at some point, if both line and curve pass through the point with the same direction.
   a. Thing
   b. Tangent0
   c. Undefined
   d. Undefined

194. _____ is a business term for the amount of money that a company receives from its activities in a given period, mostly from sales of products and/or services to customers
   a. Thing
   b. Revenue0
   c. Undefined
   d. Undefined

195. _____ is a term used in accounting, economics and finance with reference to the fact that assets with finite lives lose value over time.
   a. Depreciation0
   b. Thing
   c. Undefined
   d. Undefined

196. The _____ is the United States federal government agency that collects taxes and enforces the internal revenue laws.
   a. Internal Revenue Service0
   b. Thing
   c. Undefined
   d. Undefined

197. In mathematics and its applications, a _____ is a system for assigning an n-tuple of numbers or scalars to each point in an n-dimensional space.
   a. Coordinate system0
   b. Concept
   c. Undefined
   d. Undefined

198. In mathematics, a _____ in elementary terms is any of a variety of different functions from geometry, such as rotations, reflections and translations.
   a. Thing
   b. Transformation0
   c. Undefined
   d. Undefined

199. In physics, _____ is an influence that may cause an object to accelerate. It may be experienced as a lift, a push, or a pull. The actual acceleration of the body is determined by the vector sum of all forces acting on it, known as net _____ or resultant _____.

Chapter 1. FUNCTIONS

a. Force0
b. Thing
c. Undefined
d. Undefined

200. A _____ is a deliberate process for transforming one or more inputs into one or more results.
   a. Thing
   b. Calculation0
   c. Undefined
   d. Undefined

201. _____, usually denoted symbolically by the Greek letter phi, φ, gives the location of a place on Earth north or south of the equator. _____ is an angular measurement in degrees (marked with °) ranging from 0° at the Equator (low _____) to 90° at the poles (90° N for the North Pole or 90° S for the South Pole; high _____). The complementary angle of a _____ is called the colatitude.
   a. Thing
   b. Latitude0
   c. Undefined
   d. Undefined

202. In physics, an _____ is the path that an object makes around another object while under the influence of a source of centripetal force, such as gravity.
   a. Thing
   b. Orbit0
   c. Undefined
   d. Undefined

203. In geometry, a _____ (Greek words diairo = divide and metro = measure) of a circle is any straight line segment that passes through the centre and whose endpoints are on the circular boundary, or, in more modern usage, the length of such a line segment. When using the word in the more modern sense, one speaks of the _____ rather than a _____, because all diameters of a circle have the same length. This length is twice the radius. The _____ of a circle is also the longest chord that the circle has.
   a. Diameter0
   b. Thing
   c. Undefined
   d. Undefined

204. _____ is the difference of electrical potential between two points of an electrical or electronic circuit, expressed in volts
   a. Thing
   b. Voltage0
   c. Undefined
   d. Undefined

205. In statistics the _____ of an event i is the number n_i of times the event occurred in the experiment or the study. These frequencies are often graphically represented in histograms.
   a. Frequency0
   b. Concept
   c. Undefined
   d. Undefined

206. In regression analysis, _____, also known as ordinary _____ analysis is a method for linear regression that determines the values of unknown quantities in a statistical model by minimizing the sum of the residuals difference between the predicted and observed values squared.
   a. Least squares0
   b. Thing
   c. Undefined
   d. Undefined

207. A _____ is an abstract model that uses mathematical language to describe the behavior of a system. Eykhoff defined a _____ as 'a representation of the essential aspects of an existing system which presents knowledge of that system in usable form'.

Chapter 1. FUNCTIONS

a. Thing
b. Mathematical model0
c. Undefined
d. Undefined

208. _____ was an Italian physicist, mathematician, astronomer, and philosopher who is closely associated with the scientific revolution.
  a. Person
  b. Galileo Galilei0
  c. Undefined
  d. Undefined

209. In probability theory and statistics, _____, also called _____ coefficient, indicates the strength and direction of a linear relationship between two random variables.
  a. Thing
  b. Correlation0
  c. Undefined
  d. Undefined

210. _____ is the chance that something is likely to happen or be the case.
  a. Thing
  b. Probability0
  c. Undefined
  d. Undefined

211. _____ is a mathematical science pertaining to the collection, analysis, interpretation or explanation, and presentation of data. It is applicable to a wide variety of academic disciplines, from the physical and social sciences to the humanities.
  a. Thing
  b. Statistics0
  c. Undefined
  d. Undefined

212. The deductive-nomological model is a formalized view of scientific _____ in natural language.
  a. Explanation0
  b. Thing
  c. Undefined
  d. Undefined

213. In mathematics, a _____ set is the complement of a meager set. A meager set is one which is the countable union of nowhere dense sets.
  a. Residual0
  b. Thing
  c. Undefined
  d. Undefined

214. _____ are rectangular tables (or grids) of information, often financial information.
  a. Spreadsheets0
  b. Thing
  c. Undefined
  d. Undefined

215. There are two simple _____ the greatest common factor and least common multiple: standard factorization and prime factorization.
  a. Thing
  b. Methods for finding0
  c. Undefined
  d. Undefined

216. _____ comes from the Latin word linearis, which means created by lines.
  a. Linearity0
  b. Thing
  c. Undefined
  d. Undefined

217. In statistics, a _____ measure is one which is measuring what is supposed to measure.

a. Valid0
b. Thing
c. Undefined
d. Undefined

218. A _____ is a unit of length in the metric system, equal to one thousand metres, the current SI base unit of length
a. Thing
b. Kilometer0
c. Undefined
d. Undefined

219. A _____ is a polynomial function of the form $f(x) = ax^2 + bx + c$, where a, b, c are real numbers and a , 0.
a. Event
b. Quadratic function0
c. Undefined
d. Undefined

220. _____ systems represent systems whose behavior is not expressible as a sum of the behaviors of its descriptors.
a. Nonlinear0
b. Thing
c. Undefined
d. Undefined

221. _____ is a regression method that models the relationship between a dependent variable Y, independent variables Xp, and a random term å.
a. Linear regression0
b. Thing
c. Undefined
d. Undefined

222. In the scientific method, an _____ (Latin: ex-+-periri, "of (or from) trying"), is a set of actions and observations, performed in the context of solving a particular problem or question, in order to support or falsify a hypothesis or research concerning phenomena.
a. Thing
b. Experiment0
c. Undefined
d. Undefined

223. The _____ is defined as the summation of all particles and energy that exist and the space-time which all events occur.
a. Thing
b. Universe0
c. Undefined
d. Undefined

224. A frame of _____ is a particular perspective from which the universe is observed.
a. Thing
b. Reference0
c. Undefined
d. Undefined

225. An _____ of a product of sums expresses it as a sum of products by using the fact that multiplication distributes over addition.
a. Thing
b. Expansion0
c. Undefined
d. Undefined

226. _____ is a concept in traditional logic referring to a "type of immediate inference in which from a given proposition another proposition is inferred which has as its subject the predicate of the original proposition and as its predicate the subject of the original proposition (the quality of the proposition being retained)."

Chapter 1. FUNCTIONS 25

a. Conversion0
b. Concept
c. Undefined
d. Undefined

227. A _____ is a one-dimensional picture in which the integers are shown as specially-marked points evenly spaced on a line.
a. Number line0
b. Thing
c. Undefined
d. Undefined

228. _____ is the path a moving object follows through space.
a. Thing
b. Projectile motion0
c. Undefined
d. Undefined

229. _____ statistics are statistics that estimate population parameters.
a. Parametric0
b. Thing
c. Undefined
d. Undefined

230. In mathematics, _____ bear slight similarity to functions: they allow one to use arbitrary values, called parameters, in place of independent variables in equations, which in turn provide values for dependent variables. A simple kinematical example is when one uses a time parameter to determine the position, velocity, and other information about a body in motion.
a. Parametric equations0
b. Thing
c. Undefined
d. Undefined

231. In financial mathematics, the _____ volatility of an option contract is the volatility _____ by the market price of the option based on an option pricing model.
a. Thing
b. Implied0
c. Undefined
d. Undefined

232. _____ is a circle with a unit radius, i.e., a circle whose radius is 1.
a. Unit circle0
b. Thing
c. Undefined
d. Undefined

233. In mathematics, an _____ on a real vector space is a choice of which ordered bases are "positively" oriented, or right-handed, and which are "negatively" oriented, or left-handed.
a. Thing
b. Orientation0
c. Undefined
d. Undefined

234. In mathematics, an _____ .
a. Ellipse0
b. Thing
c. Undefined
d. Undefined

235. In mathematics, a _____ curve is the graph of the system of parametric equations, which describes complex harmonic motion.
a. Thing
b. Lissajous0
c. Undefined
d. Undefined

Chapter 1. FUNCTIONS

236. In mathematics, a _____ is a number which can be expressed as a ratio of two integers. Non-integer rational numbers (commonly called fractions) are usually written as the vulgar fraction a / b, where b is not zero.
   a. Rational Number0
   b. Concept
   c. Undefined
   d. Undefined

237. A tautochrone curve is the curve for which the time taken by a frictionless particle sliding down it under uniform gravity to its lowest point is independent of its starting point. The curve is a cycloid, and the time is equal to ð times the square root of the radius over the acceleration of gravity. The _____ is the attempt to identify this curve.
   a. Tautochrone problem0
   b. Thing
   c. Undefined
   d. Undefined

238. A _____ is 360° or 2ð radians.
   a. Turn0
   b. Thing
   c. Undefined
   d. Undefined

239. A _____ curve, or curve of fastest descent, is the curve between two points that is covered in the least time by a body that starts at the first point with zero speed and passes down along the curve to the second point, under the action of constant gravity and ignoring friction.
   a. Thing
   b. Brachistochrone0
   c. Undefined
   d. Undefined

240. A _____ is the curve between two points that is covered in the least time by a body that starts at the first point with zero speed and passes down along the curve to the second point, under the action of constant gravity and ignoring friction.
   a. Thing
   b. Brachistochrone curve0
   c. Undefined
   d. Undefined

241. A _____ is a symbol or group of symbols, or a word in a natural language that represents a number.
   a. Thing
   b. Numeral0
   c. Undefined
   d. Undefined

242. _____ numerals are a numeral system originating in ancient Rome, adapted from Etruscan numerals.
   a. Thing
   b. Roman0
   c. Undefined
   d. Undefined

243. In mathematics, science including computer science, linguistics and engineering, an _____ is, generally speaking, an independent variable or input to a function.
   a. Thing
   b. Argument0
   c. Undefined
   d. Undefined

244. A _____ signifies a point or points of probability on a subject e.g., the _____ of creativity, which allows for the formation of rule or norm or law by interpretation of the phenomena events that can be created.
   a. Principle0
   b. Thing
   c. Undefined
   d. Undefined

245. _____ is any of several theorems in probability.

Chapter 1. FUNCTIONS

a. Law of large numbers0
b. Thing
c. Undefined
d. Undefined

246. _____ is the sub-discipline of fluid mechanics dealing with fluids liquids and gases in motion.
   a. Fluid flow0
   b. Thing
   c. Undefined
   d. Undefined

247. A _____ is the sum of the elements of a sequence.
   a. Thing
   b. Series0
   c. Undefined
   d. Undefined

248. Mathematical _____ really refers to two distinct areas of research: the first is the application of the techniques of formal _____ to mathematics and mathematical reasoning, and the second, in the other direction, the application of mathematical techniques to the representation and analysis of formal _____.
   a. Thing
   b. Logic0
   c. Undefined
   d. Undefined

249. _____ is the scientific study of celestial objects such as stars, planets, comets, and galaxies; and phenomena that originate outside the Earth's atmosphere.
   a. Astronomy0
   b. Thing
   c. Undefined
   d. Undefined

250. In geometry, _____ lines are two lines that share one or more common points.
   a. Thing
   b. Intersecting0
   c. Undefined
   d. Undefined

251. Deductive _____ is the kind of _____ in which the conclusion is necessitated by, or reached from, previously known facts (the premises).
   a. Thing
   b. Reasoning0
   c. Undefined
   d. Undefined

252. _____ is the middle point of a line segment.
   a. Thing
   b. Midpoint0
   c. Undefined
   d. Undefined

253. In geometry, a _____ is defined as a quadrilateral where all four of its angles are right angles.
   a. Thing
   b. Rectangle0
   c. Undefined
   d. Undefined

254. In a mathematical proof or a syllogism, a _____ is a statement that is the logical consequence of preceding statements.
   a. Concept
   b. Conclusion0
   c. Undefined
   d. Undefined

255. Regrouping is the act of putting ones into groups of 10. For example, the 1 on the far right of 131 would be denoted _____ if the digit of the number being subtracted is larger than 1, such as 131-99.

Chapter 1. FUNCTIONS

a. Thing
b. By 100
c. Undefined
d. Undefined

256. A pair of angles is _____ if their respective measures sum to 180 degrees.
a. Supplementary0
b. Concept
c. Undefined
d. Undefined

257. _____ of Syracuse was an ancient Greek mathematician, physicist and engineer. In addition to making important discoveries in the field of mathematics and geometry, he is credited with producing machines that were well ahead of their time.
a. Archimedes0
b. Person
c. Undefined
d. Undefined

258. The State of _____ is a state located in the Rocky Mountain region of the United States of America.
a. Thing
b. Colorado0
c. Undefined
d. Undefined

259. In sociology and biology a _____ is the collection of people or organisms of a particular species living in a given geographic area or space, usually measured by a census.
a. Thing
b. Population0
c. Undefined
d. Undefined

260. _____ is a subset of a population.
a. Sample0
b. Thing
c. Undefined
d. Undefined

261. _____ is an approximation of a general function using a linear function more precisely, an affine function.
a. Linear approximation0
b. Thing
c. Undefined
d. Undefined

262. _____ is the fee paid on borrowed money.
a. Thing
b. Interest0
c. Undefined
d. Undefined

263. _____ was a Polish mathematician.
a. Thing
b. Sierpinski0
c. Undefined
d. Undefined

264. The _____ is a fractal named after Wacªaw Sierpiñski who described it in 1915. Originally constructed as a curve, this is one of the basic examples of self-similar sets, i.e. it is a mathematically generated pattern that can be reproducible at any magnification or reduction.
a. Sierpinski Triangle0
b. Thing
c. Undefined
d. Undefined

265. Mathematical _____ is used to represent ideas.

Chapter 1. FUNCTIONS

a. Notation0
b. Thing
c. Undefined
d. Undefined

266. A _____ is a simplified and structured visual representation of concepts, ideas, constructions, relations, statistical data, anatomy etc used in all aspects of human activities to visualize and clarify the topic.
   a. Thing
   b. Diagram0
   c. Undefined
   d. Undefined

267. In mathematics, a _____ is an ordered list of objects. Like a set, it contains members, also called elements or terms, and the number of terms is called the length of the _____. Unlike a set, order matters, and the exact same elements can appear multiple times at different positions in the _____.
   a. Thing
   b. Sequence0
   c. Undefined
   d. Undefined

268. _____ is a method of defining functions in which the function being defined is applied within its own definition. The term is also used more generally to describe a process of repeating objects in a self-similar way.
   a. Thing
   b. Recursion0
   c. Undefined
   d. Undefined

269. Leonardo of Pisa (1170s or 1180s – 1250), also known as Leonardo Pisano, Leonardo Bonacci, Leonardo _____, or, most commonly, simply _____, was an Italian mathematician, considered by some "the most talented mathematician of the Middle Ages."
   a. Fibonacci0
   b. Person
   c. Undefined
   d. Undefined

270. In mathematics, _____ growth occurs when the growth rate of a function is always proportional to the function's current size.
   a. Exponential0
   b. Thing
   c. Undefined
   d. Undefined

271. _____ is change in population over time, and can be quantified as the change in the number of individuals in a population per unit time.
   a. Population growth0
   b. Thing
   c. Undefined
   d. Undefined

272. In mathematics, a _____ is a condition that a solution to an optimization problem must satisfy in order to be acceptable.
   a. Thing
   b. Constraint0
   c. Undefined
   d. Undefined

273. In colloquial usage, a _____ is "a rough or fragmented geometric shape that can be subdivided in parts, each of which is, at least approximately, a reduced-size copy of the whole."
   a. Fractal0
   b. Concept
   c. Undefined
   d. Undefined

274. In mathematics, a _____ or rhodonea curve is a sinusoid plotted in polar coordinates.

a. Rose0
b. Thing
c. Undefined
d. Undefined

Chapter 2. LIMITS AND CONTINUITY

1. _____ of an object is its speed in a particular direction.
   a. Velocity0
   b. Thing
   c. Undefined
   d. Undefined

2. In mathematics, an _____, mean, or central tendency of a data set refers to a measure of the "middle" or "expected" value of the data set.
   a. Average0
   b. Concept
   c. Undefined
   d. Undefined

3. In elementary algebra, an _____ is a set that contains every real number between two indicated numbers and may contain the two numbers themselves.
   a. Thing
   b. Interval0
   c. Undefined
   d. Undefined

4. In mathematics, the concept of a _____ tries to capture the intuitive idea of a geometrical one-dimensional and continuous object. A simple example is the circle.
   a. Curve0
   b. Thing
   c. Undefined
   d. Undefined

5. _____ is often used to describe the measurement of the steepness, incline, gradient, or grade of a straight line. The _____ is defined as the ratio of the "rise" divided by the "run" between two points on a line, or in other words, the ratio of the altitude change to the horizontal distance between any two points on the line.
   a. Thing
   b. Slope0
   c. Undefined
   d. Undefined

6. _____ is the part of statistical practice concerned with the selection of individual observations intended to yield some knowledge about a population of concern, especially for the purposes of statistical inference.
   a. Sampling0
   b. Thing
   c. Undefined
   d. Undefined

7. A _____ is a symbolic representation denoting a quantity or expression. It often represents an "unknown" quantity that has the potential to change.
   a. Thing
   b. Variable0
   c. Undefined
   d. Undefined

8. In mathematics, an _____ is any of the arguments, i.e. "inputs", to a function. Thus if we have a function f(x), then x is a _____.
   a. Independent variable0
   b. Thing
   c. Undefined
   d. Undefined

9. The mathematical concept of a _____ expresses the intuitive idea of deterministic dependence between two quantities, one of which is viewed as primary and the other as secondary. A _____ then is a way to associate a unique output for each input of a specified type, for example, a real number or an element of a given set.
   a. Thing
   b. Function0
   c. Undefined
   d. Undefined

Chapter 2. LIMITS AND CONTINUITY

10. In mathematics, a _____ of a k-place relation $L \subseteq X_1 \times ... \times X_k$ is one of the sets X_j, $1 \leq j \leq k$. In the special case where k = 2 and $L \subseteq X_1 \times X_2$ is a function $L : X_1 \to X_2$, it is conventional to refer to X_1 as the _____ of the function and to refer to X_2 as the codomain of the function.
   - a. Thing
   - b. Domain0
   - c. Undefined
   - d. Undefined

11. _____ the expected value of a random variable displays the average or central value of the variable. It is a summary value of the distribution of the variable.
   - a. Determining0
   - b. Thing
   - c. Undefined
   - d. Undefined

12. In mathematics, a _____ is a mathematical statement which appears likely to be true, but has not been formally proven to be true under the rules of mathematical logic.
   - a. Concept
   - b. Conjecture0
   - c. Undefined
   - d. Undefined

13. _____ is a subset of a population.
   - a. Sample0
   - b. Thing
   - c. Undefined
   - d. Undefined

14. A _____ is 360° or 2δ radians.
   - a. Thing
   - b. Turn0
   - c. Undefined
   - d. Undefined

15. The _____ is a fundamental concept in analysis. Informally, a function f can be made as close to L as desired, by making x close enough to p.
   - a. Limit of a function0
   - b. Thing
   - c. Undefined
   - d. Undefined

16. _____ is a straight line or curve A to which another curve B the one being studied approaches closer and closer as one moves along it.
   - a. Thing
   - b. Vertical asymptote0
   - c. Undefined
   - d. Undefined

17. An _____ is a straight line or curve A to which another curve B approaches closer and closer as one moves along it. As one moves along B, the space between it and the _____ A becomes smaller and smaller, and can in fact be made as small as one could wish by going far enough along. A curve may or may not touch or cross its _____. In fact, the curve may intersect the _____ an infinite number of times.
   - a. Asymptote0
   - b. Thing
   - c. Undefined
   - d. Undefined

18. _____ is the state of being greater than any finite real or natural number, however large.
   - a. Thing
   - b. Infinite0
   - c. Undefined
   - d. Undefined

19. _____ are objects, characters, or other concrete representations of ideas, concepts, or other abstractions.

Chapter 2. LIMITS AND CONTINUITY

    a. Symbols0
    c. Undefined
    b. Thing
    d. Undefined

20. In mathematics, the _____ f is the collection of all ordered pairs. In particular, graph means the graphical representation of this collection, in the form of a curve or surface, together with axes, etc. Graphing on a Cartesian plane is sometimes referred to as curve sketching.
    a. Thing
    c. Undefined
    b. Graph of a function0
    d. Undefined

21. In astronomy, geography, geometry and related sciences and contexts, a plane is said to be _____ at a given point if it is locally perpendicular to the gradient of the gravity field, i.e., with the direction of the gravitational force at that point.
    a. Thing
    c. Undefined
    b. Horizontal0
    d. Undefined

22. _____ Any process by which a specified characteristic usually amplitude of the output of a device is prevented from exceeding a predetermined value.
    a. Limiting0
    c. Undefined
    b. Thing
    d. Undefined

23. _____ is the state of being greater than any finite number, however large.
    a. Thing
    c. Undefined
    b. Infinity0
    d. Undefined

24. In mathematics, the _____ functions are functions of an angle; they are important when studying triangles and modeling periodic phenomena, among many other applications.
    a. Trigonometric0
    c. Undefined
    b. Thing
    d. Undefined

25. The _____ are functions of an angle; they are important when studying triangles and modeling periodic phenomena, among many other applications.
    a. Thing
    c. Undefined
    b. Trigonometric functions0
    d. Undefined

26. In a mathematical proof or a syllogism, a _____ is a statement that is the logical consequence of preceding statements.
    a. Conclusion0
    c. Undefined
    b. Concept
    d. Undefined

27. In mathematics and the mathematical sciences, a _____ is a fixed, but possibly unspecified, value. This is in contrast to a variable, which is not fixed.
    a. Constant0
    c. Undefined
    b. Thing
    d. Undefined

28. In physics, _____ is an influence that may cause an object to accelerate. It may be experienced as a lift, a push, or a pull. The actual acceleration of the body is determined by the vector sum of all forces acting on it, known as net _____ or resultant _____.

34   *Chapter 2. LIMITS AND CONTINUITY*

   a. Thing   b. Force0
   c. Undefined   d. Undefined

29. In mathematics, _____ are the intuitive idea of a geometrical one-dimensional and continuous object.
   a. Thing   b. Curves0
   c. Undefined   d. Undefined

30. _____, Greek for "knowledge of nature," is the branch of science concerned with the discovery and characterization of universal laws which govern matter, energy, space, and time.
   a. Thing   b. Physics0
   c. Undefined   d. Undefined

31. A _____ is a statement or claimt that a particular event will occur in the future in more certain terms than a forecast.
   a. Thing   b. Prediction0
   c. Undefined   d. Undefined

32. _____ is a physical property of a system that underlies the common notions of hot and cold; something that is hotter has the greater _____.
   a. Thing   b. Temperature0
   c. Undefined   d. Undefined

33. _____ are a measure of time.
   a. Thing   b. Minutes0
   c. Undefined   d. Undefined

34. Equivalence is the condition of being _____ or essentially equal.
   a. Thing   b. Equivalent0
   c. Undefined   d. Undefined

35. A _____ is a deliberate process for transforming one or more inputs into one or more results.
   a. Calculation0   b. Thing
   c. Undefined   d. Undefined

36. _____ are the basic objects of study in graph theory. Informally speaking, a graph is a set of objects called points, nodes, or vertices connected by links called lines or edges.
   a. Graphs0   b. Thing
   c. Undefined   d. Undefined

37. In mathematics, a _____ is a statement that can be proved on the basis of explicitly stated or previously agreed assumptions.
   a. Theorem0   b. Thing
   c. Undefined   d. Undefined

38. _____ is a function whose values do not vary and thus are constant.

Chapter 2. LIMITS AND CONTINUITY

a. Constant function0
b. Thing
c. Undefined
d. Undefined

39. An _____ is an equality that remains true regardless of the values of any variables that appear within it, to distinguish it from an equality which is true under more particular conditions.
   a. Identity0
   b. Thing
   c. Undefined
   d. Undefined

40. An _____ is a function that does not have any effect: it always returns the same value that was used as its argument.
   a. Thing
   b. Identity function0
   c. Undefined
   d. Undefined

41. In mathematics, a _____ is the result of multiplying, or an expression that identifies factors to be multiplied.
   a. Product0
   b. Thing
   c. Undefined
   d. Undefined

42. In mathematics, a _____ is the end result of a division problem. It can also be expressed as the number of times the divisor divides into the dividend.
   a. Quotient0
   b. Thing
   c. Undefined
   d. Undefined

43. A _____ is the part of a fraction that tells how many equal parts make up a whole, and which is used in the name of the fraction: "halves", "thirds", "fourths" or "quarters", "fifths" and so on.
   a. Concept
   b. Denominator0
   c. Undefined
   d. Undefined

44. An _____ of a number a is a number b such that $b^n = a$.
   a. Thing
   b. Nth root0
   c. Undefined
   d. Undefined

45. In mathematics, a _____ of a complex-valued function f is a member x of the domain of f such that f(x) vanishes at x, that is, x : f (x) = 0.
   a. Root0
   b. Thing
   c. Undefined
   d. Undefined

46. In mathematics, a set is called _____ if there is a bijection between the set and some set of the form {1, 2, ..., n} where n is a natural number.
   a. Finite0
   b. Thing
   c. Undefined
   d. Undefined

47. In mathematics, a _____ is a demonstration that, assuming certain axioms, some statement is necessarily true.
   a. Thing
   b. Proof0
   c. Undefined
   d. Undefined

48. A _____ is a quantity that denotes the proportional amount or magnitude of one quantity relative to another.

Chapter 2. LIMITS AND CONTINUITY

    a. Thing
    c. Undefined
    b. Ratio0
    d. Undefined

49. In mathematics, a _____ number is a number which can be expressed as a ratio of two integers. Non-integer _____ numbers (commonly called fractions) are usually written as the vulgar fraction a / b, where b is not zero.
    - a. Rational0
    - b. Thing
    - c. Undefined
    - d. Undefined

50. In mathematics, a _____ is any function which can be written as the ratio of two polynomial functions.
    - a. Rational function0
    - b. Thing
    - c. Undefined
    - d. Undefined

51. In mathematics, a _____ may be described informally as a number that can be given by an infinite decimal representation.
    - a. Thing
    - b. Real number0
    - c. Undefined
    - d. Undefined

52. In mathematics, a _____ is an expression that is constructed from one or more variables and constants, using only the operations of addition, subtraction, multiplication, and constant positive whole number exponents. is a _____. Note in particular that division by an expression containing a variable is not in general allowed in polynomials. [1]
    - a. Thing
    - b. Polynomial0
    - c. Undefined
    - d. Undefined

53. In combinatorial mathematics, a _____ is an un-ordered collection of unique elements.
    - a. Concept
    - b. Combination0
    - c. Undefined
    - d. Undefined

54. A _____ is a numeral used to indicate a count. The most common use of the word today is to name the part of a fraction that tells the number or count of equal parts.
    - a. Thing
    - b. Numerator0
    - c. Undefined
    - d. Undefined

55. Two mathematical objects are equal if and only if they are precisely the same in every way. This defines a binary relation, _____, denoted by the sign of _____ "=" in such a way that the statement "x = y" means that x and y are equal.
    - a. Equality0
    - b. Thing
    - c. Undefined
    - d. Undefined

56. _____ is the largest positive integer that divides both numbers without remainder.
    - a. Common Factor0
    - b. Thing
    - c. Undefined
    - d. Undefined

57. An _____ is a combination of numbers, operators, grouping symbols and/or free variables and bound variables arranged in a meaningful way which can be evaluated..

Chapter 2. LIMITS AND CONTINUITY

    a. Thing
    b. Expression0
    c. Undefined
    d. Undefined

58. In calculus and other branches of mathematical analysis, an _____ is an algebraic expression obtained in the context of limits.
    a. Indeterminate form0
    b. Thing
    c. Undefined
    d. Undefined

59. A _____ defined function $f(x)$ of a real variable x is a function whose definition is given differently on disjoint subsets of its domain.
    a. Piecewise0
    b. Thing
    c. Undefined
    d. Undefined

60. In mathematics, the multiplicative inverse of a number x, denoted $1/x$ or x^{-1}, is the number which, when multiplied by x, yields 1. The multiplicative inverse of x is also called the _____ of x.
    a. Reciprocal0
    b. Thing
    c. Undefined
    d. Undefined

61. The _____ of a mathematical object is its size: a property by which it can be larger or smaller than other objects of the same kind; in technical terms, an ordering of the class of objects to which it belongs.
    a. Magnitude0
    b. Thing
    c. Undefined
    d. Undefined

62. A _____ is the result of the addition of a set of numbers. The numbers may be natural numbers, complex numbers, matrices, or still more complicated objects. An infinite _____ is a subtle procedure known as a series.
    a. Thing
    b. Sum0
    c. Undefined
    d. Undefined

63. In common philosophical language, a proposition or _____, is the content of an assertion, that is, it is true-or-false and defined by the meaning of a particular piece of language.
    a. Statement0
    b. Concept
    c. Undefined
    d. Undefined

64. A _____ signifies a point or points of probability on a subject e.g., the _____ of creativity, which allows for the formation of rule or norm or law by interpretation of the phenomena events that can be created.
    a. Thing
    b. Principle0
    c. Undefined
    d. Undefined

65. In mathematics, there are several meanings of _____ depending on the subject.
    a. Degree0
    b. Thing
    c. Undefined
    d. Undefined

66. In mathematics, _____ is the decomposition of an object into a product of other objects, or factors, which when multiplied together give the original.

Chapter 2. LIMITS AND CONTINUITY

    a. Factoring0
    c. Undefined
    b. Thing
    d. Undefined

67. _____ has many meanings, most of which simply .
    a. Power0
    c. Undefined
    b. Thing
    d. Undefined

68. The _____, the average in everyday English, which is also called the arithmetic _____ (and is distinguished from the geometric _____ or harmonic _____). The average is also called the sample _____. The expected value of a random variable, which is also called the population _____.
    a. Thing
    c. Undefined
    b. Mean0
    d. Undefined

69. In business, particularly accounting, a _____ is the time intervals that the accounts, statement, payments, or other calculations cover.
    a. Period0
    c. Undefined
    b. Thing
    d. Undefined

70. In set theory and its applications throughout mathematics, _____ are a collection of sets (or sometimes other mathematical objects) that can be unambiguously defined by a property that all its members share.
    a. Classes0
    c. Undefined
    b. Thing
    d. Undefined

71. Mathematical _____ are demonstrations that, assuming certain axioms, some statement is necessarily true.
    a. Thing
    c. Undefined
    b. Proofs0
    d. Undefined

72. The term _____ is used to describe an algebraic structure which in some sense cannot be divided by a smaller structure of the same type.
    a. Simple algebra0
    c. Undefined
    b. Thing
    d. Undefined

73. In mathematics, science including computer science, linguistics and engineering, an _____ is, generally speaking, an independent variable or input to a function.
    a. Argument0
    c. Undefined
    b. Thing
    d. Undefined

74. _____ is a branch of mathematics concerning the study of structure, relation and quantity.
    a. Concept
    c. Undefined
    b. Algebra0
    d. Undefined

75. In mathematics, the _____ (or modulus) of a real number is its numerical value without regard to its sign.
    a. Thing
    c. Undefined
    b. Absolute value0
    d. Undefined

76. In mathematics, _____ expressions is used to reduce the expression into the lowest possible term.

Chapter 2. LIMITS AND CONTINUITY

    a. Thing
    b. Simplifying0
    c. Undefined
    d. Undefined

77. In linear algebra, the _____ of an n-by-n square matrix A is defined to be the sum of the elements on the main diagonal of A,
    a. Trace0
    b. Thing
    c. Undefined
    d. Undefined

78. In geographic information systems, a _____ comprises an entity with a geographic location, typically determined by points, arcs, or polygons. Carriageways and cadastres exemplify _____ data.
    a. Feature0
    b. Thing
    c. Undefined
    d. Undefined

79. In mathematics, an _____ is a statement about the relative size or order of two objects.
    a. Thing
    b. Inequality0
    c. Undefined
    d. Undefined

80. A _____ is a number that is less than zero.
    a. Thing
    b. Negative number0
    c. Undefined
    d. Undefined

81. The _____ of measurement are a globally standardized and modernized form of the metric system.
    a. Thing
    b. Units0
    c. Undefined
    d. Undefined

82. In Euclidean geometry, a uniform _____ is a linear transformation that enlargers or diminishes objects, and whose _____ factor is the same in all directions. This is also called homothethy.
    a. Scale0
    b. Thing
    c. Undefined
    d. Undefined

83. In geometry, the _____ of an object is a point in some sense in the middle of the object.
    a. Center0
    b. Thing
    c. Undefined
    d. Undefined

84. In mathematics, an inequality is a statement about the relative size or order of two objects. For example 14 > 10, or 14 is _____ 10.
    a. Thing
    b. Greater than0
    c. Undefined
    d. Undefined

85. In mathematics, the _____ of a coordinate system is the point where the axes of the system intersect.
    a. Thing
    b. Origin0
    c. Undefined
    d. Undefined

86. Continuous functions are of utmost importance in mathematics and applications. However, not all functions are continuous. If a function is not continuous at a point in its domain, one says that it has a _____ there. The set of all points of _____ of a function may be a discrete set, a dense set, or even the entire domain of the function.

a. Discontinuity0
b. Thing
c. Undefined
d. Undefined

87. A _____ function is a function for which, intuitively, small changes in the input result in small changes in the output.
   a. Continuous0
   b. Event
   c. Undefined
   d. Undefined

88. In mathematics, defined and _____ are used to explain whether or not expressions have meaningful, sensible, and unambiguous values.
   a. Thing
   b. Undefined0
   c. Undefined
   d. Undefined

89. _____ (Groups, Algorithms and Programming) is a computer algebra system for computational discrete algebra with particular emphasis on, but not restricted to, computational group theory.
   a. Gap0
   b. Thing
   c. Undefined
   d. Undefined

90. In statistics, a _____ measure is one which is measuring what is supposed to measure.
   a. Thing
   b. Valid0
   c. Undefined
   d. Undefined

91. In mathematics, a _____ of a positive integer n is a way of writing n as a sum of positive integers.
   a. Composition0
   b. Thing
   c. Undefined
   d. Undefined

92. In geometry, an _____ is a point at which a line segment or ray terminates.
   a. Endpoint0
   b. Thing
   c. Undefined
   d. Undefined

93. In mathematics, the additive inverse, or _____ of a number n is the number that, when added to n, yields zero. The additive inverse of n is denoted −n. For example, 7 is −7, because 7 + (−7) = 0, and the additive inverse of −0.3 is 0.3, because −0.3 + 0.3 = 0.
   a. Opposite0
   b. Thing
   c. Undefined
   d. Undefined

94. In mathematics, the _____ of a number n is the number that, when added to n, yields zero. The _____ of n is denoted −n. For example, 7 is −7, because 7 + (−7) = 0, and the _____ of −0.3 is 0.3, because −0.3 + 0.3 = 0.
   a. Additive inverse0
   b. Thing
   c. Undefined
   d. Undefined

95. _____ is the study of terms and their use — of words and compound words that are used in specific contexts.
   a. Thing
   b. Terminology0
   c. Undefined
   d. Undefined

Chapter 2. LIMITS AND CONTINUITY

96. Deductive _____ is the kind of _____ in which the conclusion is necessitated by, or reached from, previously known facts (the premises).
 a. Thing
 b. Reasoning0
 c. Undefined
 d. Undefined

97. In sociology and biology a _____ is the collection of people or organisms of a particular species living in a given geographic area or space, usually measured by a census.
 a. Population0
 b. Thing
 c. Undefined
 d. Undefined

98. The _____ of a solid object is the three-dimensional concept of how much space it occupies, often quantified numerically.
 a. Volume0
 b. Thing
 c. Undefined
 d. Undefined

99. A _____ is a three-dimensional solid object bounded by six square faces, facets, or sides, with three meeting at each vertex.
 a. Thing
 b. Cube0
 c. Undefined
 d. Undefined

100. A _____ is a negotiable instrument instructing a financial institution to pay a specific amount of a specific currency from a specific demand account held in the maker/depositor's name with that institution. Both the maker and payee may be natural persons or legal entities.
 a. Thing
 b. Check0
 c. Undefined
 d. Undefined

101. In Euclidean geometry, a _____ is the set of all points in a plane at a fixed distance, called the radius, from a given point, the center.
 a. Circle0
 b. Thing
 c. Undefined
 d. Undefined

102. In classical geometry, a _____ of a circle or sphere is any line segment from its center to its boundary. By extension, the _____ of a circle or sphere is the length of any such segment. The _____ is half the diameter. In science and engineering the term _____ of curvature is commonly used as a synonym for _____.
 a. Radius0
 b. Thing
 c. Undefined
 d. Undefined

103. In plane geometry, a _____ is a polygon with four equal sides, four right angles, and parallel opposite sides. In algebra, the _____ of a number is that number multiplied by itself.
 a. Thing
 b. Square0
 c. Undefined
 d. Undefined

104. A _____ can refer to a line joining two nonadjacent vertices of a polygon or polyhedron, or in some contexts any upward or downward sloping line. .

Chapter 2. LIMITS AND CONTINUITY

a. Diagonal0
b. Thing
c. Undefined
d. Undefined

105. In mathematics, a _____ is a quadric surface, with the following equation in Cartesian coordinates: $(x/a)^2 + (y/b)^2 = 1$.
   a. Cylinder0
   b. Thing
   c. Undefined
   d. Undefined

106. _____ is a three-dimensional geometric shape formed by straight lines through a fixed point vertex to the points of a fixed curve directrix.
   a. Thing
   b. Right circular cone0
   c. Undefined
   d. Undefined

107. A _____ is a three-dimensional geometric shape formed by straight lines through a fixed point (vertex) to the points of a fixed curve (directrix)
   a. Cone0
   b. Concept
   c. Undefined
   d. Undefined

108. In mathematics, a _____ is the set of all points in three-dimensional space (R^3) which are at distance r from a fixed point of that space, where r is a positive real number called the radius of the _____. The fixed point is called the center or centre, and is not part of the _____ itself.
   a. Thing
   b. Sphere0
   c. Undefined
   d. Undefined

109. The _____ is a unit of plane angle. It is represented by the symbol "rad" or, more rarely, by the superscript c (for "circular measure"). For example, an angle of 1.2 radians would be written "1.2 rad" or "1.2c" (second symbol can produce confusion with centigrads).
   a. Thing
   b. Radian0
   c. Undefined
   d. Undefined

110. _____ is a unit of plane angle, equal to 180/δ degrees, or about 57.2958 degrees
   a. Radian measure0
   b. Thing
   c. Undefined
   d. Undefined

111. A _____ is a function that assigns a number to subsets of a given set.
   a. Thing
   b. Measure0
   c. Undefined
   d. Undefined

112. A _____ is a set of numbers that designate location in a given reference system, such as x,y in a planar _____ system or an x,y,z in a three-dimensional _____ system.
   a. Coordinate0
   b. Thing
   c. Undefined
   d. Undefined

113. The _____ of an angle is the ratio of the length of the adjacent side to the length of the hypotenuse.

Chapter 2. LIMITS AND CONTINUITY

a. Concept
b. Cosine0
c. Undefined
d. Undefined

114. A _____ is one of the basic shapes of geometry: a polygon with three vertices and three sides which are straight line segments.
a. Thing
b. Triangle0
c. Undefined
d. Undefined

115. _____ is a trigonemtric function that is important when studying triangles and modeling periodic phenomena, among other applications.
a. Sine0
b. Thing
c. Undefined
d. Undefined

116. _____, usually denoted symbolically by the Greek letter phi, Î¦, gives the location of a place on Earth north or south of the equator. _____ is an angular measurement in degrees (marked with Â°) ranging from 0Â° at the Equator (low _____) to 90Â° at the poles (90Â° N for the North Pole or 90Â° S for the South Pole; high _____). The complementary angle of a _____ is called the colatitude.
a. Thing
b. Latitude0
c. Undefined
d. Undefined

117. In mathematics, factorization (British English: factorisation) or factoring is the decomposition of an object (for example, a number, a polynomial, or a matrix) into a product of other objects, or _____, which when multiplied together give the original.
a. Thing
b. Factors0
c. Undefined
d. Undefined

118. _____ is defined as the rate of change or derivative with respect to time of velocity.
a. Thing
b. Acceleration0
c. Undefined
d. Undefined

119. A pair of angles is _____ if their respective measures sum to 180 degrees.
a. Supplementary0
b. Concept
c. Undefined
d. Undefined

120. In mathematics, a _____ is a number which can be expressed as a ratio of two integers. Non-integer rational numbers (commonly called fractions) are usually written as the vulgar fraction a / b, where b is not zero.
a. Concept
b. Rational Number0
c. Undefined
d. Undefined

121. In mathematics, an _____ number is any real number that is not a rational number- that is, it is a number which cannot be expressed as a fraction m/n, where m and n are integers.
a. Irrational0
b. Thing
c. Undefined
d. Undefined

122. In mathematics, an _____ is any real number that is not a rational number ¡ª that is, it is a number which cannot be expressed as m/n, where m and n are integers.

44   *Chapter 2. LIMITS AND CONTINUITY*

   a. Thing   b. Irrational number0
   c. Undefined   d. Undefined

123. _____ is the difference of electrical potential between two points of an electrical or electronic circuit, expressed in volts
   a. Voltage0   b. Thing
   c. Undefined   d. Undefined

124. The _____, in practice often shortened to amp, is a unit of electric current, or amount of electric charge per second.
   a. Amperes0   b. Thing
   c. Undefined   d. Undefined

125. A _____ is a function for which, intuitively, small changes in the input result in small changes in the output.
   a. Continuous function0   b. Event
   c. Undefined   d. Undefined

126. _____, or Rationalisation in mathematics is the process of removing a square root or imaginary number from the denominator of a fraction.
   a. Rationalizing0   b. Thing
   c. Undefined   d. Undefined

127. Initial objects are also called _____, and terminal objects are also called final.
   a. Coterminal0   b. Thing
   c. Undefined   d. Undefined

128. In mathematics and its applications, a _____ is a system for assigning an n-tuple of numbers or scalars to each point in an n-dimensional space.
   a. Coordinate system0   b. Concept
   c. Undefined   d. Undefined

Chapter 3. THE DERIVATIVE

1. _____ is the difference of electrical potential between two points of an electrical or electronic circuit, expressed in volts
   a. Voltage0
   b. Thing
   c. Undefined
   d. Undefined

2. In mainstream economics, the word _____ refers to a general rise in prices measured against a standard level of purchasing power.
   a. Inflation0
   b. Thing
   c. Undefined
   d. Undefined

3. A _____ is a vehicle, missile or aircraft which obtains thrust by the reaction to the ejection of fast moving fluid from within a _____ engine.
   a. Thing
   b. Rocket0
   c. Undefined
   d. Undefined

4. The _____ is a measurement of how a function changes when the values of its inputs change.
   a. Derivative0
   b. Thing
   c. Undefined
   d. Undefined

5. An _____ is the result from the sudden release of stored energy in the Earth's crust that creates seismic waves.
   a. Thing
   b. Earthquake0
   c. Undefined
   d. Undefined

6. _____ of an object is its speed in a particular direction.
   a. Velocity0
   b. Thing
   c. Undefined
   d. Undefined

7. _____ is often used to describe the measurement of the steepness, incline, gradient, or grade of a straight line. The _____ is defined as the ratio of the "rise" divided by the "run" between two points on a line, or in other words, the ratio of the altitude change to the horizontal distance between any two points on the line.
   a. Slope0
   b. Thing
   c. Undefined
   d. Undefined

8. In mathematics, the concept of a _____ tries to capture the intuitive idea of a geometrical one-dimensional and continuous object. A simple example is the circle.
   a. Curve0
   b. Thing
   c. Undefined
   d. Undefined

9. In mathematics, an _____, mean, or central tendency of a data set refers to a measure of the "middle" or "expected" value of the data set.
   a. Average0
   b. Concept
   c. Undefined
   d. Undefined

10. A _____ is a special kind of ratio, indicating a relationship between two measurements with different units, such as miles to gallons or cents to pounds.

a. Rate0
b. Thing
c. Undefined
d. Undefined

11. _____, a field in mathematics, is the study of how functions change when their inputs change. The primary object of study in _____ is the derivative.
   a. Thing
   b. Differential calculus0
   c. Undefined
   d. Undefined

12. _____ systems represent systems whose behavior is not expressible as a sum of the behaviors of its descriptors.
   a. Nonlinear0
   b. Thing
   c. Undefined
   d. Undefined

13. The word _____ comes from the Latin word linearis, which means created by lines.
   a. Linear0
   b. Thing
   c. Undefined
   d. Undefined

14. A _____ is a first degree polynomial mathematical function of the form: f(x) = mx + b where m and b are real constants and x is a real variable.
   a. Thing
   b. Linear function0
   c. Undefined
   d. Undefined

15. _____ is a mathematical subject that includes the study of limits, derivatives, integrals, and power series and constitutes a major part of modern university curriculum.
   a. Calculus0
   b. Thing
   c. Undefined
   d. Undefined

16. The mathematical concept of a _____ expresses the intuitive idea of deterministic dependence between two quantities, one of which is viewed as primary and the other as secondary. A _____ then is a way to associate a unique output for each input of a specified type, for example, a real number or an element of a given set.
   a. Function0
   b. Thing
   c. Undefined
   d. Undefined

17. In mathematics, a _____ is an algebraic structure in which addition and multiplication are defined and have properties listed below.
   a. Thing
   b. Ring0
   c. Undefined
   d. Undefined

18. _____ is the transport of people on a trip/journey or the process or time involved in a person or object moving from one location to another.
   a. Travel0
   b. Thing
   c. Undefined
   d. Undefined

19. A _____ is a function that assigns a number to subsets of a given set.

Chapter 3. THE DERIVATIVE

    a. Thing
    b. Measure0
    c. Undefined
    d. Undefined

20. In Euclidean geometry, a _____ is the set of all points in a plane at a fixed distance, called the radius, from a given point, the center.
    a. Thing
    b. Circle0
    c. Undefined
    d. Undefined

21. _____ is bother the congnitive process of transferring information from a particular subject, and a linguistic expression corresponding to such a process.
    a. Thing
    b. Analogy0
    c. Undefined
    d. Undefined

22. _____ is a trigonometric function that is the reciprocal of cosine.
    a. Thing
    b. Secant0
    c. Undefined
    d. Undefined

23. _____ of a curve is a line that intersects two or more points on the curve.
    a. Thing
    b. Secant line0
    c. Undefined
    d. Undefined

24. _____ is a physical property of a system that underlies the common notions of hot and cold; something that is hotter has the greater _____.
    a. Temperature0
    b. Thing
    c. Undefined
    d. Undefined

25. In mathematics, a _____ is the result of multiplying, or an expression that identifies factors to be multiplied.
    a. Thing
    b. Product0
    c. Undefined
    d. Undefined

26. In classical geometry, a _____ of a circle or sphere is any line segment from its center to its boundary. By extension, the _____ of a circle or sphere is the length of any such segment. The _____ is half the diameter. In science and engineering the term _____ of curvature is commonly used as a synonym for _____.
    a. Radius0
    b. Thing
    c. Undefined
    d. Undefined

27. In elementary algebra, an _____ is a set that contains every real number between two indicated numbers and may contain the two numbers themselves.
    a. Thing
    b. Interval0
    c. Undefined
    d. Undefined

28. The _____ of measurement are a globally standardized and modernized form of the metric system.
    a. Units0
    b. Thing
    c. Undefined
    d. Undefined

Chapter 3. THE DERIVATIVE

29. In mathematics, the additive inverse, or _____ of a number n is the number that, when added to n, yields zero. The additive inverse of n is denoted −n. For example, 7 is −7, because 7 + (−7) = 0, and the additive inverse of −0.3 is 0.3, because −0.3 + 0.3 = 0.
    a. Opposite0
    b. Thing
    c. Undefined
    d. Undefined

30. In mathematics, the _____ of a number n is the number that, when added to n, yields zero. The _____ of n is denoted −n. For example, 7 is −7, because 7 + (−7) = 0, and the _____ of −0.3 is 0.3, because −0.3 + 0.3 = 0.
    a. Additive inverse0
    b. Thing
    c. Undefined
    d. Undefined

31. In mathematics, _____ expressions is used to reduce the expression into the lowest possible term.
    a. Simplifying0
    b. Thing
    c. Undefined
    d. Undefined

32. _____ is a branch of mathematics concerning the study of structure, relation and quantity.
    a. Algebra0
    b. Concept
    c. Undefined
    d. Undefined

33. _____ is the volume of blood being pumped by the heart, in particular a ventricle in a minute.
    a. Thing
    b. Cardiac output0
    c. Undefined
    d. Undefined

34. In geometry, a line _____ is a part of a line that is bounded by two end points, and contains every point on the line between its end points.
    a. Segment0
    b. Concept
    c. Undefined
    d. Undefined

35. A _____ is a part of a line that is bounded by two end points, and contains every point on the line between its end points.
    a. Thing
    b. Line segment0
    c. Undefined
    d. Undefined

36. Acid _____ ratio measures the ability of a company to use its near cash or quick assets to immediately extinguish its current liabilities.
    a. Thing
    b. Test0
    c. Undefined
    d. Undefined

37. The act of _____ is the calculated approximation of a result which is usable even if input data may be incomplete, uncertain, or noisy.
    a. Estimating0
    b. Thing
    c. Undefined
    d. Undefined

38. In mathematics, the _____ of a coordinate system is the point where the axes of the system intersect.

Chapter 3. THE DERIVATIVE

a. Thing
b. Origin0
c. Undefined
d. Undefined

39. In astronomy, geography, geometry and related sciences and contexts, a plane is said to be _____ at a given point if it is locally perpendicular to the gradient of the gravity field, i.e., with the direction of the gravitational force at that point.
a. Thing
b. Horizontal0
c. Undefined
d. Undefined

40. In mathematics, _____ are the intuitive idea of a geometrical one-dimensional and continuous object.
a. Curves0
b. Thing
c. Undefined
d. Undefined

41. In business, particularly accounting, a _____ is the time intervals that the accounts, statement, payments, or other calculations cover.
a. Thing
b. Period0
c. Undefined
d. Undefined

42. Initial objects are also called _____, and terminal objects are also called final.
a. Coterminal0
b. Thing
c. Undefined
d. Undefined

43. A _____ is a unit of length, usually used to measure distance, in a number of different systems, including Imperial units, United States customary units and Norwegian/Swedish mil. Its size can vary from system to system, but in each is between 1 and 10 kilometers. In contemporary English contexts _____ refers to either:
a. Thing
b. Mile0
c. Undefined
d. Undefined

44. _____ are a measure of time.
a. Thing
b. Minutes0
c. Undefined
d. Undefined

45. In mathematics, a _____ is the end result of a division problem. It can also be expressed as the number of times the divisor divides into the dividend.
a. Quotient0
b. Thing
c. Undefined
d. Undefined

46. The function difference divided by the point difference is known as the _____
a. Difference quotient0
b. Thing
c. Undefined
d. Undefined

47. An _____ is a combination of numbers, operators, grouping symbols and/or free variables and bound variables arranged in a meaningful way which can be evaluated..
a. Thing
b. Expression0
c. Undefined
d. Undefined

50 Chapter 3. THE DERIVATIVE

48. In mathematics, a _____ of a k-place relation L ⊆ X$_1$ × ... × X$_k$ is one of the sets X$_j$, 1 ≤ j ≤ k. In the special case where k = 2 and L ⊆ X$_1$ × X$_2$ is a function L : X$_1$ → X$_2$, it is conventional to refer to X$_1$ as the _____ of the function and to refer to X$_2$ as the codomain of the function.
- a. Thing
- b. Domain0
- c. Undefined
- d. Undefined

49. In trigonometry, the _____ is a function defined as tan x = $^{\sin x}/_{\cos x}$. The function is so-named because it can be defined as the length of a certain segment of a _____ (in the geometric sense) to the unit circle. In plane geometry, a line is _____ to a curve, at some point, if both line and curve pass through the point with the same direction.
- a. Tangent0
- b. Thing
- c. Undefined
- d. Undefined

50. _____ has two distinct but etymologically-related meanings: one in geometry and one in trigonometry.
- a. Tangent line0
- b. Thing
- c. Undefined
- d. Undefined

51. In mathematics, the _____ f is the collection of all ordered pairs . In particular, graph means the graphical representation of this collection, in the form of a curve or surface, together with axes, etc. Graphing on a Cartesian plane is sometimes referred to as curve sketching.
- a. Graph of a function0
- b. Thing
- c. Undefined
- d. Undefined

52. _____ are the basic objects of study in graph theory. Informally speaking, a graph is a set of objects called points, nodes, or vertices connected by links called lines or edges.
- a. Thing
- b. Graphs0
- c. Undefined
- d. Undefined

53. In linear algebra, the _____ of an n-by-n square matrix A is defined to be the sum of the elements on the main diagonal of A,
- a. Trace0
- b. Thing
- c. Undefined
- d. Undefined

54. Mathematical _____ is used to represent ideas.
- a. Notation0
- b. Thing
- c. Undefined
- d. Undefined

55. A _____ is a symbolic representation denoting a quantity or expression. It often represents an "unknown" quantity that has the potential to change.
- a. Thing
- b. Variable0
- c. Undefined
- d. Undefined

56. A frame of _____ is a particular perspective from which the universe is observed.
- a. Thing
- b. Reference0
- c. Undefined
- d. Undefined

57. _____ is the state of being greater than any finite real or natural number, however large.

Chapter 3. THE DERIVATIVE

a. Thing
c. Undefined

b. Infinite0
d. Undefined

58. Continuous functions are of utmost importance in mathematics and applications. However, not all functions are continuous. If a function is not continuous at a point in its domain, one says that it has a _____ there. The set of all points of _____ of a function may be a discrete set, a dense set, or even the entire domain of the function.

a. Discontinuity0
c. Undefined

b. Thing
d. Undefined

59. A _____ function is a function for which, intuitively, small changes in the input result in small changes in the output.

a. Continuous0
c. Undefined

b. Event
d. Undefined

60. A _____ defined function $f(x)$ of a real variable x is a function whose definition is given differently on disjoint subsets of its domain.

a. Piecewise0
c. Undefined

b. Thing
d. Undefined

61. In mathematics, a _____ is a countable collection of open covers of a topological space that satisfies certain separation axioms.

a. Development0
c. Undefined

b. Thing
d. Undefined

62. A _____ is the sum of the elements of a sequence.

a. Series0
c. Undefined

b. Thing
d. Undefined

63. A _____ is a function for which, intuitively, small changes in the input result in small changes in the output.

a. Continuous function0
c. Undefined

b. Event
d. Undefined

64. In mathematics, a _____ is a demonstration that, assuming certain axioms, some statement is necessarily true.

a. Thing
c. Undefined

b. Proof0
d. Undefined

65. In colloquial usage, a _____ is "a rough or fragmented geometric shape that can be subdivided in parts, each of which is, at least approximately, a reduced-size copy of the whole."

a. Fractal0
c. Undefined

b. Concept
d. Undefined

66. In economics, supply and _____ describe market relations between prospective sellers and buyers of a good.

a. Thing
c. Undefined

b. Demand0
d. Undefined

Chapter 3. THE DERIVATIVE

67. In common philosophical language, a proposition or _____, is the content of an assertion, that is, it is true-or-false and defined by the meaning of a particular piece of language.
    a. Concept
    b. Statement0
    c. Undefined
    d. Undefined

68. _____ is a set, with some particular properties and usually some additional structure, such as the operations of addition or multiplication, for instance.
    a. Space0
    b. Thing
    c. Undefined
    d. Undefined

69. In physics, _____ is an influence that may cause an object to accelerate. It may be experienced as a lift, a push, or a pull. The actual acceleration of the body is determined by the vector sum of all forces acting on it, known as net _____ or resultant _____.
    a. Force0
    b. Thing
    c. Undefined
    d. Undefined

70. In mathematics, an _____ is any of the arguments, i.e. "inputs", to a function. Thus if we have a function f(x), then x is a _____.
    a. Independent variable0
    b. Thing
    c. Undefined
    d. Undefined

71. In a function the _____, is the variable which is the value, i.e. the "output", of the function.
    a. Thing
    b. Dependent variable0
    c. Undefined
    d. Undefined

72. In geometry, an _____ is a point at which a line segment or ray terminates.
    a. Thing
    b. Endpoint0
    c. Undefined
    d. Undefined

73. Equivalence is the condition of being _____ or essentially equal.
    a. Thing
    b. Equivalent0
    c. Undefined
    d. Undefined

74. In mathematics, the _____ of a function is the set of all "output" values produced by that function. Given a function $f : A \to B$, the _____ of f, is defined to be the set $\{x \in B : x = f(a) \text{ for some } a \in A\}$.
    a. Range0
    b. Thing
    c. Undefined
    d. Undefined

75. In mathematics and the mathematical sciences, a _____ is a fixed, but possibly unspecified, value. This is in contrast to a variable, which is not fixed.
    a. Thing
    b. Constant0
    c. Undefined
    d. Undefined

76. In mathematics, science including computer science, linguistics and engineering, an _____ is, generally speaking, an independent variable or input to a function.

Chapter 3. THE DERIVATIVE

a. Thing
b. Argument0
c. Undefined
d. Undefined

77. _____ is the application of tools and a processing medium to the transformation of raw materials into finished goods for sale.
a. Thing
b. Manufacturing0
c. Undefined
d. Undefined

78. U.S. liquid _____ is legally defined as 231 cubic inches, and is equal to 3.785411784 litres or abotu 0.13368 cubic feet. This is the most common definition of a _____. The U.S. fluid ounce is defined as 1/128 of a U.S. _____.
a. Thing
b. Gallon0
c. Undefined
d. Undefined

79. In mathematics, a _____ is a quadric surface, with the following equation in Cartesian coordinates: $(x/_a)^2 + (y/_b)^2 = 1$.
a. Thing
b. Cylinder0
c. Undefined
d. Undefined

80. The _____ of a mathematical object is its size: a property by which it can be larger or smaller than other objects of the same kind; in technical terms, an ordering of the class of objects to which it belongs.
a. Magnitude0
b. Thing
c. Undefined
d. Undefined

81. The _____ is a unit of plane angle. It is represented by the symbol "rad" or, more rarely, by the superscript c (for "circular measure"). For example, an angle of 1.2 radians would be written "1.2 rad" or "1.2c" (second symbol can produce confusion with centigrads).
a. Radian0
b. Thing
c. Undefined
d. Undefined

82. In mathematics, a _____ is a constant multiplicative factor of a certain object. The object can be such things as a variable, a vector, a function, etc. For example, the _____ of $9x^2$ is 9.
a. Thing
b. Coefficient0
c. Undefined
d. Undefined

83. _____ is the force that opposes the relative motion or tendency toward such motion of two surfaces in contact.
a. Thing
b. Friction0
c. Undefined
d. Undefined

84. The _____ is the total number of human beings alive on the planet Earth at a given time.
a. World population0
b. Thing
c. Undefined
d. Undefined

85. In sociology and biology a _____ is the collection of people or organisms of a particular species living in a given geographic area or space, usually measured by a census.

a. Population0
b. Thing
c. Undefined
d. Undefined

86. A _____ fraction is a fraction in which the absolute value of the numerator is less than the denominator--hence, the absolute value of the fraction is less than 1.
   a. Thing
   b. Proper0
   c. Undefined
   d. Undefined

87. Sir Isaac _____, was an English physicist, mathematician, astronomer, natural philosopher, and alchemist, regarded by many as the greatest figure in the history of science
   a. Newton0
   b. Person
   c. Undefined
   d. Undefined

88. In mathematics, two quantities are called _____ if they vary in such a way that one of the quantities is a constant multiple of the other, or equivalently if they have a constant ratio.
   a. Proportional0
   b. Thing
   c. Undefined
   d. Undefined

89. _____ is a temperature scale named after the German physicist Daniel Gabriel _____ , who proposed it in 1724.
   a. Thing
   b. Fahrenheit0
   c. Undefined
   d. Undefined

90. In mathematics, there are several meanings of _____ depending on the subject.
   a. Thing
   b. Degree0
   c. Undefined
   d. Undefined

91. _____ is a special mathematical relationship between two quantities. Two quantities are called proportional if they vary in such a way that one of the quantities is a constant multiple of the other, or equivalently if they have a constant ratio.
   a. Thing
   b. Proportionality0
   c. Undefined
   d. Undefined

92. The _____, the average in everyday English, which is also called the arithmetic _____ (and is distinguished from the geometric _____ or harmonic _____). The average is also called the sample _____. The expected value of a random variable, which is also called the population _____.
   a. Mean0
   b. Thing
   c. Undefined
   d. Undefined

93. _____ is a function whose values do not vary and thus are constant.
   a. Constant function0
   b. Thing
   c. Undefined
   d. Undefined

94. In mathematics, a _____ may be described informally as a number that can be given by an infinite decimal representation.

Chapter 3. THE DERIVATIVE

a. Real number0
b. Thing
c. Undefined
d. Undefined

95. In mathematics, a _____ is a statement that can be proved on the basis of explicitly stated or previously agreed assumptions.
    a. Theorem0
    b. Thing
    c. Undefined
    d. Undefined

96. A _____ is the result of the addition of a set of numbers. The numbers may be natural numbers, complex numbers, matrices, or still more complicated objects. An infinite _____ is a subtle procedure known as a series.
    a. Sum0
    b. Thing
    c. Undefined
    d. Undefined

97. In chemistry, a _____ is substance made by combining two or more different materials in such a way that no chemical reaction occurs.
    a. Mixture0
    b. Thing
    c. Undefined
    d. Undefined

98. The _____ governs the differentiation of products of differentiable functions.
    a. Thing
    b. Product rule0
    c. Undefined
    d. Undefined

99. The _____ is a method of finding the derivative of a function that is the quotient of two other functions for which derivatives exist.
    a. Quotient rule0
    b. Thing
    c. Undefined
    d. Undefined

100. A _____ is a numeral used to indicate a count. The most common use of the word today is to name the part of a fraction that tells the number or count of equal parts.
    a. Thing
    b. Numerator0
    c. Undefined
    d. Undefined

101. The _____ of a solid object is the three-dimensional concept of how much space it occupies, often quantified numerically.
    a. Thing
    b. Volume0
    c. Undefined
    d. Undefined

102. In mathematics, a _____ is a mathematical statement which appears likely to be true, but has not been formally proven to be true under the rules of mathematical logic.
    a. Concept
    b. Conjecture0
    c. Undefined
    d. Undefined

103. A _____ is a set of numbers that designate location in a given reference system, such as x,y in a planar _____ system or an x,y,z in a three-dimensional _____ system.

a. Coordinate0
b. Thing
c. Undefined
d. Undefined

104. In mathematics, the _____ is a conic section generated by the intersection of a right circular conical surface and a plane parallel to a generating straight line of that surface. It can also be defined as locus of points in a plane which are equidistant from a given point.
   a. Parabola0
   b. Thing
   c. Undefined
   d. Undefined

105. An _____ is when two lines intersect somewhere on a plane creating a right angle at intersection
   a. Thing
   b. Axes0
   c. Undefined
   d. Undefined

106. A _____ is one of the basic shapes of geometry: a polygon with three vertices and three sides which are straight line segments.
   a. Thing
   b. Triangle0
   c. Undefined
   d. Undefined

107. In plane geometry, a _____ is a polygon with four equal sides, four right angles, and parallel opposite sides. In algebra, the _____ of a number is that number multiplied by itself.
   a. Square0
   b. Thing
   c. Undefined
   d. Undefined

108. In mathematics, a _____ is an expression that is constructed from one or more variables and constants, using only the operations of addition, subtraction, multiplication, and constant positive whole number exponents. is a _____. Note in particular that division by an expression containing a variable is not in general allowed in polynomials. [1]
   a. Polynomial0
   b. Thing
   c. Undefined
   d. Undefined

109. _____ algebra (sometimes called General algebra) is the field of mathematics that studies the ideas common to all algebraic structures.
   a. Universal0
   b. Thing
   c. Undefined
   d. Undefined

110. _____ is the property of a physical object that quantifies the amount of matter and energy it is equivalent to.
   a. Mass0
   b. Thing
   c. Undefined
   d. Undefined

111. _____ is, or relates to, the _____ temperature scale .
   a. Thing
   b. Celsius0
   c. Undefined
   d. Undefined

112. In mathematics, the _____ functions are functions of an angle; they are important when studying triangles and modeling periodic phenomena, among many other applications.

Chapter 3. THE DERIVATIVE

a. Trigonometric0
b. Thing
c. Undefined
d. Undefined

113. The _____ are functions of an angle; they are important when studying triangles and modeling periodic phenomena, among many other applications.
    a. Trigonometric functions0
    b. Thing
    c. Undefined
    d. Undefined

114. _____ is a trigonemtric function that is important when studying triangles and modeling periodic phenomena, among other applications.
    a. Sine0
    b. Thing
    c. Undefined
    d. Undefined

115. The _____ of a geographic location is its height above a fixed reference point, often the mean sea level.
    a. Thing
    b. Elevation0
    c. Undefined
    d. Undefined

116. The plus and _____ signs are mathematical symbols used to represent the notions of positive and negative as well as the operations of addition and subtraction.
    a. Minus0
    b. Thing
    c. Undefined
    d. Undefined

117. _____ is electromagnetic radiation with a wavelength that is visible to the eye (visible _____) or, in a technical or scientific context, electromagnetic radiation of any wavelength.
    a. Thing
    b. Light0
    c. Undefined
    d. Undefined

118. In calculus, the _____ is a formula for the derivative of the composite of two functions.
    a. Chain rule0
    b. Concept
    c. Undefined
    d. Undefined

119. A _____ is a negotiable instrument instructing a financial institution to pay a specific amount of a specific currency from a specific demand account held in the maker/depositor's name with that institution. Both the maker and payee may be natural persons or legal entities.
    a. Check0
    b. Thing
    c. Undefined
    d. Undefined

120. In economics, economic _____ is simply a state of the world where economic forces are balanced and in the absence of external influences the values of economic variables will not change.
    a. Equilibrium0
    b. Thing
    c. Undefined
    d. Undefined

121. In acoustics and telecommunication, the _____ of a wave is a component frequency of the signal that is an integer multiple of the fundamental frequency.

Chapter 3. THE DERIVATIVE

a. Harmonic0
b. Thing
c. Undefined
d. Undefined

122. Simple _____ is the motion of a simple harmonic oscillator, a motion that is neither driven nor damped. Complex _____ is the superposition — linear combination — of several simultaneous simple harmonic motions.
    a. Thing
    b. Harmonic motion0
    c. Undefined
    d. Undefined

123. _____ is a kind of property which exists as magnitude or multitude. It is among the basic classes of things along with quality, substance, change, and relation.
    a. Thing
    b. Amount0
    c. Undefined
    d. Undefined

124. The _____ is a nonnegative scalar measure of a wave's magnitude of oscillation, that is, the magnitude of the maximum disturbance in the medium during one wave cycle.
    a. Amplitude0
    b. Thing
    c. Undefined
    d. Undefined

125. In physics, the _____ momentum of an object rotating about some reference point is the measure of the extent to which the object will continue to rotate about that point unless acted upon by an external torque.
    a. Thing
    b. Angular0
    c. Undefined
    d. Undefined

126. _____ is a scalar measure of rotation rate. It is the magnitude of the vector quantity angular velocity.
    a. Thing
    b. Angular frequency0
    c. Undefined
    d. Undefined

127. In statistics the _____ of an event i is the number n_i of times the event occurred in the experiment or the study. These frequencies are often graphically represented in histograms.
    a. Concept
    b. Frequency0
    c. Undefined
    d. Undefined

128. In geometry, an _____ of a triangle is a straight line through a vertex and perpendicular to (i.e. forming a right angle with) the opposite side or an extension of the opposite side.
    a. Altitude0
    b. Concept
    c. Undefined
    d. Undefined

129. _____ is to give an equation $R(x,y) = S(x,y)$ that at least in part has the same graph as $y = f(x)$.
    a. Implicit differentiation0
    b. Thing
    c. Undefined
    d. Undefined

130. The deductive-nomological model is a formalized view of scientific _____ in natural language.
    a. Thing
    b. Explanation0
    c. Undefined
    d. Undefined

Chapter 3. THE DERIVATIVE

131. In physics, an _____ is the path that an object makes around another object while under the influence of a source of centripetal force, such as gravity.
    a. Thing
    b. Orbit0
    c. Undefined
    d. Undefined

132. In geometry, the _____ of an object is a point in some sense in the middle of the object.
    a. Thing
    b. Center0
    c. Undefined
    d. Undefined

133. _____ is the point at which an object in orbit around the Earth makes its closest approach to the Earth.
    a. Thing
    b. Perigee0
    c. Undefined
    d. Undefined

134. The _____ is the point in the Moon's orbit that is farthest from the Earth.
    a. Apogee0
    b. Thing
    c. Undefined
    d. Undefined

135. In geometry, a _____ (Greek words diairo = divide and metro = measure) of a circle is any straight line segment that passes through the centre and whose endpoints are on the circular boundary, or, in more modern usage, the length of such a line segment. When using the word in the more modern sense, one speaks of the _____ rather than a _____, because all diameters of a circle have the same length. This length is twice the radius. The _____ of a circle is also the longest chord that the circle has.
    a. Thing
    b. Diameter0
    c. Undefined
    d. Undefined

136. In differential calculus, _____ problems involve finding the rate at which a quantity is changing by relating that quantity to other quantities whose rates of change are known.
    a. Related rates0
    b. Thing
    c. Undefined
    d. Undefined

137. _____ is the path a moving object follows through space.
    a. Projectile motion0
    b. Thing
    c. Undefined
    d. Undefined

138. In geometry, two lines or planes if one falls on the other in such a way as to create congruent adjacent angles. The term may be used as a noun or adjective. Thus, referring to Figure 1, the line AB is the _____ to CD through the point B.
    a. Perpendicular0
    b. Thing
    c. Undefined
    d. Undefined

139. The _____ of an angle is the ratio of the length of the adjacent side to the length of the hypotenuse.
    a. Concept
    b. Cosine0
    c. Undefined
    d. Undefined

140. The _____ is a statement about a general triangle which relates the lengths of its sides to the cosine of one of its angles.

Chapter 3. THE DERIVATIVE

a. Thing
b. Law of cosines0
c. Undefined
d. Undefined

141. In mathematics, _____ is a part of the set theoretic notion of function.
a. Thing
b. Image0
c. Undefined
d. Undefined

142. _____, Greek for "knowledge of nature," is the branch of science concerned with the discovery and characterization of universal laws which govern matter, energy, space, and time.
a. Thing
b. Physics0
c. Undefined
d. Undefined

143. In geometry, a _____ is a special kind of point, usually a corner of a polygon, polyhedron, or higher dimensional polytope. In the geometry of curves a _____ is a point of where the first derivative of curvature is zero. In graph theory, a _____ is the fundamental unit out of which graphs are formed
a. Vertex0
b. Thing
c. Undefined
d. Undefined

144. A _____ is a three-dimensional geometric shape formed by straight lines through a fixed point (vertex) to the points of a fixed curve (directrix)
a. Cone0
b. Concept
c. Undefined
d. Undefined

145. _____ is an approximation of a general function using a linear function more precisely, an affine function.
a. Linear approximation0
b. Thing
c. Undefined
d. Undefined

146. _____ is a unit of plane angle, equal to 180/δ degrees, or about 57.2958 degrees
a. Thing
b. Radian measure0
c. Undefined
d. Undefined

147. _____ was a German mathematician and philosopher. He invented calculus independently of Newton, and his notation is the one in general use since.
a. Person
b. Leibniz0
c. Undefined
d. Undefined

148. A _____ is traditionally an infinitesimally small change in a variable.
a. Thing
b. Differential0
c. Undefined
d. Undefined

149. _____ named in honor of the 17th century German philosopher and mathematician Gottfried Wilhelm Leibniz, was originally the use of expressions such as dx and dy and to represent "infinitely small" or infinitesimal increments of quantities x and y, just as Äx and Äy represent finite increments of x and y respectively.
a. Leibniz notation0
b. Thing
c. Undefined
d. Undefined

Chapter 3. THE DERIVATIVE

150. A _____ is a quantity that denotes the proportional amount or magnitude of one quantity relative to another.
  a. Thing
  b. Ratio0
  c. Undefined
  d. Undefined

151. _____ are objects, characters, or other concrete representations of ideas, concepts, or other abstractions.
  a. Thing
  b. Symbols0
  c. Undefined
  d. Undefined

152. A _____ is a number, figure, or indicator that appears below the normal line of type, typically used in a formula, mathematical expression, or description of a chemical compound.
  a. Subscript0
  b. Thing
  c. Undefined
  d. Undefined

153. An _____ is an increase, either of some fixed amount, for example added regularly, or of a variable amount.
  a. Increment0
  b. Thing
  c. Undefined
  d. Undefined

154. A _____ is 360° or 2δ radians.
  a. Thing
  b. Turn0
  c. Undefined
  d. Undefined

155. _____ is the estimation of a physical quantity such as distance, energy, temperature, or time.
  a. Thing
  b. Measurement0
  c. Undefined
  d. Undefined

156. The term _____ is defined dually as an element of P which is lesser than or equal to every element of S.
  a. Thing
  b. Lower bound0
  c. Undefined
  d. Undefined

157. In the mathematical field of numerical analysis, the _____ in some data is the discrepancy between an exact value and some approximation to it.
  a. Thing
  b. Approximation Error0
  c. Undefined
  d. Undefined

158. A _____ is a deliberate process for transforming one or more inputs into one or more results.
  a. Calculation0
  b. Thing
  c. Undefined
  d. Undefined

159. In mathematics, a _____ is the set of all points in three-dimensional space (R^3) which are at distance r from a fixed point of that space, where r is a positive real number called the radius of the _____. The fixed point is called the center or centre, and is not part of the _____ itself.
  a. Sphere0
  b. Thing
  c. Undefined
  d. Undefined

160. A _____ is a three-dimensional solid object bounded by six square faces, facets, or sides, with three meeting at each vertex.

Chapter 3. THE DERIVATIVE

    a. Cube0   b. Thing
    c. Undefined   d. Undefined

161. The _____ of a right triangle is the triangle's longest side; the side opposite the right angle.
    a. Hypotenuse0   b. Thing
    c. Undefined   d. Undefined

162. _____ has one 90° internal angle a right angle.
    a. Thing   b. Right triangle0
    c. Undefined   d. Undefined

163. Angles smaller than a right angle are called _____ angles (less than 90 degrees).
    a. Acute0   b. Concept
    c. Undefined   d. Undefined

164. In geometry, _____ angles are angles that have a common ray coming out of the vertex going between two other rays.
    a. Concept   b. Adjacent0
    c. Undefined   d. Undefined

165. _____ is a way of expressing a number as a fraction of 100 per cent meaning "per hundred".
    a. Percent0   b. Thing
    c. Undefined   d. Undefined

166. A _____ is an object that is attached to a pivot point so that it can swing freely.
    a. Thing   b. Pendulum0
    c. Undefined   d. Undefined

167. _____ is defined as the rate of change or derivative with respect to time of velocity.
    a. Thing   b. Acceleration0
    c. Undefined   d. Undefined

168. An _____ of a product of sums expresses it as a sum of products by using the fact that multiplication distributes over addition.
    a. Thing   b. Expansion0
    c. Undefined   d. Undefined

169. In mathematics, _____ geometry was the traditional name for the geometry of three-dimensional Euclidean space — for practical purposes the kind of space we live in.
    a. Solid0   b. Thing
    c. Undefined   d. Undefined

170. A pair of angles is _____ if their respective measures sum to 180 degrees.
    a. Concept   b. Supplementary0
    c. Undefined   d. Undefined

Chapter 3. THE DERIVATIVE

171. An n-sided _____ is a polyhedron formed by connecting an n-sided polygonal base and a point, called the apex, by n triangular faces. In other words, it is a conic solid with polygonal base.
   a. Pyramid0
   b. Thing
   c. Undefined
   d. Undefined

172. The metre (or _____, see spelling differences) is a measure of length. It is the basic unit of length in the metric system and in the International System of Units (SI), used around the world for general and scientific purposes.
   a. Concept
   b. Meter0
   c. Undefined
   d. Undefined

173. _____ is the science and technology of robots, their design, manufacture, and application
   a. Thing
   b. Robotics0
   c. Undefined
   d. Undefined

174. _____ is the design, analysis, and/or construction of works for practical purposes.
   a. Engineering0
   b. Thing
   c. Undefined
   d. Undefined

175. _____ statistics are statistics that estimate population parameters.
   a. Parametric0
   b. Thing
   c. Undefined
   d. Undefined

176. In mathematics, _____ bear slight similarity to functions: they allow one to use arbitrary values, called parameters, in place of independent variables in equations, which in turn provide values for dependent variables. A simple kinematical example is when one uses a time parameter to determine the position, velocity, and other information about a body in motion.
   a. Parametric equations0
   b. Thing
   c. Undefined
   d. Undefined

177. An _____ is an equality that remains true regardless of the values of any variables that appear within it, to distinguish it from an equality which is true under more particular conditions.
   a. Thing
   b. Identity0
   c. Undefined
   d. Undefined

178. A _____ is a movement of an object in a circular motion. A two-dimensional object rotates around a center (or point) of _____. A three-dimensional object rotates around a line called an axis. If the axis of _____ is within the body, the body is said to rotate upon itself, or spin—which implies relative speed and perhaps free-movement with angular momentum. A circular motion about an external point, e.g. the Earth about the Sun, is called an orbit or more properly an orbital revolution.
   a. Rotation0
   b. Thing
   c. Undefined
   d. Undefined

Chapter 4. THE DERIVATIVE IN GRAPHING AND APPLICATIONS

1. _____ is a mathematical subject that includes the study of limits, derivatives, integrals, and power series and constitutes a major part of modern university curriculum.
   a. Calculus0
   b. Thing
   c. Undefined
   d. Undefined

2. The mathematical concept of a _____ expresses the intuitive idea of deterministic dependence between two quantities, one of which is viewed as primary and the other as secondary. A _____ then is a way to associate a unique output for each input of a specified type, for example, a real number or an element of a given set.
   a. Thing
   b. Function0
   c. Undefined
   d. Undefined

3. In computer science, an _____ is the problem of finding the best solution from all feasible solutions.
   a. Thing
   b. Optimization problem0
   c. Undefined
   d. Undefined

4. The _____ is a measurement of how a function changes when the values of its inputs change.
   a. Derivative0
   b. Thing
   c. Undefined
   d. Undefined

5. _____ the expected value of a random variable displays the average or central value of the variable. It is a summary value of the distribution of the variable.
   a. Thing
   b. Determining0
   c. Undefined
   d. Undefined

6. In elementary algebra, an _____ is a set that contains every real number between two indicated numbers and may contain the two numbers themselves.
   a. Thing
   b. Interval0
   c. Undefined
   d. Undefined

7. The word _____ means curving in or hollowed inward.
   a. Concavity0
   b. Thing
   c. Undefined
   d. Undefined

8. The _____, the average in everyday English, which is also called the arithmetic _____ (and is distinguished from the geometric _____ or harmonic _____). The average is also called the sample _____. The expected value of a random variable, which is also called the population _____.
   a. Thing
   b. Mean0
   c. Undefined
   d. Undefined

9. _____ is the transport of people on a trip/journey or the process or time involved in a person or object moving from one location to another.
   a. Travel0
   b. Thing
   c. Undefined
   d. Undefined

10. In mathematics and the mathematical sciences, a _____ is a fixed, but possibly unspecified, value. This is in contrast to a variable, which is not fixed.

Chapter 4. THE DERIVATIVE IN GRAPHING AND APPLICATIONS

    a. Thing
    b. Constant0
    c. Undefined
    d. Undefined

11. _____ is often used to describe the measurement of the steepness, incline, gradient, or grade of a straight line. The _____ is defined as the ratio of the "rise" divided by the "run" between two points on a line, or in other words, the ratio of the altitude change to the horizontal distance between any two points on the line.
    a. Slope0
    b. Thing
    c. Undefined
    d. Undefined

12. A _____ function is a function for which, intuitively, small changes in the input result in small changes in the output.
    a. Event
    b. Continuous0
    c. Undefined
    d. Undefined

13. In mathematics, a _____ is a statement that can be proved on the basis of explicitly stated or previously agreed assumptions.
    a. Thing
    b. Theorem0
    c. Undefined
    d. Undefined

14. In a mathematical proof or a syllogism, a _____ is a statement that is the logical consequence of preceding statements.
    a. Conclusion0
    b. Concept
    c. Undefined
    d. Undefined

15. In mathematics, a _____ is a mathematical statement which appears likely to be true, but has not been formally proven to be true under the rules of mathematical logic.
    a. Concept
    b. Conjecture0
    c. Undefined
    d. Undefined

16. In mathematics, _____ refers to a number of loosely related concepts in different areas of geometry. Intuitively, _____ is the amount by which a geometric object deviates from being flat, but this is defined in different ways depending on the context
    a. Thing
    b. Curvature0
    c. Undefined
    d. Undefined

17. In trigonometry, the _____ is a function defined as $\tan x = \sin x / \cos x$. The function is so-named because it can be defined as the length of a certain segment of a _____ (in the geometric sense) to the unit circle. In plane geometry, a line is _____ to a curve, at some point, if both line and curve pass through the point with the same direction.
    a. Thing
    b. Tangent0
    c. Undefined
    d. Undefined

18. _____ has two distinct but etymologically-related meanings: one in geometry and one in trigonometry.
    a. Tangent line0
    b. Thing
    c. Undefined
    d. Undefined

19. _____ is the study of terms and their use — of words and compound words that are used in specific contexts.

Chapter 4. THE DERIVATIVE IN GRAPHING AND APPLICATIONS

a. Terminology0
b. Thing
c. Undefined
d. Undefined

20. A _____ is a negotiable instrument instructing a financial institution to pay a specific amount of a specific currency from a specific demand account held in the maker/depositor's name with that institution. Both the maker and payee may be natural persons or legal entities.
    a. Check0
    b. Thing
    c. Undefined
    d. Undefined

21. _____ is a a point on a curve at which the tangent crosses the curve itself.
    a. Thing
    b. Inflection point0
    c. Undefined
    d. Undefined

22. In mathematics, the concept of a _____ tries to capture the intuitive idea of a geometrical one-dimensional and continuous object. A simple example is the circle.
    a. Curve0
    b. Thing
    c. Undefined
    d. Undefined

23. A _____ is a special kind of ratio, indicating a relationship between two measurements with different units, such as miles to gallons or cents to pounds.
    a. Rate0
    b. Thing
    c. Undefined
    d. Undefined

24. In geometry, a _____ (Greek words diairo = divide and metro = measure) of a circle is any straight line segment that passes through the centre and whose endpoints are on the circular boundary, or, in more modern usage, the length of such a line segment. When using the word in the more modern sense, one speaks of the _____ rather than a _____, because all diameters of a circle have the same length. This length is twice the radius. The _____ of a circle is also the longest chord that the circle has.
    a. Diameter0
    b. Thing
    c. Undefined
    d. Undefined

25. In mathematics, the _____ of a coordinate system is the point where the axes of the system intersect.
    a. Thing
    b. Origin0
    c. Undefined
    d. Undefined

26. In mathematics, the _____ functions are functions of an angle; they are important when studying triangles and modeling periodic phenomena, among many other applications.
    a. Thing
    b. Trigonometric0
    c. Undefined
    d. Undefined

27. A _____ is a set of numbers that designate location in a given reference system, such as x,y in a planar _____ system or an x,y,z in a three-dimensional _____ system.
    a. Thing
    b. Coordinate0
    c. Undefined
    d. Undefined

Chapter 4. THE DERIVATIVE IN GRAPHING AND APPLICATIONS

28. _____ are the basic objects of study in graph theory. Informally speaking, a graph is a set of objects called points, nodes, or vertices connected by links called lines or edges.
   a. Graphs0
   b. Thing
   c. Undefined
   d. Undefined

29. In common philosophical language, a proposition or _____, is the content of an assertion, that is, it is true-or-false and defined by the meaning of a particular piece of language.
   a. Statement0
   b. Concept
   c. Undefined
   d. Undefined

30. In mathematics, a _____ is an expression that is constructed from one or more variables and constants, using only the operations of addition, subtraction, multiplication, and constant positive whole number exponents. is a _____. Note in particular that division by an expression containing a variable is not in general allowed in polynomials. [1]
   a. Polynomial0
   b. Thing
   c. Undefined
   d. Undefined

31. In mathematics, an _____, mean, or central tendency of a data set refers to a measure of the "middle" or "expected" value of the data set.
   a. Average0
   b. Concept
   c. Undefined
   d. Undefined

32. Any point where a graph makes contact with an coordinate axis is called an _____ of the graph
   a. Thing
   b. Intercept0
   c. Undefined
   d. Undefined

33. A _____ is a landform that extends above the surrounding terrain in a limited area. A _____ is generally steeper than a hill, but there is no universally accepted standard definition for the height of a _____ or a hill although a _____ usually has an identifiable summit.
   a. Thing
   b. Mountain0
   c. Undefined
   d. Undefined

34. In mathematics, the _____ f is the collection of all ordered pairs . In particular, graph means the graphical representation of this collection, in the form of a curve or surface, together with axes, etc. Graphing on a Cartesian plane is sometimes referred to as curve sketching.
   a. Graph of a function0
   b. Thing
   c. Undefined
   d. Undefined

35. In mathematics, the _____ of a function is the set of all "output" values produced by that function. Given a function $f : A \to B$, the _____ of f, is defined to be the set $\{x \in B : x = f(a)$ for some $a \in A\}$.
   a. Thing
   b. Range0
   c. Undefined
   d. Undefined

36. _____ is a free computer algebra system based on a 1982 version of Macsyma
   a. Thing
   b. Maxima0
   c. Undefined
   d. Undefined

Chapter 4. THE DERIVATIVE IN GRAPHING AND APPLICATIONS

37. In mathematics, maxima and _____, known collectively as extrema, are points in the domain of a function at which the function takes a largest value.
   a. Minima0
   b. Thing
   c. Undefined
   d. Undefined

38. The _____ is the highest point in a certain portion of a graph.
   a. Thing
   b. Relative maximum0
   c. Undefined
   d. Undefined

39. In mathematics, maxima and minima, known collectively as extrema, are the largest value maximum or smallest value minimum, that a function takes in a point either within a given neighborhood local _____ or on the function domain in its entirety global _____.
   a. Thing
   b. Extremum0
   c. Undefined
   d. Undefined

40. The _____ is the lowest point in a certain portion of a graph.
   a. Relative minimum0
   b. Thing
   c. Undefined
   d. Undefined

41. in mathematics, maxima and minima, known collectively as _____, are the largest value maximum or smallest value minimum, that a function takes in a point either within a given neighborhood or on the function domain in its entirety global extremum.
   a. Extrema0
   b. Thing
   c. Undefined
   d. Undefined

42. A _____ of a number is the product of that number with any integer.
   a. Thing
   b. Multiple0
   c. Undefined
   d. Undefined

43. A _____ is a function for which, intuitively, small changes in the input result in small changes in the output.
   a. Event
   b. Continuous function0
   c. Undefined
   d. Undefined

44. In astronomy, geography, geometry and related sciences and contexts, a plane is said to be _____ at a given point if it is locally perpendicular to the gradient of the gravity field, i.e., with the direction of the gravitational force at that point.
   a. Horizontal0
   b. Thing
   c. Undefined
   d. Undefined

45. The term _____ refers to the largest and the smallest element of a set.
   a. Thing
   b. Extreme value0
   c. Undefined
   d. Undefined

46. In mathematics, a _____ of a k-place relation $L \subseteq X_1 \times ... \times X_k$ is one of the sets X_j, $1 \leq j \leq k$. In the special case where k = 2 and $L \subseteq X_1 \times X_2$ is a function $L : X_1 \to X_2$, it is conventional to refer to X_1 as the _____ of the function and to refer to X_2 as the codomain of the function.

Chapter 4. THE DERIVATIVE IN GRAPHING AND APPLICATIONS

a. Domain0
b. Thing
c. Undefined
d. Undefined

47. Acid _____ ratio measures the ability of a company to use its near cash or quick assets to immediately extinguish its current liabilities.
    a. Test0
    b. Thing
    c. Undefined
    d. Undefined

48. _____ determines whether a given critical point of a function is a maximum, a minimum, or neither.
    a. Thing
    b. First Derivative Test0
    c. Undefined
    d. Undefined

49. The easiest _____ prime numbers resides in the use of the Sieve of Eratosthenes, an algorithm that discovers all prime numbers to a specified integer.
    a. Thing
    b. Method for finding0
    c. Undefined
    d. Undefined

50. In mathematics, a _____ is a demonstration that, assuming certain axioms, some statement is necessarily true.
    a. Proof0
    b. Thing
    c. Undefined
    d. Undefined

51. Two mathematical objects are equal if and only if they are precisely the same in every way. This defines a binary relation, _____, denoted by the sign of _____ "=" in such a way that the statement "x = y" means that x and y are equal.
    a. Equality0
    b. Thing
    c. Undefined
    d. Undefined

52. _____ consists either of a suggested explanation for a phenomenon or of a reasoned proposal suggesting a possible correlation between multiple phenomena.
    a. Event
    b. Hypotheses0
    c. Undefined
    d. Undefined

53. _____ are points in the domain of a function at which the function takes a largest value or smallest value, either within a given neighborhood or on the function domain in its entirety.
    a. Thing
    b. Maxima and minima0
    c. Undefined
    d. Undefined

54. _____ determines whether a given stationary point of a function is a maximum or a minimum.
    a. Second derivative test0
    b. Thing
    c. Undefined
    d. Undefined

55. In mathematics, _____ are the intuitive idea of a geometrical one-dimensional and continuous object.
    a. Thing
    b. Curves0
    c. Undefined
    d. Undefined

Chapter 4. THE DERIVATIVE IN GRAPHING AND APPLICATIONS

56. The _____ are functions of an angle; they are important when studying triangles and modeling periodic phenomena, among many other applications.
   a. Trigonometric functions0
   b. Thing
   c. Undefined
   d. Undefined

57. The _____ of a ring R is defined to be the smallest positive integer n such that $n\,a = 0$, for all a in R.
   a. Thing
   b. Characteristic0
   c. Undefined
   d. Undefined

58. In mathematics, a _____ number is a number which can be expressed as a ratio of two integers. Non-integer _____ numbers (commonly called fractions) are usually written as the vulgar fraction a / b, where b is not zero.
   a. Thing
   b. Rational0
   c. Undefined
   d. Undefined

59. In mathematics, a _____ is any function which can be written as the ratio of two polynomial functions.
   a. Rational function0
   b. Thing
   c. Undefined
   d. Undefined

60. An _____ is a straight line or curve A to which another curve B approaches closer and closer as one moves along it. As one moves along B, the space between it and the _____ A becomes smaller and smaller, and can in fact be made as small as one could wish by going far enough along. A curve may or may not touch or cross its _____. In fact, the curve may intersect the _____ an infinite number of times.
   a. Asymptote0
   b. Thing
   c. Undefined
   d. Undefined

61. _____ is the fee paid on borrowed money.
   a. Thing
   b. Interest0
   c. Undefined
   d. Undefined

62. _____ means "constancy", i.e. if something retains a certain feature even after we change a way of looking at it, then it is symmetric.
   a. Thing
   b. Symmetry0
   c. Undefined
   d. Undefined

63. _____ is a straight line or curve A to which another curve B the one being studied approaches closer and closer as one moves along it.
   a. Thing
   b. Vertical asymptote0
   c. Undefined
   d. Undefined

64. In geographic information systems, a _____ comprises an entity with a geographic location, typically determined by points, arcs, or polygons. Carriageways and cadastres exemplify _____ data.
   a. Thing
   b. Feature0
   c. Undefined
   d. Undefined

65. In mathematics, _____ is an elementary arithmetic operation. When one of the numbers is a whole number, _____ is the repeated sum of the other number.

Chapter 4. THE DERIVATIVE IN GRAPHING AND APPLICATIONS

    a. Thing
    b. Multiplication0
    c. Undefined
    d. Undefined

66. In mathematics, there are several meanings of _____ depending on the subject.
    a. Degree0
    b. Thing
    c. Undefined
    d. Undefined

67. In mathematics, an inequality is a statement about the relative size or order of two objects. For example 14 > 10, or 14 is _____ 10.
    a. Thing
    b. Greater than0
    c. Undefined
    d. Undefined

68. In mathematics, a _____ of a complex-valued function f is a member x of the domain of f such that f(x) vanishes at x, that is, x : f (x) = 0.
    a. Root0
    b. Thing
    c. Undefined
    d. Undefined

69. The _____ of a member of a multiset is how many memberships in the multiset it has.
    a. Thing
    b. Multiplicity0
    c. Undefined
    d. Undefined

70. A _____ is a quantity that denotes the proportional amount or magnitude of one quantity relative to another.
    a. Thing
    b. Ratio0
    c. Undefined
    d. Undefined

71. Continuous functions are of utmost importance in mathematics and applications. However, not all functions are continuous. If a function is not continuous at a point in its domain, one says that it has a _____ there. The set of all points of _____ of a function may be a discrete set, a dense set, or even the entire domain of the function.
    a. Thing
    b. Discontinuity0
    c. Undefined
    d. Undefined

72. An _____ is a straight line around which a geometric figure can be rotated.
    a. Axis0
    b. Thing
    c. Undefined
    d. Undefined

73. A _____ is a numeral used to indicate a count. The most common use of the word today is to name the part of a fraction that tells the number or count of equal parts.
    a. Numerator0
    b. Thing
    c. Undefined
    d. Undefined

74. A _____ is the part of a fraction that tells how many equal parts make up a whole, and which is used in the name of the fraction: "halves", "thirds", "fourths" or "quarters", "fifths" and so on.
    a. Denominator0
    b. Concept
    c. Undefined
    d. Undefined

75. An _____ or member of a set is an object that when collected together make up the set.

Chapter 4. THE DERIVATIVE IN GRAPHING AND APPLICATIONS

a. Element0
b. Thing
c. Undefined
d. Undefined

76. In mathematics, the _____, or members of a set or more generally a class are all those objects which when collected together make up the set or class.
   a. Thing
   b. Elements0
   c. Undefined
   d. Undefined

77. _____ is the symbol used to indicate the nth root of a number
   a. Thing
   b. Radical0
   c. Undefined
   d. Undefined

78. In mathematics, _____ are used to indicate the square root of a number.
   a. Radicals0
   b. Thing
   c. Undefined
   d. Undefined

79. _____ is a mathematical operation, written a^n, involving two numbers, the base a and the exponent n.
   a. Thing
   b. Exponentiating0
   c. Undefined
   d. Undefined

80. _____ is a mathematical operation, written a^n, involving two numbers, the base a and the exponent n.
   a. Exponentiation0
   b. Thing
   c. Undefined
   d. Undefined

81. _____ is a trigonometric function that is the reciprocal of cosine.
   a. Secant0
   b. Thing
   c. Undefined
   d. Undefined

82. _____ of a curve is a line that intersects two or more points on the curve.
   a. Thing
   b. Secant line0
   c. Undefined
   d. Undefined

83. In Euclidean geometry, a _____ is moving every point a constant distance in a specified direction.
   a. Translation0
   b. Concept
   c. Undefined
   d. Undefined

84. The _____ of measurement are a globally standardized and modernized form of the metric system.
   a. Units0
   b. Thing
   c. Undefined
   d. Undefined

85. An _____ is when two lines intersect somewhere on a plane creating a right angle at intersection
   a. Axes0
   b. Thing
   c. Undefined
   d. Undefined

86. In geometry, an _____ angle is an angle that is not a 90 degree angle, or an angle that is divisible by 90: 180, 270, 360/0

Chapter 4. THE DERIVATIVE IN GRAPHING AND APPLICATIONS

    a. Thing
    b. Oblique0
    c. Undefined
    d. Undefined

87. _____ is a trigonemtric function that is important when studying triangles and modeling periodic phenomena, among other applications.
    a. Thing
    b. Sine0
    c. Undefined
    d. Undefined

88. In mathematics, a _____ is the end result of a division problem. It can also be expressed as the number of times the divisor divides into the dividend.
    a. Thing
    b. Quotient0
    c. Undefined
    d. Undefined

89. A _____ is the part of the dividend that is left over when the dividend is not evenly divisible by the divisor.
    a. Remainder0
    b. Thing
    c. Undefined
    d. Undefined

90. _____ is a method of describing limiting behavior.
    a. Thing
    b. Asymptotic0
    c. Undefined
    d. Undefined

91. In geometry, a _____ is defined as a quadrilateral where all four of its angles are right angles.
    a. Rectangle0
    b. Thing
    c. Undefined
    d. Undefined

92. The _____ of a solid object is the three-dimensional concept of how much space it occupies, often quantified numerically.
    a. Thing
    b. Volume0
    c. Undefined
    d. Undefined

93. In plane geometry, a _____ is a polygon with four equal sides, four right angles, and parallel opposite sides. In algebra, the _____ of a number is that number multiplied by itself.
    a. Square0
    b. Thing
    c. Undefined
    d. Undefined

94. In Euclidean geometry, a uniform _____ is a linear transformation that enlargers or diminishes objects, and whose _____ factor is the same in all directions. This is also called homothethy.
    a. Thing
    b. Scale0
    c. Undefined
    d. Undefined

95. A _____ is a symbolic representation denoting a quantity or expression. It often represents an "unknown" quantity that has the potential to change.
    a. Variable0
    b. Thing
    c. Undefined
    d. Undefined

96. _____ of an object is its speed in a particular direction.

Chapter 4. THE DERIVATIVE IN GRAPHING AND APPLICATIONS

    a. Velocity0
    c. Undefined
    b. Thing
    d. Undefined

97. A _____ is 360° or 2δ radians.
    a. Turn0
    c. Undefined
    b. Thing
    d. Undefined

98. In mathematics, the additive inverse, or _____ of a number n is the number that, when added to n, yields zero. The additive inverse of n is denoted −n. For example, 7 is −7, because 7 + (−7) = 0, and the additive inverse of −0.3 is 0.3, because −0.3 + 0.3 = 0.
    a. Opposite0
    c. Undefined
    b. Thing
    d. Undefined

99. In mathematics, the _____ (or modulus) of a real number is its numerical value without regard to its sign.
    a. Absolute value0
    c. Undefined
    b. Thing
    d. Undefined

100. In mathematics, the _____ of a number n is the number that, when added to n, yields zero. The _____ of n is denoted −n. For example, 7 is −7, because 7 + (−7) = 0, and the _____ of −0.3 is 0.3, because −0.3 + 0.3 = 0.
    a. Thing
    c. Undefined
    b. Additive inverse0
    d. Undefined

101. The metre (or _____, see spelling differences) is a measure of length. It is the basic unit of length in the metric system and in the International System of Units (SI), used around the world for general and scientific purposes.
    a. Concept
    c. Undefined
    b. Meter0
    d. Undefined

102. _____ is defined as the rate of change or derivative with respect to time of velocity.
    a. Acceleration0
    c. Undefined
    b. Thing
    d. Undefined

103. _____ is the weakest of the four fundamental forces of bature, as described by Issac Newton
    a. Gravitational force0
    c. Undefined
    b. Thing
    d. Undefined

104. In physics, _____ is an influence that may cause an object to accelerate. It may be experienced as a lift, a push, or a pull. The actual acceleration of the body is determined by the vector sum of all forces acting on it, known as net _____ or resultant _____.
    a. Force0
    c. Undefined
    b. Thing
    d. Undefined

105. _____ is the largest city in the state of Texas and the fourth-largest in the United States. As of the 2005 U.S. Census estimate, it had a population of more than 2 million.
    a. Thing
    c. Undefined
    b. Houston0
    d. Undefined

Chapter 4. THE DERIVATIVE IN GRAPHING AND APPLICATIONS

106. Deductive _____ is the kind of _____ in which the conclusion is necessitated by, or reached from, previously known facts (the premises).
   a. Thing
   b. Reasoning0
   c. Undefined
   d. Undefined

107. Initial objects are also called _____, and terminal objects are also called final.
   a. Thing
   b. Coterminal0
   c. Undefined
   d. Undefined

108. A _____ is any object propelled through space by the applicationp of a force.
   a. Projectile0
   b. Thing
   c. Undefined
   d. Undefined

109. _____, in economics and political economy, are the distributions or payments awarded to the various suppliers of the factors of production.
   a. Thing
   b. Returns0
   c. Undefined
   d. Undefined

110. In calculus, the _____ is a formula for the derivative of the composite of two functions.
   a. Chain rule0
   b. Concept
   c. Undefined
   d. Undefined

111. _____ is the state of being greater than any finite real or natural number, however large.
   a. Thing
   b. Infinite0
   c. Undefined
   d. Undefined

112. In mathematics, a set is called _____ if there is a bijection between the set and some set of the form {1, 2, ..., n} where n is a natural number.
   a. Thing
   b. Finite0
   c. Undefined
   d. Undefined

113. _____ is bother the congnitive process of transferring information from a particular subject , and a linguistic expression corresponding to such a process.
   a. Thing
   b. Analogy0
   c. Undefined
   d. Undefined

114. In statistics, a _____ measure is one which is measuring what is supposed to measure.
   a. Thing
   b. Valid0
   c. Undefined
   d. Undefined

115. In geometry, an _____ is a point at which a line segment or ray terminates.
   a. Thing
   b. Endpoint0
   c. Undefined
   d. Undefined

116. In mathematics, a _____ is a constant multiplicative factor of a certain object. The object can be such things as a variable, a vector, a function, etc. For example, the _____ of $9x^2$ is 9.

a. Coefficient0
b. Thing
c. Undefined
d. Undefined

117. _____ is the path a moving object follows through space.
a. Thing
b. Projectile motion0
c. Undefined
d. Undefined

118. In business, particularly accounting, a _____ is the time intervals that the accounts, statement, payments, or other calculations cover.
a. Thing
b. Period0
c. Undefined
d. Undefined

119. A _____ is a function that repeats its values after some definite period has been added to its independent variable.
a. Periodic function0
b. Thing
c. Undefined
d. Undefined

120. The _____ integers are all the integers from zero on upwards.
a. Nonnegative0
b. Thing
c. Undefined
d. Undefined

121. In mathematics, an _____ is a statement about the relative size or order of two objects.
a. Inequality0
b. Thing
c. Undefined
d. Undefined

122. A _____ is traditionally an infinitesimally small change in a variable.
a. Differential0
b. Thing
c. Undefined
d. Undefined

123. _____, a field in mathematics, is the study of how functions change when their inputs change. The primary object of study in _____ is the derivative.
a. Differential calculus0
b. Thing
c. Undefined
d. Undefined

124. Sir Isaac _____, was an English physicist, mathematician, astronomer, natural philosopher, and alchemist, regarded by many as the greatest figure in the history of science
a. Newton0
b. Person
c. Undefined
d. Undefined

125. _____ was a German mathematician and philosopher. He invented calculus independently of Newton, and his notation is the one in general use since.
a. Leibniz0
b. Person
c. Undefined
d. Undefined

Chapter 4. THE DERIVATIVE IN GRAPHING AND APPLICATIONS

126. _____ is the distance around a given two-dimensional object. As a general rule, the _____ of a polygon can always be calculated by adding all the length of the sides together. So, the formula for triangles is P = a + b + c, where a, b and c stand for each side of it. For quadrilaterals the equation is P = a + b + c + d. For equilateral polygons, P = na, where n is the number of sides and a is the side length.
- a. Thing
- b. Perimeter0
- c. Undefined
- d. Undefined

127. _____ is the study of geometry using the principles of algebra. _____ can be explained more simply: it is concerned with defining geometrical shapes in a numerical way and extracting numerical information from that representation.
- a. Thing
- b. Analytic geometry0
- c. Undefined
- d. Undefined

128. _____ was a highly influential French philosopher, mathematician, scientist, and writer. Dubbed the "Founder of Modern Philosophy", and the "Father of Modern Mathematics". His theories provided the basis for the calculus of Newton and Leibniz, by applying infinitesimal calculus to the tangent line problem, thus permitting the evolution of that branch of modern mathematics
- a. Person
- b. Descartes0
- c. Undefined
- d. Undefined

129. _____ is the branch of pure mathematics concerned with the properties of numbers in general, and integers in particular, as well as the wider classes of problems that arise from their study.
- a. Number theory0
- b. Thing
- c. Undefined
- d. Undefined

130. In mathematics, a _____ can mean either an element of the set {1, 2, 3, ...} (i.e the positive integers) or an element of the set {0, 1, 2, 3, ...} (i.e. the non-negative integers).
- a. Concept
- b. Whole number0
- c. Undefined
- d. Undefined

131. _____ is the chance that something is likely to happen or be the case.
- a. Probability0
- b. Thing
- c. Undefined
- d. Undefined

132. _____ is a kind of property which exists as magnitude or multitude. It is among the basic classes of things along with quality, substance, change, and relation.
- a. Thing
- b. Amount0
- c. Undefined
- d. Undefined

133. In finance, a _____ is collateral that the holder of a position in securities, options, or futures contracts has to deposit to cover the credit risk of his counterparty.
- a. Thing
- b. Margin0
- c. Undefined
- d. Undefined

134. _____ of Alexandria, sometimes called the father of algebra was a Hellenistic mathematician.

Chapter 4. THE DERIVATIVE IN GRAPHING AND APPLICATIONS

    a. Person
    b. Diophantus0
    c. Undefined
    d. Undefined

135. In mathematics, a _____ is the result of multiplying, or an expression that identifies factors to be multiplied.
    a. Product0
    b. Thing
    c. Undefined
    d. Undefined

136. An _____ is a combination of numbers, operators, grouping symbols and/or free variables and bound variables arranged in a meaningful way which can be evaluated..
    a. Expression0
    b. Thing
    c. Undefined
    d. Undefined

137. _____ was an Greek philosopher. He is best known for a theorem in trigonometry that bears his name.
    a. Pythagoras0
    b. Person
    c. Undefined
    d. Undefined

138. A _____ is a unit of length in the metric system, equal to one thousand metres, the current SI base unit of length
    a. Thing
    b. Kilometer0
    c. Undefined
    d. Undefined

139. In classical geometry, a _____ of a circle or sphere is any line segment from its center to its boundary. By extension, the _____ of a circle or sphere is the length of any such segment. The _____ is half the diameter. In science and engineering the term _____ of curvature is commonly used as a synonym for _____.
    a. Thing
    b. Radius0
    c. Undefined
    d. Undefined

140. In mathematics, a _____ is a quadric surface, with the following equation in Cartesian coordinates: $(x/_a)^2 + (y/_b)^2 = 1$.
    a. Cylinder0
    b. Thing
    c. Undefined
    d. Undefined

141. A _____ is one of the basic shapes of geometry: a polygon with three vertices and three sides which are straight line segments.
    a. Triangle0
    b. Thing
    c. Undefined
    d. Undefined

142. A _____ is a three-dimensional geometric shape formed by straight lines through a fixed point (vertex) to the points of a fixed curve (directrix)
    a. Cone0
    b. Concept
    c. Undefined
    d. Undefined

143. In mathematics, a _____ is a polynomial equation of the second degree. The general form is $ax^2 + bx + c = 0$.
    a. Quadratic equation0
    b. Thing
    c. Undefined
    d. Undefined

Chapter 4. THE DERIVATIVE IN GRAPHING AND APPLICATIONS

144. A quadratic equation with real solutions, called roots, which may be real or complex, is given by the _____ : $x = \frac{-b \pm \sqrt{b^2 - 4ac}}{2a}$.
- a. Quadratic formula0
- b. Thing
- c. Undefined
- d. Undefined

145. _____, from Latin meaning "to make progress", is defined in two different ways. Pure economic _____ is the increase in wealth that an investor has from making an investment, taking into consideration all costs associated with that investment including the opportunity cost of capital.
- a. Thing
- b. Profit0
- c. Undefined
- d. Undefined

146. _____ is a business term for the amount of money that a company receives from its activities in a given period, mostly from sales of products and/or services to customers
- a. Thing
- b. Revenue0
- c. Undefined
- d. Undefined

147. A _____ is the result of the addition of a set of numbers. The numbers may be natural numbers, complex numbers, matrices, or still more complicated objects. An infinite _____ is a subtle procedure known as a series.
- a. Sum0
- b. Thing
- c. Undefined
- d. Undefined

148. In business, _____, _____ cost or _____ expense refers to an ongoing expense of operating a business.
- a. Overhead0
- b. Thing
- c. Undefined
- d. Undefined

149. _____ is the application of tools and a processing medium to the transformation of raw materials into finished goods for sale.
- a. Thing
- b. Manufacturing0
- c. Undefined
- d. Undefined

150. _____, in law and economics, is a form of risk management primarily used to hedge against the risk of a contingent loss.
- a. Insurance0
- b. Thing
- c. Undefined
- d. Undefined

Chapter 4. THE DERIVATIVE IN GRAPHING AND APPLICATIONS

151. Fixed costs are expenses whose total does not change in proportion to the activity of a business.Unit fixed costs decline with volume following a retangular hyperbola as the volume of production.Variable costs by contrast change in relation to the activity of a business such as sales or production volume.Along with variable costs,fixed costs make up one of the two components of total cost. In the most simple production function total cost is equal to fixed costs plus variable costs.In accounting terminology, fixed costs will broadly include all costs which are not included in cost of goods sold, and variable costs are those captured in costs of goods sold. The implicit assumption required to make the equivalence between the accounting and economics terminology is that the accounting period is equal to the period in which fixed costs do not vary in relation to production. In practice, this equivalence does not always hold and depending on the period under consideration by management, some overhead expenses can be adjusted by management, and the specific allocation of each expense to each category will be decided under cost accounting.In business planning and management accounting, usage of the terms fixed costs, variable costs and others will often differ from usage in economics, and may depend on the intended use. For example, costs may be segregated into per unit costs fixed costs per period, and variable costs as a proportion of revenue. Capital expenditures will usually be allocated separately, and depending on the purpose, a portion may be regularly allocated to expenses as depreciation and amortization and seen as a _____ per period, or the entire amount may be considered upfront fixed costs.
- a. Fixed cost0
- b. Thing
- c. Undefined
- d. Undefined

152. _____ are expenses whose total does not change in proportion to the activity of a business, within the relevant time period or scale of production
- a. Fixed costs0
- b. Thing
- c. Undefined
- d. Undefined

153. In mathematics, _____ expressions is used to reduce the expression into the lowest possible term.
- a. Simplifying0
- b. Thing
- c. Undefined
- d. Undefined

154. In mathematics, factorization (British English: factorisation) or factoring is the decomposition of an object (for example, a number, a polynomial, or a matrix) into a product of other objects, or _____, which when multiplied together give the original.
- a. Thing
- b. Factors0
- c. Undefined
- d. Undefined

155. A _____ signifies a point or points of probability on a subject e.g., the _____ of creativity, which allows for the formation of rule or norm or law by interpretation of the phenomena events that can be created.
- a. Thing
- b. Principle0
- c. Undefined
- d. Undefined

156. _____ is the use of marginal concepts within economics. Marginal concepts include marginal cost, marginal productivity and marginal utility, the law of diminishing rates of substitution, and the law of diminishing marginal utility.
- a. Thing
- b. Marginal analysis0
- c. Undefined
- d. Undefined

157. _____ is the ability to hold, receive or absorb, or a measure thereof, similar to the concept of volume.

Chapter 4. THE DERIVATIVE IN GRAPHING AND APPLICATIONS

a. Capacity0
b. Concept
c. Undefined
d. Undefined

158. In mathematics, the multiplicative inverse of a number x, denoted 1/x or x^{-1}, is the number which, when multiplied by x, yields 1. The multiplicative inverse of x is also called the _____ of x.
   a. Reciprocal0
   b. Thing
   c. Undefined
   d. Undefined

159. _____ has one 90° internal angle a right angle.
   a. Right triangle0
   b. Thing
   c. Undefined
   d. Undefined

160. In Euclidean geometry, a _____ is the set of all points in a plane at a fixed distance, called the radius, from a given point, the center.
   a. Circle0
   b. Thing
   c. Undefined
   d. Undefined

161. In mathematical analysis and related areas of mathematics, a set is called _____, if it is, in a certain sense, of finite size.
   a. Thing
   b. Bounded0
   c. Undefined
   d. Undefined

162. An _____ triange is a triangle with at least two sides of equal length.
   a. Isosceles0
   b. Thing
   c. Undefined
   d. Undefined

163. A _____, or stained glass window refers either to the material of colored glass or to the art and craft of working with it.
   a. Thing
   b. Church window0
   c. Undefined
   d. Undefined

164. _____ are cubes in which all sides are of the same length and all face perpendicular to each other including an atom at each corner of the unigt cell.
   a. Thing
   b. Cubic units0
   c. Undefined
   d. Undefined

165. In mathematics, a _____ is the set of all points in three-dimensional space (R^3) which are at distance r from a fixed point of that space, where r is a positive real number called the radius of the _____. The fixed point is called the center or centre, and is not part of the _____ itself.
   a. Thing
   b. Sphere0
   c. Undefined
   d. Undefined

166. _____ is a three-dimensional geometric shape formed by straight lines through a fixed point vertex to the points of a fixed curve directrix.

Chapter 4. THE DERIVATIVE IN GRAPHING AND APPLICATIONS

    a. Right circular cone0   b. Thing
    c. Undefined   d. Undefined

167. A _____ is a three-dimensional solid object bounded by six square faces, facets, or sides, with three meeting at each vertex.
    a. Thing   b. Cube0
    c. Undefined   d. Undefined

168. The _____ of a right circular cone is the distance from any point on the circle to the apex of the cone.
    a. Thing   b. Slant height0
    c. Undefined   d. Undefined

169. A _____ is a quadrilateral, which is defined as a shape with four sides, which has a pair of parallel sides.
    a. Trapezoid0   b. Thing
    c. Undefined   d. Undefined

170. In geometry, a _____ planar shape or solid is one that encloses and "fits snugly" around another geometric shape or solid.
    a. Thing   b. Circumscribed0
    c. Undefined   d. Undefined

171. In geometry, a _____ planar shape or solid is one that encloses and "fits snugly" around another geometric shape or solid.
    a. Circumscribed about0   b. Thing
    c. Undefined   d. Undefined

172. _____ is electromagnetic radiation with a wavelength that is visible to the eye (visible _____) or, in a technical or scientific context, electromagnetic radiation of any wavelength.
    a. Light0   b. Thing
    c. Undefined   d. Undefined

173. _____ is the production of food, feed, fiber, fuel and other goods by the systematic raizing of plants and animals.
    a. Thing   b. Agriculture0
    c. Undefined   d. Undefined

174. A central concept in science and the scientific method is that all evidence must be _____, or empirically based, that is, dependent on evidence or consequences that are observable by the senses.
    a. Empirical0   b. Thing
    c. Undefined   d. Undefined

175. A _____ is a unit of length, usually used to measure distance, in a number of different systems, including Imperial units, United States customary units and Norwegian/Swedish mil. Its size can vary from system to system, but in each is between 1 and 10 kilometers. In contemporary English contexts _____ refers to either:
    a. Mile0   b. Thing
    c. Undefined   d. Undefined

Chapter 4. THE DERIVATIVE IN GRAPHING AND APPLICATIONS

176. _____ is a unit of speed, expressing the number of international miles covered per hour.
   a. Miles per hour0
   b. Thing
   c. Undefined
   d. Undefined

177. In mathematics, the _____ is a conic section generated by the intersection of a right circular conical surface and a plane parallel to a generating straight line of that surface. It can also be defined as locus of points in a plane which are equidistant from a given point.
   a. Parabola0
   b. Thing
   c. Undefined
   d. Undefined

178. _____ is the estimation of a physical quantity such as distance, energy, temperature, or time.
   a. Measurement0
   b. Thing
   c. Undefined
   d. Undefined

179. _____ is a physical property of a system that underlies the common notions of hot and cold; something that is hotter has the greater _____.
   a. Thing
   b. Temperature0
   c. Undefined
   d. Undefined

180. In regression analysis, _____, also known as ordinary _____ analysis is a method for linear regression that determines the values of unknown quantities in a statistical model by minimizing the sum of the residuals difference between the predicted and observed values squared.
   a. Thing
   b. Least squares0
   c. Undefined
   d. Undefined

181. _____ is a measure of difference for interval and ratio variables between the observed value and the mean.
   a. Deviation0
   b. Thing
   c. Undefined
   d. Undefined

182. _____ or arithmetics is the oldest and most elementary branch of mathematics, used by almost everyone, for tasks ranging from simple daily counting to advanced science and business calculations.
   a. Arithmetic0
   b. Thing
   c. Undefined
   d. Undefined

183. In linear algebra, a _____ of a matrix A is the determinant of some smaller square matrix, cut down from A.
   a. Thing
   b. Minor0
   c. Undefined
   d. Undefined

184. A _____ given two distinct points A and B on the _____, is the set of points C on the line containing points A and B such that A is not strictly between C and B.
   a. Thing
   b. Ray0
   c. Undefined
   d. Undefined

185. In geometry and physics, _____ are half-lines that continue forever in one direction.

a. Thing
b. Rays0
c. Undefined
d. Undefined

186. In mathematics, a _____ (also spelled reflexion) is a map that transforms an object into its mirror image.
a. Reflection0
b. Concept
c. Undefined
d. Undefined

187. In geometry, the relations of _____ are those such as 'lies on' between points and lines (as in 'point P lies on line L'), and 'intersects' (as in 'line L_1 intersects line L_2', in three-dimensional space). That is, they are the binary relations describing how subsets meet.
a. Incidence0
b. Thing
c. Undefined
d. Undefined

188. The _____ in a vacuum is an important physical constant denoted by the letter c for constant or the Latin word celeritas meaning "swiftness
a. Thing
b. Speed of light0
c. Undefined
d. Undefined

189. _____ is a branch of mathematics concerning the study of structure, relation and quantity.
a. Algebra0
b. Concept
c. Undefined
d. Undefined

190. A _____ fraction is a fraction in which the absolute value of the numerator is less than the denominator--hence, the absolute value of the fraction is less than 1.
a. Proper0
b. Thing
c. Undefined
d. Undefined

191. Claudius Ptolemaeus, known in English as _____, was a Hellenistic mathematician, geographer, astronomer, and astrologer. The Almagest is widely held to be the first systematic treatise on astronomy in antiquity. Babylonian astronomers had developed arithmetical techniques for calculating astronomical phenomena; Greek astronomers such as Hipparchus had produced geometric models for calculating celestial motions; _____, however, clearly derived his geometrical models from selected astronomical observations by his predecessors spanning more than 800 years.
a. Person
b. Ptolemy0
c. Undefined
d. Undefined

192. In trigonometry and elementary geometry, _____ is the process of finding coordinates and distance to a point by calculating the length of one side of a triangle, given measurements of angles and sides of the triangle formed by that point and two other known reference points, using the law of sines.
a. Triangulation0
b. Thing
c. Undefined
d. Undefined

193. Leonhard _____ was a pioneering Swiss mathematician and physicist, who spent most of his life in Russia and Germany.
a. Person
b. Euler0
c. Undefined
d. Undefined

Chapter 4. THE DERIVATIVE IN GRAPHING AND APPLICATIONS

194. A _____ is a form of periodic payment from an employer to an employee, which is specified in an employment contract.
- a. Thing
- b. Salary0
- c. Undefined
- d. Undefined

195. In mathematics, a _____ number is a real or complex number which is not algebraic, that is, not a solution of a non-zero polynomial equation, with rational coefficients.
- a. Transcendental0
- b. Thing
- c. Undefined
- d. Undefined

196. The _____ is a learned society, founded in 1666 by Louis XIV at the suggestion of Jean-Baptiste Colbert, to encourage and protect the spirit of French scientific research. It was at the forefront of scientific developments in Europe in the 17th and 18th centuries. It is one of the earliest academies of sciences.
- a. French Academy of Sciences0
- b. Place
- c. Undefined
- d. Undefined

197. The word _____ comes from the Latin word linearis, which means created by lines.
- a. Thing
- b. Linear0
- c. Undefined
- d. Undefined

198. _____ is an approximation of a general function using a linear function more precisely, an affine function.
- a. Linear approximation0
- b. Thing
- c. Undefined
- d. Undefined

199. The _____ is a unit of plane angle. It is represented by the symbol "rad" or, more rarely, by the superscript c (for "circular measure"). For example, an angle of 1.2 radians would be written "1.2 rad" or "1.2c" (second symbol can produce confusion with centigrads).
- a. Thing
- b. Radian0
- c. Undefined
- d. Undefined

200. _____ is a professional society that focuses on undergraduate mathematics education.
- a. Mathematical Association of America0
- b. Person
- c. Undefined
- d. Undefined

201. In mathematics, the _____ of two sets A and B is the set that contains all elements of A that also belong to B (or equivalently, all elements of B that also belong to A), but no other elements.
- a. Thing
- b. Intersection0
- c. Undefined
- d. Undefined

202. In mathematics, a _____ of a number x is a number r such that $r^2 = x$, or in words, a number r whose square (the result of multiplying the number by itself) is x.
- a. Thing
- b. Square root0
- c. Undefined
- d. Undefined

Chapter 4. THE DERIVATIVE IN GRAPHING AND APPLICATIONS

203. In mathematics, a _____ is an ordered list of objects. Like a set, it contains members, also called elements or terms, and the number of terms is called the length of the _____. Unlike a set, order matters, and the exact same elements can appear multiple times at different positions in the _____.
   a. Thing
   b. Sequence0
   c. Undefined
   d. Undefined

204. In mathematics, a _____ function in the sense of algebraic geometry is an everywhere-defined, polynomial function on an algebraic variety V with values in the field K over which V is defined.
   a. Regular0
   b. Thing
   c. Undefined
   d. Undefined

205. _____ is the income from capital investment paid in a series of regular payments.
   a. Thing
   b. Annuity0
   c. Undefined
   d. Undefined

206. In banking and accountancy, the outstanding _____ is the amount of money owned, or due, that remains in a deposit account or a loan account at a given date, after all past remittances, payments and withdrawal have been accounted for.
   a. Balance0
   b. Thing
   c. Undefined
   d. Undefined

207. An _____ is the fee paid on borrow money.
   a. Interest rate0
   b. Concept
   c. Undefined
   d. Undefined

208. A _____ consists either of a suggested explanation for a phenomenon or of a reasoned proposal suggesting a possible correlation between multiple phenomena.
   a. Thing
   b. Hypothesis0
   c. Undefined
   d. Undefined

209. _____ is a form of periodic payment from an employer to an employee, which is specified in an employment contract.
   a. Thing
   b. Gross pay0
   c. Undefined
   d. Undefined

210. Mathematical _____ is used to represent ideas.
   a. Thing
   b. Notation0
   c. Undefined
   d. Undefined

211. An _____ of a number a is a number b such that $b^n = a$.
   a. Nth root0
   b. Thing
   c. Undefined
   d. Undefined

212. A _____ is a number that is less than zero.

Chapter 4. THE DERIVATIVE IN GRAPHING AND APPLICATIONS

a. Thing
b. Negative number0
c. Undefined
d. Undefined

213. Mathematical _____ are demonstrations that, assuming certain axioms, some statement is necessarily true.
a. Thing
b. Proofs0
c. Undefined
d. Undefined

214. _____ Logic is a concept in traditional logic referring to a "type of immediate inference in which from a given proposition another proposition is inferred which has as its subject the predicate of the original proposition and as its predicate the subject of the original proposition (the quality of the proposition being retained)."
a. Concept
b. Converse0
c. Undefined
d. Undefined

215. In mathematics and its applications, a _____ is a system for assigning an n-tuple of numbers or scalars to each point in an n-dimensional space.
a. Coordinate system0
b. Concept
c. Undefined
d. Undefined

216. An _____ is an equality that remains true regardless of the values of any variables that appear within it, to distinguish it from an equality which is true under more particular conditions.
a. Thing
b. Identity0
c. Undefined
d. Undefined

217. _____ is to give an equation $R(x,y) = S(x,y)$ that at least in part has the same graph as $y = f(x)$.
a. Thing
b. Implicit differentiation0
c. Undefined
d. Undefined

218. In mathematics, an _____ .
a. Thing
b. Ellipse0
c. Undefined
d. Undefined

219. In physics, an _____ is the path that an object makes around another object while under the influence of a source of centripetal force, such as gravity.
a. Orbit0
b. Thing
c. Undefined
d. Undefined

220. A _____, as defined by the International Astronomical Union, is a celestial body orbiting a star or stellar remnant that is massive enough to be rounded by its own gravity, not massive enough to cause thermonuclear fusion in its core, and has cleared its neighboring region of planetesimals.
a. Thing
b. Planet0
c. Undefined
d. Undefined

221. In geometry, the _____ of an object is a point in some sense in the middle of the object.
a. Thing
b. Center0
c. Undefined
d. Undefined

222. A _____ is a function that assigns a number to subsets of a given set.
   a. Thing
   b. Measure0
   c. Undefined
   d. Undefined

Chapter 5. INTEGRATION

1. A _____ is a special kind of ratio, indicating a relationship between two measurements with different units, such as miles to gallons or cents to pounds.
   a. Thing
   b. Rate0
   c. Undefined
   d. Undefined

2. In trigonometry, the _____ is a function defined as $\tan x = \sin x / \cos x$. The function is so-named because it can be defined as the length of a certain segment of a _____ (in the geometric sense) to the unit circle. In plane geometry, a line is _____ to a curve, at some point, if both line and curve pass through the point with the same direction.
   a. Tangent0
   b. Thing
   c. Undefined
   d. Undefined

3. _____ has two distinct but etymologically-related meanings: one in geometry and one in trigonometry.
   a. Thing
   b. Tangent line0
   c. Undefined
   d. Undefined

4. The _____ of a function is an extension of the concept of a sum, and are identified or found through the use of integration.
   a. Integral0
   b. Thing
   c. Undefined
   d. Undefined

5. _____ is a mathematical subject that includes the study of limits, derivatives, integrals, and power series and constitutes a major part of modern university curriculum.
   a. Thing
   b. Calculus0
   c. Undefined
   d. Undefined

6. A _____ is traditionally an infinitesimally small change in a variable.
   a. Differential0
   b. Thing
   c. Undefined
   d. Undefined

7. _____, a field in mathematics, is the study of how functions change when their inputs change. The primary object of study in _____ is the derivative.
   a. Thing
   b. Differential calculus0
   c. Undefined
   d. Undefined

8. In Euclidean geometry, a _____ is the set of all points in a plane at a fixed distance, called the radius, from a given point, the center.
   a. Thing
   b. Circle0
   c. Undefined
   d. Undefined

9. In classical geometry, a _____ of a circle or sphere is any line segment from its center to its boundary. By extension, the _____ of a circle or sphere is the length of any such segment. The _____ is half the diameter. In science and engineering the term _____ of curvature is commonly used as a synonym for _____.
   a. Thing
   b. Radius0
   c. Undefined
   d. Undefined

10. In mathematics, a _____ function in the sense of algebraic geometry is an everywhere-defined, polynomial function on an algebraic variety V with values in the field K over which V is defined.

a. Regular0
b. Thing
c. Undefined
d. Undefined

11. In geometry a _____ is a plane figure that is bounded by a closed path or circuit, composed of a finite number of sequential line segments.
   a. Polygon0
   b. Thing
   c. Undefined
   d. Undefined

12. In geometry, _____ are plane figures that are bounded by a closed path or circuit, composed of a finite number of sequential line segments.
   a. Thing
   b. Polygons0
   c. Undefined
   d. Undefined

13. _____ of Syracuse was an ancient Greek mathematician, physicist and engineer. In addition to making important discoveries in the field of mathematics and geometry, he is credited with producing machines that were well ahead of their time.
   a. Person
   b. Archimedes0
   c. Undefined
   d. Undefined

14. _____ numerals are a numeral system originating in ancient Rome, adapted from Etruscan numerals.
   a. Roman0
   b. Thing
   c. Undefined
   d. Undefined

15. Sir Isaac _____, was an English physicist, mathematician, astronomer, natural philosopher, and alchemist, regarded by many as the greatest figure in the history of science
   a. Newton0
   b. Person
   c. Undefined
   d. Undefined

16. _____ is a set of numbers, in the broadest sense of the word, together with one or more operations, such as addition or multiplication.
   a. Number system0
   b. Thing
   c. Undefined
   d. Undefined

17. _____ is a branch of mathematics concerning the study of structure, relation and quantity.
   a. Algebra0
   b. Concept
   c. Undefined
   d. Undefined

18. In geometry, a line _____ is a part of a line that is bounded by two end points, and contains every point on the line between its end points.
   a. Concept
   b. Segment0
   c. Undefined
   d. Undefined

19. The _____ of a solid object is the three-dimensional concept of how much space it occupies, often quantified numerically.

Chapter 5. INTEGRATION

    a. Volume0
    c. Undefined
    b. Thing
    d. Undefined

20. In mathematics, a _____ is the set of all points in three-dimensional space (R^3) which are at distance r from a fixed point of that space, where r is a positive real number called the radius of the _____. The fixed point is called the center or centre, and is not part of the _____ itself.
    a. Sphere0
    c. Undefined
    b. Thing
    d. Undefined

21. In mathematics, a _____ are a curve which emanates from a central point, getting progressively farther away as it revolves around the point.
    a. Spirals0
    c. Undefined
    b. Thing
    d. Undefined

22. In mathematics, a _____ is a quadric surface, with the following equation in Cartesian coordinates: $(x/_a)^2 + (y/_b)^2 = 1$.
    a. Cylinder0
    c. Undefined
    b. Thing
    d. Undefined

23. In mathematics, the _____ is a conic section generated by the intersection of a right circular conical surface and a plane parallel to a generating straight line of that surface. It can also be defined as locus of points in a plane which are equidistant from a given point.
    a. Thing
    c. Undefined
    b. Parabola0
    d. Undefined

24. _____ is a quadric
    a. Thing
    c. Undefined
    b. Paraboloid0
    d. Undefined

25. In mathematical analysis and related areas of mathematics, a set is called _____, if it is, in a certain sense, of finite size.
    a. Bounded0
    c. Undefined
    b. Thing
    d. Undefined

26. The easiest _____ prime numbers resides in the use of the Sieve of Eratosthenes, an algorithm that discovers all prime numbers to a specified integer.
    a. Method for finding0
    c. Undefined
    b. Thing
    d. Undefined

27. In economics, economic _____ is simply a state of the world where economic forces are balanced and in the absence of external influences the values of economic variables will not change.
    a. Equilibrium0
    c. Undefined
    b. Thing
    d. Undefined

28. _____ is the design, analysis, and/or construction of works for practical purposes.

a. Engineering0
b. Thing
c. Undefined
d. Undefined

29. In geometry, a _____ is defined as a quadrilateral where all four of its angles are right angles.
   a. Rectangle0
   b. Thing
   c. Undefined
   d. Undefined

30. An _____ of a function f is a function F whose derivative is equal to f, i.e., F' = f.
   a. Antiderivative0
   b. Thing
   c. Undefined
   d. Undefined

31. There are two simple _____ the greatest common factor and least common multiple: standard factorization and prime factorization.
   a. Methods for finding0
   b. Thing
   c. Undefined
   d. Undefined

32. In geometry, the _____ of an object is a point in some sense in the middle of the object.
   a. Thing
   b. Center0
   c. Undefined
   d. Undefined

33. In geometry, an _____ is a point at which a line segment or ray terminates.
   a. Endpoint0
   b. Thing
   c. Undefined
   d. Undefined

34. In mathematics, the concept of a _____ tries to capture the intuitive idea of a geometrical one-dimensional and continuous object. A simple example is the circle.
   a. Curve0
   b. Thing
   c. Undefined
   d. Undefined

35. In elementary algebra, an _____ is a set that contains every real number between two indicated numbers and may contain the two numbers themselves.
   a. Interval0
   b. Thing
   c. Undefined
   d. Undefined

36. _____ is a process of combining or accumulating. It may also refer to:
   a. Thing
   b. Integration0
   c. Undefined
   d. Undefined

37. _____ is the eighteenth letter of the Greek alphabet.
   a. Thing
   b. Sigma0
   c. Undefined
   d. Undefined

38. _____ is used as the symbol for summation. Summation is the addition of a set of numbers; the result is their sum. The "numbers" to be summed may be natural numbers, complex numbers, matrices, or still more complicated objects. An infinite sum is a subtle procedure known as a series.

Chapter 5. INTEGRATION

a. Sigma notation0
b. Thing
c. Undefined
d. Undefined

39. Mathematical _____ is used to represent ideas.
   a. Thing
   b. Notation0
   c. Undefined
   d. Undefined

40. A _____ is the result of the addition of a set of numbers. The numbers may be natural numbers, complex numbers, matrices, or still more complicated objects. An infinite _____ is a subtle procedure known as a series.
   a. Thing
   b. Sum0
   c. Undefined
   d. Undefined

41. The mathematical concept of a _____ expresses the intuitive idea of deterministic dependence between two quantities, one of which is viewed as primary and the other as secondary. A _____ then is a way to associate a unique output for each input of a specified type, for example, a real number or an element of a given set.
   a. Thing
   b. Function0
   c. Undefined
   d. Undefined

42. _____ was a German mathematician and philosopher. He invented calculus independently of Newton, and his notation is the one in general use since.
   a. Leibniz0
   b. Person
   c. Undefined
   d. Undefined

43. _____ was an English divine, scholar and mathematician who is generally given minor credit for his role in the development of modern calculus; in particular, for his work regarding the tangent; for example, Barrow is given credit for being the first to calculate the tangents of the kappa curve. Isaac Newton was a student of Barrow's. Lunar crater Barrow is named after him.
   a. Isaac Barrow0
   b. Thing
   c. Undefined
   d. Undefined

44. Sir _____ was an English physicist, mathematician, astronomer, natural philosopher, and alchemist, regarded by many as the greatest figure in the history of science.
   a. Person
   b. Isaac Newton0
   c. Undefined
   d. Undefined

45. In logic, Modus tollens (or Modus ponendo tollens) means to affirm by denying. It is the formal name for _____ proof or proof by contrapositive (contrapositive inference), often abbreviated to MT.
   a. Indirect0
   b. Thing
   c. Undefined
   d. Undefined

46. The _____ is a measurement of how a function changes when the values of its inputs change.
   a. Derivative0
   b. Thing
   c. Undefined
   d. Undefined

47. A _____ is a quadrilateral, which is defined as a shape with four sides, which has a pair of parallel sides.

a. Thing
b. Trapezoid0
c. Undefined
d. Undefined

48. A _____ is one of the basic shapes of geometry: a polygon with three vertices and three sides which are straight line segments.
   a. Thing
   b. Triangle0
   c. Undefined
   d. Undefined

49. _____ has one 90° internal angle a right angle.
   a. Thing
   b. Right triangle0
   c. Undefined
   d. Undefined

50. In geometry, an _____ of a triangle is a straight line through a vertex and perpendicular to (i.e. forming a right angle with) the opposite side or an extension of the opposite side.
   a. Altitude0
   b. Concept
   c. Undefined
   d. Undefined

51. The _____ (symbol _____) and the millibar (symbol mbar, also mb) are units of pressure.
   a. Thing
   b. Bar0
   c. Undefined
   d. Undefined

52. An _____ triange is a triangle with at least two sides of equal length.
   a. Isosceles0
   b. Thing
   c. Undefined
   d. Undefined

53. In mathematics, a _____ is a statement that can be proved on the basis of explicitly stated or previously agreed assumptions.
   a. Theorem0
   b. Thing
   c. Undefined
   d. Undefined

54. In mathematics and the mathematical sciences, a _____ is a fixed, but possibly unspecified, value. This is in contrast to a variable, which is not fixed.
   a. Thing
   b. Constant0
   c. Undefined
   d. Undefined

55. _____ in calculus is primitive or indefinite integral of a function f is a function F whose derivative is equal to f, i.e., F Œ = f. The process of solving for antiderivatives is _____.
   a. Thing
   b. Antidifferentiation0
   c. Undefined
   d. Undefined

56. _____ is an extension of the concept of a sum.
   a. Definite integral0
   b. Thing
   c. Undefined
   d. Undefined

57. _____ is a method for approximating the values of integrals.

Chapter 5. INTEGRATION

a. Thing
b. Riemann sum0
c. Undefined
d. Undefined

58. In mathematics, _____ are the intuitive idea of a geometrical one-dimensional and continuous object.
a. Curves0
b. Thing
c. Undefined
d. Undefined

59. The _____, the average in everyday English, which is also called the arithmetic _____ (and is distinguished from the geometric _____ or harmonic _____). The average is also called the sample _____. The expected value of a random variable, which is also called the population _____.
a. Mean0
b. Thing
c. Undefined
d. Undefined

60. _____ is the fee paid on borrowed money.
a. Interest0
b. Thing
c. Undefined
d. Undefined

61. In number theory, the _____ of arithmetic (or unique factorization theorem) states that every natural number greater than 1 can be written as a unique product of prime numbers.
a. Concept
b. Fundamental theorem0
c. Undefined
d. Undefined

62. _____ of calculus is the statement that the two central operations of calculus, differentiation and integration, are inverse operations: if a continuous function is first integrated and then differentiated, the original function is retrieved.
a. Fundamental Theorem of Calculus0
b. Thing
c. Undefined
d. Undefined

63. _____ has many meanings, most of which simply .
a. Thing
b. Power0
c. Undefined
d. Undefined

64. _____ is the addition of a set of numbers; the result is their sum. The "numbers" to be summed may be natural numbers, complex numbers, matrices, or still more complicated objects. An infinite sum is a subtle procedure known as a series.
a. Thing
b. Summation0
c. Undefined
d. Undefined

65. The _____ integers are all the integers from zero on upwards.
a. Thing
b. Nonnegative0
c. Undefined
d. Undefined

66. The word _____ comes from the Latin word linearis, which means created by lines.
a. Linear0
b. Thing
c. Undefined
d. Undefined

67. A _____ is a first degree polynomial mathematical function of the form: f(x) = mx + b where m and b are real constants and x is a real variable.
   a. Thing
   b. Linear function0
   c. Undefined
   d. Undefined

68. _____ is a function that extends the concept of an ordinary sum
   a. Integrand0
   b. Thing
   c. Undefined
   d. Undefined

69. In calculus, the indefinite integral of a given function i.e. the set of all antiderivatives of the function is always written with a constant, the _____.
   a. Constant of integration0
   b. Thing
   c. Undefined
   d. Undefined

70. A _____ is a symbolic representation denoting a quantity or expression. It often represents an "unknown" quantity that has the potential to change.
   a. Thing
   b. Variable0
   c. Undefined
   d. Undefined

71. In mathematics, an _____ is any of the arguments, i.e. "inputs", to a function. Thus if we have a function f(x), then x is a _____.
   a. Independent variable0
   b. Thing
   c. Undefined
   d. Undefined

72. A _____ is a mathematical equation for an unknown function of one or several variables which relates the values of the function itself and of its derivatives of various orders.
   a. Differential equation0
   b. Thing
   c. Undefined
   d. Undefined

73. Initial objects are also called _____, and terminal objects are also called final.
   a. Coterminal0
   b. Thing
   c. Undefined
   d. Undefined

74. _____ is often used to describe the measurement of the steepness, incline, gradient, or grade of a straight line. The _____ is defined as the ratio of the "rise" divided by the "run" between two points on a line, or in other words, the ratio of the altitude change to the horizontal distance between any two points on the line.
   a. Slope0
   b. Thing
   c. Undefined
   d. Undefined

75. In mathematics, in the field of differential equations, an initial value problem is a differential equation together with specified value, called the _____, of the unknown function at a given point in the domain of the solution.
   a. Thing
   b. Initial condition0
   c. Undefined
   d. Undefined

76. A _____ is a graphical tool to qualitatively visualize, or aid in numerical approximation of, solutions to differential equations.

Chapter 5. INTEGRATION

a. Thing
c. Undefined
b. Slope field0
d. Undefined

77. A _____ is a negotiable instrument instructing a financial institution to pay a specific amount of a specific currency from a specific demand account held in the maker/depositor's name with that institution. Both the maker and payee may be natural persons or legal entities.
a. Check0
c. Undefined
b. Thing
d. Undefined

78. One of the three formats applicable to a quadratic function is the _____ which is defined as $f = ax^2 + bx + c$.
a. General form0
c. Undefined
b. Thing
d. Undefined

79. In plane geometry, a _____ is a polygon with four equal sides, four right angles, and parallel opposite sides. In algebra, the _____ of a number is that number multiplied by itself.
a. Thing
c. Undefined
b. Square0
d. Undefined

80. _____ is a physical property of a system that underlies the common notions of hot and cold; something that is hotter has the greater _____.
a. Thing
c. Undefined
b. Temperature0
d. Undefined

81. In mathematics, _____ expressions is used to reduce the expression into the lowest possible term.
a. Thing
c. Undefined
b. Simplifying0
d. Undefined

82. In mathematics, the _____ functions are functions of an angle; they are important when studying triangles and modeling periodic phenomena, among many other applications.
a. Trigonometric0
c. Undefined
b. Thing
d. Undefined

83. An _____ is an equality that remains true regardless of the values of any variables that appear within it, to distinguish it from an equality which is true under more particular conditions.
a. Thing
c. Undefined
b. Identity0
d. Undefined

84. A _____ defined function $f(x)$ of a real variable x is a function whose definition is given differently on disjoint subsets of its domain.
a. Piecewise0
c. Undefined
b. Thing
d. Undefined

85. The _____ is a thermodynamic (absolute) temperature scale where absolute zero—the coldest possible temperature—is defined as being equivalent to zero kelvin (0 K).

a. Kelvin scale0
b. Thing
c. Undefined
d. Undefined

86. In Euclidean geometry, a uniform _____ is a linear transformation that enlargers or diminishes objects, and whose _____ factor is the same in all directions. This is also called homothethy.
    a. Thing
    b. Scale0
    c. Undefined
    d. Undefined

87. In calculus, the _____ is a formula for the derivative of the composite of two functions.
    a. Chain rule0
    b. Concept
    c. Undefined
    d. Undefined

88. An _____ is a combination of numbers, operators, grouping symbols and/or free variables and bound variables arranged in a meaningful way which can be evaluated..
    a. Thing
    b. Expression0
    c. Undefined
    d. Undefined

89. In mathematics, a _____ of a positive integer n is a way of writing n as a sum of positive integers.
    a. Thing
    b. Composition0
    c. Undefined
    d. Undefined

90. _____ is a tool for finding antiderivatives and integrals. Using the fundamental theorem of calculus often requires finding an antiderivative. For this and other reasons, this rule is a relatively important tool for mathematicians. It is the counterpart to the chain rule of differentiation.
    a. Integration by substitution0
    b. Thing
    c. Undefined
    d. Undefined

91. Two mathematical objects are equal if and only if they are precisely the same in every way. This defines a binary relation, _____, denoted by the sign of _____ "=" in such a way that the statement "x = y" means that x and y are equal.
    a. Equality0
    b. Thing
    c. Undefined
    d. Undefined

92. _____ is a trigonemtric function that is important when studying triangles and modeling periodic phenomena, among other applications.
    a. Sine0
    b. Thing
    c. Undefined
    d. Undefined

93. Equivalence is the condition of being _____ or essentially equal.
    a. Thing
    b. Equivalent0
    c. Undefined
    d. Undefined

94. A _____ function is a function for which, intuitively, small changes in the input result in small changes in the output.

Chapter 5. INTEGRATION

a. Event
b. Continuous0
c. Undefined
d. Undefined

95. In sociology and biology a _____ is the collection of people or organisms of a particular species living in a given geographic area or space, usually measured by a census.
   a. Population0
   b. Thing
   c. Undefined
   d. Undefined

96. The word _____ is used in a variety of ways in mathematics.
   a. Thing
   b. Index0
   c. Undefined
   d. Undefined

97. In mathematics, a _____ is a demonstration that, assuming certain axioms, some statement is necessarily true.
   a. Proof0
   b. Thing
   c. Undefined
   d. Undefined

98. In mathematics, the notion of _____ is a generalization of the notion of invertible.
   a. Cancellation0
   b. Thing
   c. Undefined
   d. Undefined

99. In mathematics, the _____(e) for L-functions are a class of summation formulae, expressing sums taken over the complex number zeroes of a given L-function, typically in terms of quantities studied by number theory by use of the theory of special functions.
   a. Thing
   b. Explicit formula0
   c. Undefined
   d. Undefined

100. In set theory and other branches of mathematics, the _____ of a collection of sets is the set that contains everything that belongs to any of the sets, but nothing else.
   a. Thing
   b. Union0
   c. Undefined
   d. Undefined

101. _____ is used in mathematics, and throughout the physical sciences, engineering, and economics. The complexity of such notation ranges from relatively simple symbolic representations, such as numbers 1 and 2; function symbols sin and +, to conceptual symbols, such as lim and dy/dx; to equations and variables.
   a. Thing
   b. Mathematical notation0
   c. Undefined
   d. Undefined

102. _____ is the middle point of a line segment.
   a. Midpoint0
   b. Thing
   c. Undefined
   d. Undefined

103. In topology and related areas of mathematics a _____ or Moore-Smith sequence is a generalization of a sequence, intended to unify the various notions of limit and generalize them to arbitrary topological spaces.
   a. Net0
   b. Thing
   c. Undefined
   d. Undefined

Chapter 5. INTEGRATION

104. The plus and _____ signs are mathematical symbols used to represent the notions of positive and negative as well as the operations of addition and subtraction.
   a. Minus0
   b. Thing
   c. Undefined
   d. Undefined

105. A _____ is a function for which, intuitively, small changes in the input result in small changes in the output.
   a. Continuous function0
   b. Event
   c. Undefined
   d. Undefined

106. The _____ are the only integral domain whose positive elements are well-ordered, and in which order is preserved by addition. Like the natural numbers, the _____ form a countably infinite set. The set of all _____ is usually denoted in mathematics by a boldface Z .
   a. Integers0
   b. Thing
   c. Undefined
   d. Undefined

107. In geographic information systems, a _____ comprises an entity with a geographic location, typically determined by points, arcs, or polygons. Carriageways and cadastres exemplify _____ data.
   a. Feature0
   b. Thing
   c. Undefined
   d. Undefined

108. In mathematics, science including computer science, linguistics and engineering, an _____ is, generally speaking, an independent variable or input to a function.
   a. Thing
   b. Argument0
   c. Undefined
   d. Undefined

109. Generally, a _____ is a splitting of something into parts.
   a. Partition0
   b. Thing
   c. Undefined
   d. Undefined

110. A _____ is a function that assigns a number to subsets of a given set.
   a. Thing
   b. Measure0
   c. Undefined
   d. Undefined

111. The _____ of a mathematical object is its size: a property by which it can be larger or smaller than other objects of the same kind; in technical terms, an ordering of the class of objects to which it belongs.
   a. Thing
   b. Magnitude0
   c. Undefined
   d. Undefined

112. In mathematics, a set is called _____ if there is a bijection between the set and some set of the form {1, 2, ..., n} where n is a natural number.
   a. Thing
   b. Finite0
   c. Undefined
   d. Undefined

113. A _____ is the part of the dividend that is left over when the dividend is not evenly divisible by the divisor.

Chapter 5. INTEGRATION

    a. Remainder0   b. Thing
    c. Undefined   d. Undefined

114. _____, Greek for "knowledge of nature," is the branch of science concerned with the discovery and characterization of universal laws which govern matter, energy, space, and time.
    a. Physics0   b. Thing
    c. Undefined   d. Undefined

115. _____ is a function whose values do not vary and thus are constant.
    a. Thing   b. Constant function0
    c. Undefined   d. Undefined

116. In mathematics, a _____ is a two-dimensional manifold or surface that is perfectly flat.
    a. Thing   b. Plane0
    c. Undefined   d. Undefined

117. In mathematics, the _____ of a coordinate system is the point where the axes of the system intersect.
    a. Thing   b. Origin0
    c. Undefined   d. Undefined

118. In astronomy, geography, geometry and related sciences and contexts, a plane is said to be _____ at a given point if it is locally perpendicular to the gradient of the gravity field, i.e., with the direction of the gravitational force at that point.
    a. Thing   b. Horizontal0
    c. Undefined   d. Undefined

119. In mathematics, an inequality is a statement about the relative size or order of two objects. For example 14 > 10, or 14 is _____ 10.
    a. Greater than0   b. Thing
    c. Undefined   d. Undefined

120. Continuous functions are of utmost importance in mathematics and applications. However, not all functions are continuous. If a function is not continuous at a point in its domain, one says that it has a _____ there. The set of all points of _____ of a function may be a discrete set, a dense set, or even the entire domain of the function.
    a. Discontinuity0   b. Thing
    c. Undefined   d. Undefined

121. _____ is a technique used in algebra to solve quadratic equations, in analytic geometry for determining the shapes of graphs, and in calculus for computing integrals, including, but hardly limited to, the integrals that define Laplace transforms. The essential objective is to reduce a quadratic polynomial in a variable in an equation or expression to a squared polynomial of linear order. This can reduce an equation or integral to one that is more easily solved or evaluated.
    a. Completing the square0   b. Thing
    c. Undefined   d. Undefined

122. In mathematics, a _____ number is a number which can be expressed as a ratio of two integers. Non-integer _____ numbers (commonly called fractions) are usually written as the vulgar fraction a / b, where b is not zero.

Chapter 5. INTEGRATION

a. Thing
b. Rational0
c. Undefined
d. Undefined

123. In mathematics, an _____ number is any real number that is not a rational number- that is, it is a number which cannot be expressed as a fraction m/n, where m and n are integers.
   a. Irrational0
   b. Thing
   c. Undefined
   d. Undefined

124. In mathematics, an _____ is any real number that is not a rational number ¡ª that is, it is a number which cannot be expressed as m/n, where m and n are integers.
   a. Thing
   b. Irrational number0
   c. Undefined
   d. Undefined

125. In mathematics, _____ are any real number that is not a rational number ¡ª that is, it is a number which cannot be expressed as m/n, where m and n are integers.
   a. Thing
   b. Irrational numbers0
   c. Undefined
   d. Undefined

126. In mathematics, a _____ is a mathematical statement which appears likely to be true, but has not been formally proven to be true under the rules of mathematical logic.
   a. Concept
   b. Conjecture0
   c. Undefined
   d. Undefined

127. _____ constitutes a broad family of algorithms for calculating the numerical value of a definite integral, and by extension, the term is also sometimes used to describe the numerical solution of differential equations.
   a. Thing
   b. Numerical integration0
   c. Undefined
   d. Undefined

128. In common philosophical language, a proposition or _____, is the content of an assertion, that is, it is true-or-false and defined by the meaning of a particular piece of language.
   a. Concept
   b. Statement0
   c. Undefined
   d. Undefined

129. In mathematics, an _____, mean, or central tendency of a data set refers to a measure of the "middle" or "expected" value of the data set.
   a. Concept
   b. Average0
   c. Undefined
   d. Undefined

130. _____ of an object is its speed in a particular direction.
   a. Thing
   b. Velocity0
   c. Undefined
   d. Undefined

131. _____ is defined as the rate of change or derivative with respect to time of velocity.
   a. Acceleration0
   b. Thing
   c. Undefined
   d. Undefined

Chapter 5. INTEGRATION

132. A _____ is a set of numbers that designate location in a given reference system, such as x,y in a planar _____ system or an x,y,z in a three-dimensional _____ system.
   a. Coordinate0
   b. Thing
   c. Undefined
   d. Undefined

133. _____ is the transport of people on a trip/journey or the process or time involved in a person or object moving from one location to another.
   a. Travel0
   b. Thing
   c. Undefined
   d. Undefined

134. In mathematics, a _____ is a polynomial equation of the second degree. The general form is $ax^2 + bx + c = 0$.
   a. Thing
   b. Quadratic equation0
   c. Undefined
   d. Undefined

135. A quadratic equation with real solutions, called roots, which may be real or complex, is given by the _____: $x = \frac{-b \pm \sqrt{b^2 - 4ac}}{2a}$.
   a. Quadratic formula0
   b. Thing
   c. Undefined
   d. Undefined

136. In physics, _____ is an influence that may cause an object to accelerate. It may be experienced as a lift, a push, or a pull. The actual acceleration of the body is determined by the vector sum of all forces acting on it, known as net _____ or resultant _____.
   a. Thing
   b. Force0
   c. Undefined
   d. Undefined

137. The metre (or _____, see spelling differences) is a measure of length. It is the basic unit of length in the metric system and in the International System of Units (SI), used around the world for general and scientific purposes.
   a. Concept
   b. Meter0
   c. Undefined
   d. Undefined

138. _____, usually denoted symbolically by the Greek letter phi, Ï¦, gives the location of a place on Earth north or south of the equator. _____ is an angular measurement in degrees (marked with Â°) ranging from 0Â° at the Equator (low _____) to 90Â° at the poles (90Â° N for the North Pole or 90Â° S for the South Pole; high _____). The complementary angle of a _____ is called the colatitude.
   a. Latitude0
   b. Thing
   c. Undefined
   d. Undefined

139. In mathematics, the additive inverse, or _____ of a number n is the number that, when added to n, yields zero. The additive inverse of n is denoted −n. For example, 7 is −7, because 7 + (−7) = 0, and the additive inverse of −0.3 is 0.3, because −0.3 + 0.3 = 0.
   a. Opposite0
   b. Thing
   c. Undefined
   d. Undefined

140. In mathematics, the _____ of a number n is the number that, when added to n, yields zero. The _____ of n is denoted −n. For example, 7 is −7, because 7 + (−7) = 0, and the _____ of −0.3 is 0.3, because −0.3 + 0.3 = 0.

a. Additive inverse0
b. Thing
c. Undefined
d. Undefined

141. A _____ signifies a point or points of probability on a subject e.g., the _____ of creativity, which allows for the formation of rule or norm or law by interpretation of the phenomena events that can be created.
a. Thing
b. Principle0
c. Undefined
d. Undefined

142. The _____ of measurement are a globally standardized and modernized form of the metric system.
a. Thing
b. Units0
c. Undefined
d. Undefined

143. In business, particularly accounting, a _____ is the time intervals that the accounts, statement, payments, or other calculations cover.
a. Period0
b. Thing
c. Undefined
d. Undefined

144. _____ is a synonym for information.
a. Data0
b. Thing
c. Undefined
d. Undefined

145. _____ or arithmetics is the oldest and most elementary branch of mathematics, used by almost everyone, for tasks ranging from simple daily counting to advanced science and business calculations.
a. Arithmetic0
b. Thing
c. Undefined
d. Undefined

146. _____ of a list of numbers is the sum of all the members of the list divided by the number of items in the list.
a. Arithmetic mean0
b. Thing
c. Undefined
d. Undefined

147. _____ is a trigonometric function that is the reciprocal of cosine.
a. Thing
b. Secant0
c. Undefined
d. Undefined

148. _____ of a curve is a line that intersects two or more points on the curve.
a. Thing
b. Secant line0
c. Undefined
d. Undefined

149. _____ are the basic objects of study in graph theory. Informally speaking, a graph is a set of objects called points, nodes, or vertices connected by links called lines or edges.
a. Graphs0
b. Thing
c. Undefined
d. Undefined

150. In botany, _____ are above-ground plant organs specialized for photosynthesis. Their characteristics are typically analyzed by using Fiobonacci's sequences.

Chapter 5. INTEGRATION

a. Leaves0
b. Thing
c. Undefined
d. Undefined

151. A _____ is any object propelled through space by the applicationp of a force.
a. Thing
b. Projectile0
c. Undefined
d. Undefined

152. In mathematics and more specifically set theory, the _____ set is the unique set which contains no elements.
a. Empty0
b. Thing
c. Undefined
d. Undefined

153. _____ is mass m per unit volume V.
a. Density0
b. Thing
c. Undefined
d. Undefined

154. _____ is the difference of electrical potential between two points of an electrical or electronic circuit, expressed in volts
a. Voltage0
b. Thing
c. Undefined
d. Undefined

155. The _____ is a nonnegative scalar measure of a wave's magnitude of oscillation, that is, the magnitude of the maximum disturbance in the medium during one wave cycle.
a. Thing
b. Amplitude0
c. Undefined
d. Undefined

156. In statistics the _____ of an event i is the number n_i of times the event occurred in the experiment or the study. These frequencies are often graphically represented in histograms.
a. Frequency0
b. Concept
c. Undefined
d. Undefined

157. In mathematics, a _____ of a number x is a number r such that $r^2 = x$, or in words, a number r whose square (the result of multiplying the number by itself) is x.
a. Thing
b. Square root0
c. Undefined
d. Undefined

158. In mathematics, a _____ of a complex-valued function f is a member x of the domain of f such that f(x) vanishes at x, that is, x : f (x) = 0.
a. Thing
b. Root0
c. Undefined
d. Undefined

159. A _____ is a deliberate process for transforming one or more inputs into one or more results.
a. Calculation0
b. Thing
c. Undefined
d. Undefined

160. A pair of angles is _____ if their respective measures sum to 180 degrees.

Chapter 5. INTEGRATION

a. Concept
b. Supplementary0
c. Undefined
d. Undefined

161. _____ are functions which satisfy particular symmetry relations, with respect to taking additive inverses.
a. Thing
b. Even function0
c. Undefined
d. Undefined

162. The deductive-nomological model is a formalized view of scientific _____ in natural language.
a. Explanation0
b. Thing
c. Undefined
d. Undefined

163. _____ are objects, characters, or other concrete representations of ideas, concepts, or other abstractions.
a. Thing
b. Symbols0
c. Undefined
d. Undefined

164. _____ element of an element x with respect to a binary operation * with identity element e is an element y such that x * y = y * x = e. In particular,
a. Inverse0
b. Thing
c. Undefined
d. Undefined

165. _____ means in succession or back-to-back
a. Thing
b. Consecutive0
c. Undefined
d. Undefined

166. Deductive _____ is the kind of _____ in which the conclusion is necessitated by, or reached from, previously known facts (the premises).
a. Reasoning0
b. Thing
c. Undefined
d. Undefined

167. in mathematics, maxima and minima, known collectively as _____, are the largest value maximum or smallest value minimum, that a function takes in a point either within a given neighborhood or on the function domain in its entirety global extremum.
a. Extrema0
b. Thing
c. Undefined
d. Undefined

168. The term _____ refers to the largest and the smallest element of a set.
a. Thing
b. Extreme value0
c. Undefined
d. Undefined

169. A _____ consists of one quarter of the coordinate plane.
a. Quadrant0
b. Thing
c. Undefined
d. Undefined

170. _____ first defined by the mathematician Daniel Bernoulli and generalized by Friedrich Bessel, are canonical solutions y(x) of Bessel's differential equation:

Chapter 5. INTEGRATION

    a. Thing
    c. Undefined
    b. Bessel function0
    d. Undefined

171. _____ is the path a moving object follows through space.
    a. Projectile motion0
    b. Thing
    c. Undefined
    d. Undefined

172. The _____ of a geographic location is its height above a fixed reference point, often the mean sea level.
    a. Elevation0
    b. Thing
    c. Undefined
    d. Undefined

173. In mathematics, in the field of group theory, a _____ of a group is a quasisimple subnormal subgroup.
    a. Component0
    b. Concept
    c. Undefined
    d. Undefined

174. _____ statistics are statistics that estimate population parameters.
    a. Thing
    b. Parametric0
    c. Undefined
    d. Undefined

175. In mathematics, _____ bear slight similarity to functions: they allow one to use arbitrary values, called parameters, in place of independent variables in equations, which in turn provide values for dependent variables. A simple kinematical example is when one uses a time parameter to determine the position, velocity, and other information about a body in motion.
    a. Thing
    b. Parametric equations0
    c. Undefined
    d. Undefined

176. A _____ is the quantity that defines certain relatively constant characteristics of systems or functions..
    a. Thing
    b. Parameter0
    c. Undefined
    d. Undefined

177. In mathematics, the _____ of a function is the set of all "output" values produced by that function. Given a function $f : A \to B$, the _____ of f, is defined to be the set $\{x \in B : x = f(a)$ for some $a \in A\}$.
    a. Thing
    b. Range0
    c. Undefined
    d. Undefined

178. An _____ is an increase, either of some fixed amount, for example added regularly, or of a variable amount.
    a. Increment0
    b. Thing
    c. Undefined
    d. Undefined

179. _____, in economics and political economy, are the distributions or payments awarded to the various suppliers of the factors of production.
    a. Returns0
    b. Thing
    c. Undefined
    d. Undefined

Chapter 6. APPLICATIONS OF THE DEFINITE INTEGRAL IN GEOMETRY, SCIENCE, AND ENGINEERING

1. _____ is the design, analysis, and/or construction of works for practical purposes.
   a. Thing
   b. Engineering0
   c. Undefined
   d. Undefined

2. A _____ is the result of the addition of a set of numbers. The numbers may be natural numbers, complex numbers, matrices, or still more complicated objects. An infinite _____ is a subtle procedure known as a series.
   a. Thing
   b. Sum0
   c. Undefined
   d. Undefined

3. _____ is an extension of the concept of a sum.
   a. Definite integral0
   b. Thing
   c. Undefined
   d. Undefined

4. The _____ of a function is an extension of the concept of a sum, and are identified or found through the use of integration.
   a. Integral0
   b. Thing
   c. Undefined
   d. Undefined

5. _____ is a method for approximating the values of integrals.
   a. Riemann sum0
   b. Thing
   c. Undefined
   d. Undefined

6. A _____ is a deliberate process for transforming one or more inputs into one or more results.
   a. Thing
   b. Calculation0
   c. Undefined
   d. Undefined

7. In mathematics, the concept of a _____ tries to capture the intuitive idea of a geometrical one-dimensional and continuous object. A simple example is the circle.
   a. Thing
   b. Curve0
   c. Undefined
   d. Undefined

8. In mathematics, _____ are the intuitive idea of a geometrical one-dimensional and continuous object.
   a. Curves0
   b. Thing
   c. Undefined
   d. Undefined

9. In elementary algebra, an _____ is a set that contains every real number between two indicated numbers and may contain the two numbers themselves.
   a. Thing
   b. Interval0
   c. Undefined
   d. Undefined

10. A _____ function is a function for which, intuitively, small changes in the input result in small changes in the output.
    a. Event
    b. Continuous0
    c. Undefined
    d. Undefined

11. The _____ integers are all the integers from zero on upwards.

Chapter 6. APPLICATIONS OF THE DEFINITE INTEGRAL IN GEOMETRY, SCIENCE, AND ENGINEERING

a. Thing
b. Nonnegative0
c. Undefined
d. Undefined

12. In geometry, a _____ is defined as a quadrilateral where all four of its angles are right angles.
    a. Thing
    b. Rectangle0
    c. Undefined
    d. Undefined

13. _____ is a process of combining or accumulating. It may also refer to:
    a. Integration0
    b. Thing
    c. Undefined
    d. Undefined

14. In geometry, a line _____ is a part of a line that is bounded by two end points, and contains every point on the line between its end points.
    a. Segment0
    b. Concept
    c. Undefined
    d. Undefined

15. In geometry, an _____ is a point at which a line segment or ray terminates.
    a. Thing
    b. Endpoint0
    c. Undefined
    d. Undefined

16. A _____ is a part of a line that is bounded by two end points, and contains every point on the line between its end points.
    a. Thing
    b. Line segment0
    c. Undefined
    d. Undefined

17. _____ is a function that extends the concept of an ordinary sum
    a. Thing
    b. Integrand0
    c. Undefined
    d. Undefined

18. In topology, the _____ are subsets S of a topological space X is the set of points which can be approached both from S and from the outside of S.
    a. Thing
    b. Boundaries0
    c. Undefined
    d. Undefined

19. In geometry, a _____ is the intersection of a body in 2-dimensional space with a line, or of a body in 3-dimensional space with a plane
    a. Thing
    b. Cross section0
    c. Undefined
    d. Undefined

20. In mathematical analysis and related areas of mathematics, a set is called _____, if it is, in a certain sense, of finite size.
    a. Thing
    b. Bounded0
    c. Undefined
    d. Undefined

Chapter 6. APPLICATIONS OF THE DEFINITE INTEGRAL IN GEOMETRY, SCIENCE, AND ENGINEERING

21. In mathematics, the _____ of two sets A and B is the set that contains all elements of A that also belong to B (or equivalently, all elements of B that also belong to A), but no other elements.
    a. Thing
    b. Intersection0
    c. Undefined
    d. Undefined

22. _____ traditionally refers to the statistical process of determining comparable scores on different forms of an exam
    a. Thing
    b. Equating0
    c. Undefined
    d. Undefined

23. An _____ is a combination of numbers, operators, grouping symbols and/or free variables and bound variables arranged in a meaningful way which can be evaluated..
    a. Expression0
    b. Thing
    c. Undefined
    d. Undefined

24. The mathematical concept of a _____ expresses the intuitive idea of deterministic dependence between two quantities, one of which is viewed as primary and the other as secondary. A _____ then is a way to associate a unique output for each input of a specified type, for example, a real number or an element of a given set.
    a. Thing
    b. Function0
    c. Undefined
    d. Undefined

25. _____ are the basic objects of study in graph theory. Informally speaking, a graph is a set of objects called points, nodes, or vertices connected by links called lines or edges.
    a. Graphs0
    b. Thing
    c. Undefined
    d. Undefined

26. _____ of an object is its speed in a particular direction.
    a. Thing
    b. Velocity0
    c. Undefined
    d. Undefined

27. In astronomy, geography, geometry and related sciences and contexts, a plane is said to be _____ at a given point if it is locally perpendicular to the gradient of the gravity field, i.e., with the direction of the gravitational force at that point.
    a. Horizontal0
    b. Thing
    c. Undefined
    d. Undefined

28. In mathematics, the _____ is a conic section generated by the intersection of a right circular conical surface and a plane parallel to a generating straight line of that surface. It can also be defined as locus of points in a plane which are equidistant from a given point.
    a. Thing
    b. Parabola0
    c. Undefined
    d. Undefined

29. A _____ consists of one quarter of the coordinate plane.
    a. Thing
    b. Quadrant0
    c. Undefined
    d. Undefined

Chapter 6. APPLICATIONS OF THE DEFINITE INTEGRAL IN GEOMETRY, SCIENCE, AND ENGINEERING

30. In mathematics, a _____ is a mathematical statement which appears likely to be true, but has not been formally proven to be true under the rules of mathematical logic.
    a. Conjecture0
    b. Concept
    c. Undefined
    d. Undefined

31. Sir Isaac _____, was an English physicist, mathematician, astronomer, natural philosopher, and alchemist, regarded by many as the greatest figure in the history of science
    a. Person
    b. Newton0
    c. Undefined
    d. Undefined

32. In geometry, a _____ is a special kind of point, usually a corner of a polygon, polyhedron, or higher dimensional polytope. In the geometry of curves a _____ is a point of where the first derivative of curvature is zero. In graph theory, a _____ is the fundamental unit out of which graphs are formed
    a. Thing
    b. Vertex0
    c. Undefined
    d. Undefined

33. A _____ is a set of numbers that designate location in a given reference system, such as x,y in a planar _____ system or an x,y,z in a three-dimensional _____ system.
    a. Coordinate0
    b. Thing
    c. Undefined
    d. Undefined

34. An _____ is when two lines intersect somewhere on a plane creating a right angle at intersection
    a. Thing
    b. Axes0
    c. Undefined
    d. Undefined

35. In mathematics, the additive inverse, or _____ of a number n is the number that, when added to n, yields zero. The additive inverse of n is denoted −n. For example, 7 is −7, because 7 + (−7) = 0, and the additive inverse of −0.3 is 0.3, because −0.3 + 0.3 = 0.
    a. Thing
    b. Opposite0
    c. Undefined
    d. Undefined

36. In mathematics, the _____ of a coordinate system is the point where the axes of the system intersect.
    a. Origin0
    b. Thing
    c. Undefined
    d. Undefined

37. In mathematics, the _____ of a number n is the number that, when added to n, yields zero. The _____ of n is denoted −n. For example, 7 is −7, because 7 + (−7) = 0, and the _____ of −0.3 is 0.3, because −0.3 + 0.3 = 0.
    a. Additive inverse0
    b. Thing
    c. Undefined
    d. Undefined

38. In mathematics, an _____ .
    a. Ellipse0
    b. Thing
    c. Undefined
    d. Undefined

Chapter 6. APPLICATIONS OF THE DEFINITE INTEGRAL IN GEOMETRY, SCIENCE, AND ENGINEERING

39. The _____ of a solid object is the three-dimensional concept of how much space it occupies, often quantified numerically.
  a. Volume0
  b. Thing
  c. Undefined
  d. Undefined

40. In mathematics, a _____ is a two-dimensional manifold or surface that is perfectly flat.
  a. Thing
  b. Plane0
  c. Undefined
  d. Undefined

41. A _____ signifies a point or points of probability on a subject e.g., the _____ of creativity, which allows for the formation of rule or norm or law by interpretation of the phenomena events that can be created.
  a. Principle0
  b. Thing
  c. Undefined
  d. Undefined

42. In mathematics, _____ geometry was the traditional name for the geometry of three-dimensional Euclidean space — for practical purposes the kind of space we live in.
  a. Thing
  b. Solid0
  c. Undefined
  d. Undefined

43. In classical geometry, a _____ of a circle or sphere is any line segment from its center to its boundary. By extension, the _____ of a circle or sphere is the length of any such segment. The _____ is half the diameter. In science and engineering the term _____ of curvature is commonly used as a synonym for _____.
  a. Thing
  b. Radius0
  c. Undefined
  d. Undefined

44. In mathematics, a _____ is a quadric surface, with the following equation in Cartesian coordinates: $(x/_a)^2 + (y/_b)^2 = 1$.
  a. Thing
  b. Cylinder0
  c. Undefined
  d. Undefined

45. An _____ is a straight line around which a geometric figure can be rotated.
  a. Axis0
  b. Thing
  c. Undefined
  d. Undefined

46. In geometry, two lines or planes if one falls on the other in such a way as to create congruent adjacent angles. The term may be used as a noun or adjective. Thus, referring to Figure 1, the line AB is the _____ to CD through the point B.
  a. Thing
  b. Perpendicular0
  c. Undefined
  d. Undefined

47. In mathematics, _____ are two-dimensional manifolds or surfaces that are perfectly flat.
  a. Thing
  b. Planes0
  c. Undefined
  d. Undefined

48. An n-sided _____ is a polyhedron formed by connecting an n-sided polygonal base and a point, called the apex, by n triangular faces. In other words, it is a conic solid with polygonal base.

Chapter 6. APPLICATIONS OF THE DEFINITE INTEGRAL IN GEOMETRY, SCIENCE, AND ENGINEERING

a. Pyramid0   b. Thing
c. Undefined   d. Undefined

49. In plane geometry, a _____ is a polygon with four equal sides, four right angles, and parallel opposite sides. In algebra, the _____ of a number is that number multiplied by itself.
 a. Square0
 b. Thing
 c. Undefined
 d. Undefined

50. In geometry, an _____ of a triangle is a straight line through a vertex and perpendicular to (i.e. forming a right angle with) the opposite side or an extension of the opposite side.
 a. Altitude0
 b. Concept
 c. Undefined
 d. Undefined

51. A _____ is one of the basic shapes of geometry: a polygon with three vertices and three sides which are straight line segments.
 a. Thing
 b. Triangle0
 c. Undefined
 d. Undefined

52. In mathematics, a _____ is the set of all points in three-dimensional space (R^3) which are at distance r from a fixed point of that space, where r is a positive real number called the radius of the _____. The fixed point is called the center or centre, and is not part of the _____ itself.
 a. Thing
 b. Sphere0
 c. Undefined
 d. Undefined

53. In Euclidean geometry, a uniform _____ is a linear transformation that enlargers or diminishes objects, and whose _____ factor is the same in all directions. This is also called homothethy.
 a. Thing
 b. Scale0
 c. Undefined
 d. Undefined

54. An _____ is an equality that remains true regardless of the values of any variables that appear within it, to distinguish it from an equality which is true under more particular conditions.
 a. Identity0
 b. Thing
 c. Undefined
 d. Undefined

55. In Euclidean geometry, a _____ is the set of all points in a plane at a fixed distance, called the radius, from a given point, the center.
 a. Circle0
 b. Thing
 c. Undefined
 d. Undefined

56. _____ is a set, with some particular properties and usually some additional structure, such as the operations of addition or multiplication, for instance.
 a. Thing
 b. Space0
 c. Undefined
 d. Undefined

Chapter 6. APPLICATIONS OF THE DEFINITE INTEGRAL IN GEOMETRY, SCIENCE, AND ENGINEERING

57. _____ means "constancy", i.e. if something retains a certain feature even after we change a way of looking at it, then it is symmetric.
   a. Symmetry0
   b. Thing
   c. Undefined
   d. Undefined

58. _____ of a two-dimensional figure is a line such that, if a perpendicular is constructed, any two points lying on the perpendicular at equal distances from the _____ are identical.
   a. Axis of symmetry0
   b. Thing
   c. Undefined
   d. Undefined

59. A _____ is a three-dimensional geometric shape formed by straight lines through a fixed point (vertex) to the points of a fixed curve (directrix)
   a. Cone0
   b. Concept
   c. Undefined
   d. Undefined

60. In geometry, a _____ (Greek words diairo = divide and metro = measure) of a circle is any straight line segment that passes through the centre and whose endpoints are on the circular boundary, or, in more modern usage, the length of such a line segment. When using the word in the more modern sense, one speaks of the _____ rather than a _____, because all diameters of a circle have the same length. This length is twice the radius. The _____ of a circle is also the longest chord that the circle has.
   a. Thing
   b. Diameter0
   c. Undefined
   d. Undefined

61. In geometry, an _____ polygon is a polygon which has all sides of the same length.
   a. Equilateral0
   b. Thing
   c. Undefined
   d. Undefined

62. An _____ is a triangle in which all sides are of equal length.
   a. Thing
   b. Equilateral triangle0
   c. Undefined
   d. Undefined

63. In geometry, the _____ of an object is a point in some sense in the middle of the object.
   a. Center0
   b. Thing
   c. Undefined
   d. Undefined

64. In geometry, a _____ is a surface of revolution generated by revolving a circle in three dimensional space about an axis coplanar with the circle, which does not touch the circle. Examples of tori include the surfaces of doughnuts and inner tubes. A circle rotated about a chord of the circle is called a _____ in some contexts, but this is not a common usage in mathematics. The shape produced when a circle is rotated about a chord resembles a round cushion. _____ was the Latin word for a cushion of this shape.
   a. Torus0
   b. Thing
   c. Undefined
   d. Undefined

65. In Euclidean geometry, an _____ is a closed segment of a differentiable curve in the two-dimensional plane; for example, a circular _____ is a segment of a circle.

Chapter 6. APPLICATIONS OF THE DEFINITE INTEGRAL IN GEOMETRY, SCIENCE, AND ENGINEERING

a. Arc0
b. Concept
c. Undefined
d. Undefined

66. A _____ is the curve defined by the path of a point on the edge of circular wheel as the wheel rolls along a straight line.
a. Thing
b. Cycloid0
c. Undefined
d. Undefined

67. _____ also called rectification of a curve—was historically difficult.
a. Arc length0
b. Thing
c. Undefined
d. Undefined

68. A _____ is a function for which, intuitively, small changes in the input result in small changes in the output.
a. Continuous function0
b. Event
c. Undefined
d. Undefined

69. _____ statistics are statistics that estimate population parameters.
a. Thing
b. Parametric0
c. Undefined
d. Undefined

70. In mathematics, _____ bear slight similarity to functions: they allow one to use arbitrary values, called parameters, in place of independent variables in equations, which in turn provide values for dependent variables. A simple kinematical example is when one uses a time parameter to determine the position, velocity, and other information about a body in motion.
a. Thing
b. Parametric equations0
c. Undefined
d. Undefined

71. The _____ is the distance around a closed curve. _____ is a kind of perimeter.
a. Thing
b. Circumference0
c. Undefined
d. Undefined

72. _____ was an Greek philosopher. He is best known for a theorem in trigonometry that bears his name.
a. Pythagoras0
b. Person
c. Undefined
d. Undefined

73. A _____ is a negotiable instrument instructing a financial institution to pay a specific amount of a specific currency from a specific demand account held in the maker/depositor's name with that institution. Both the maker and payee may be natural persons or legal entities.
a. Check0
b. Thing
c. Undefined
d. Undefined

74. In mathematics, a _____ is a statement that can be proved on the basis of explicitly stated or previously agreed assumptions.

Chapter 6. APPLICATIONS OF THE DEFINITE INTEGRAL IN GEOMETRY, SCIENCE, AND ENGINEERING

a. Theorem0
b. Thing
c. Undefined
d. Undefined

75. A _____ is the quantity that defines certain relatively constant characteristics of systems or functions..
a. Thing
b. Parameter0
c. Undefined
d. Undefined

76. _____ is the middle point of a line segment.
a. Midpoint0
b. Thing
c. Undefined
d. Undefined

77. _____ constitutes a broad family of algorithms for calculating the numerical value of a definite integral, and by extension, the term is also sometimes used to describe the numerical solution of differential equations.
a. Thing
b. Numerical integration0
c. Undefined
d. Undefined

78. In mathematics, an _____ is a statement about the relative size or order of two objects.
a. Inequality0
b. Thing
c. Undefined
d. Undefined

79. _____ is the transport of people on a trip/journey or the process or time involved in a person or object moving from one location to another.
a. Travel0
b. Thing
c. Undefined
d. Undefined

80. The _____ of measurement are a globally standardized and modernized form of the metric system.
a. Thing
b. Units0
c. Undefined
d. Undefined

81. In mathematics, a _____ is a curve in a Euclidian plane. The most frequently studied types are the smooth _____, and the algebraic _____.
a. Plane curve0
b. Thing
c. Undefined
d. Undefined

82. _____ is the portion of a solid – normally a cone or pyramid – which lies between two parallel planes cutting the solid.
a. Truncated pyramid0
b. Thing
c. Undefined
d. Undefined

83. The _____ of a right circular cone is the distance from any point on the circle to the apex of the cone.
a. Thing
b. Slant height0
c. Undefined
d. Undefined

84. A _____ surface is the surface or face of a solid on its sides. It can also be defined as any face or surface that is not a base.

Chapter 6. APPLICATIONS OF THE DEFINITE INTEGRAL IN GEOMETRY, SCIENCE, AND ENGINEERING

a. Lateral0
b. Thing
c. Undefined
d. Undefined

85. _____ is a three-dimensional geometric shape formed by straight lines through a fixed point vertex to the points of a fixed curve directrix.
   a. Right circular cone0
   b. Thing
   c. Undefined
   d. Undefined

86. A _____ is a symbolic representation denoting a quantity or expression. It often represents an "unknown" quantity that has the potential to change.
   a. Thing
   b. Variable0
   c. Undefined
   d. Undefined

87. In mathematics, an _____, mean, or central tendency of a data set refers to a measure of the "middle" or "expected" value of the data set.
   a. Average0
   b. Concept
   c. Undefined
   d. Undefined

88. The _____ of an object is the extra energy which it possesses due to its motion.
   a. Kinetic energy0
   b. Thing
   c. Undefined
   d. Undefined

89. _____, Greek for "knowledge of nature," is the branch of science concerned with the discovery and characterization of universal laws which govern matter, energy, space, and time.
   a. Thing
   b. Physics0
   c. Undefined
   d. Undefined

90. The _____ of a mathematical object is its size: a property by which it can be larger or smaller than other objects of the same kind; in technical terms, an ordering of the class of objects to which it belongs.
   a. Thing
   b. Magnitude0
   c. Undefined
   d. Undefined

91. In mathematics and the mathematical sciences, a _____ is a fixed, but possibly unspecified, value. This is in contrast to a variable, which is not fixed.
   a. Thing
   b. Constant0
   c. Undefined
   d. Undefined

92. In physics, _____ is an influence that may cause an object to accelerate. It may be experienced as a lift, a push, or a pull. The actual acceleration of the body is determined by the vector sum of all forces acting on it, known as net _____ or resultant _____.
   a. Force0
   b. Thing
   c. Undefined
   d. Undefined

93. _____ is the property of a physical object that quantifies the amount of matter and energy it is equivalent to.

Chapter 6. APPLICATIONS OF THE DEFINITE INTEGRAL IN GEOMETRY, SCIENCE, AND ENGINEERING

    a. Thing
    b. Mass0
    c. Undefined
    d. Undefined

94. _____ is defined as the rate of change or derivative with respect to time of velocity.
    a. Acceleration0
    b. Thing
    c. Undefined
    d. Undefined

95. _____ is the weakest of the four fundamental forces of bature, as described by Issac Newton
    a. Thing
    b. Gravitational force0
    c. Undefined
    d. Undefined

96. The metre (or _____, see spelling differences) is a measure of length. It is the basic unit of length in the metric system and in the International System of Units (SI), used around the world for general and scientific purposes.
    a. Concept
    b. Meter0
    c. Undefined
    d. Undefined

97. Initial objects are also called _____, and terminal objects are also called final.
    a. Thing
    b. Coterminal0
    c. Undefined
    d. Undefined

98. _____ is mass m per unit volume V.
    a. Density0
    b. Thing
    c. Undefined
    d. Undefined

99. In geometry, a _____ is a three-dimensional figure formed by six parallelograms.
    a. Parallelepiped0
    b. Thing
    c. Undefined
    d. Undefined

100. A _____ is a vehicle, missile or aircraft which obtains thrust by the reaction to the ejection of fast moving fluid from within a _____ engine.
    a. Thing
    b. Rocket0
    c. Undefined
    d. Undefined

101. A _____ is a special kind of ratio, indicating a relationship between two measurements with different units, such as miles to gallons or cents to pounds.
    a. Rate0
    b. Thing
    c. Undefined
    d. Undefined

102. In mathematics, two quantities are called _____ if they vary in such a way that one of the quantities is a constant multiple of the other, or equivalently if they have a constant ratio.
    a. Proportional0
    b. Thing
    c. Undefined
    d. Undefined

103. Acid _____ ratio measures the ability of a company to use its near cash or quick assets to immediately extinguish its current liabilities.

Chapter 6. APPLICATIONS OF THE DEFINITE INTEGRAL IN GEOMETRY, SCIENCE, AND ENGINEERING

a. Test0
b. Thing
c. Undefined
d. Undefined

104. The _____ of a ring R is defined to be the smallest positive integer n such that $n\,a = 0$, for all a in R.
a. Characteristic0
b. Thing
c. Undefined
d. Undefined

105. _____ is a subset of a population.
a. Thing
b. Sample0
c. Undefined
d. Undefined

106. Blaise _____ was a French mathematician, physicist, and religious philosopher.
a. Person
b. Pascal0
c. Undefined
d. Undefined

107. _____, also known as _____ of Alexandria, was a Greek mathematician. His Elements is the most successful textbook in the history of mathematics. In it, the principles of geometry are deduced from a small set of axioms. His method of proving mathematical theorems by logical reasoning from accepted first principles remains the backbone of mathematics and is responsible for the field's characteristic rigor
a. Person
b. Euclid0
c. Undefined
d. Undefined

108. _____ was a highly influential French philosopher, mathematician, scientist, and writer. Dubbed the "Founder of Modern Philosophy", and the "Father of Modern Mathematics". His theories provided the basis for the calculus of Newton and Leibniz, by applying infinitesimal calculus to the tangent line problem, thus permitting the evolution of that branch of modern mathematics
a. Descartes0
b. Person
c. Undefined
d. Undefined

109. _____ is the level of functional and/or metabolic efficiency of an organism at both the micro level.
a. Health0
b. Thing
c. Undefined
d. Undefined

110. _____ is the chance that something is likely to happen or be the case.
a. Probability0
b. Thing
c. Undefined
d. Undefined

111. _____ is a non-metrical form of geometry.
a. Thing
b. Projective geometry0
c. Undefined
d. Undefined

112. A _____ is the sum of the elements of a sequence.
a. Series0
b. Thing
c. Undefined
d. Undefined

Chapter 6. APPLICATIONS OF THE DEFINITE INTEGRAL IN GEOMETRY, SCIENCE, AND ENGINEERING

113. _____ is a mathematical subject that includes the study of limits, derivatives, integrals, and power series and constitutes a major part of modern university curriculum.
    a. Thing
    b. Calculus0
    c. Undefined
    d. Undefined

114. The _____ is one of the classical simple machines; as the name suggests, it is a flat surface whose endpoints are at different heights. By moving an object up an _____ rather than directly from one height to another, the amount of force required is reduced, at the expense of increasing the distance the object must travel. The mechanical advantage of an _____ is the ratio of the length of the sloped surface to the height it spans; this may also be expressed as the cosecant of the angle between the plane and the horizontal.
    a. Inclined plane0
    b. Thing
    c. Undefined
    d. Undefined

115. In common philosophical language, a proposition or _____, is the content of an assertion, that is, it is true-or-false and defined by the meaning of a particular piece of language.
    a. Concept
    b. Statement0
    c. Undefined
    d. Undefined

116. A pair of angles is _____ if their respective measures sum to 180 degrees.
    a. Concept
    b. Supplementary0
    c. Undefined
    d. Undefined

Chapter 7. EXPONENTIAL, LOGARITHMIC, AND INVERSE TRIGONOMETRIC FUNCTIONS

1. In mathematics, the _____ functions are functions of an angle; they are important when studying triangles and modeling periodic phenomena, among many other applications.
   - a. Thing
   - b. Trigonometric0
   - c. Undefined
   - d. Undefined

2. The _____ are functions of an angle; they are important when studying triangles and modeling periodic phenomena, among many other applications.
   - a. Thing
   - b. Trigonometric functions0
   - c. Undefined
   - d. Undefined

3. The mathematical concept of a _____ expresses the intuitive idea of deterministic dependence between two quantities, one of which is viewed as primary and the other as secondary. A _____ then is a way to associate a unique output for each input of a specified type, for example, a real number or an element of a given set.
   - a. Function0
   - b. Thing
   - c. Undefined
   - d. Undefined

4. In mathematics, _____ growth occurs when the growth rate of a function is always proportional to the function's current size.
   - a. Thing
   - b. Exponential0
   - c. Undefined
   - d. Undefined

5. _____ element of an element x with respect to a binary operation * with identity element e is an element y such that x * y = y * x = e. In particular,
   - a. Inverse0
   - b. Thing
   - c. Undefined
   - d. Undefined

6. In mathematics, the _____ are the inverse functions of the trigonometric functions.
   - a. Inverse trigonometric functions0
   - b. Thing
   - c. Undefined
   - d. Undefined

7. An _____ is a function which does the reverse of a given function.
   - a. Thing
   - b. Inverse function0
   - c. Undefined
   - d. Undefined

8. In mathematics, a _____ of a positive integer n is a way of writing n as a sum of positive integers.
   - a. Thing
   - b. Composition0
   - c. Undefined
   - d. Undefined

9. In mathematics, the conjugate _____ or adjoint matrix of an m-by-n matrix A with complex entries is the n-by-m matrix A* obtained from A by taking the transpose and then taking the complex conjugate of each entry.
   - a. Thing
   - b. Pairs0
   - c. Undefined
   - d. Undefined

10. _____ is the study of terms and their use — of words and compound words that are used in specific contexts.
    - a. Terminology0
    - b. Thing
    - c. Undefined
    - d. Undefined

Chapter 7. EXPONENTIAL, LOGARITHMIC, AND INVERSE TRIGONOMETRIC FUNCTIONS

11. In mathematics, a _____ of a k-place relation $L \subseteq X_1 \times ... \times X_k$ is one of the sets X_j, $1 \leq j \leq k$. In the special case where k = 2 and $L \subseteq X_1 \times X_2$ is a function $L : X_1 \to X_2$, it is conventional to refer to X_1 as the _____ of the function and to refer to X_2 as the codomain of the function.
   - a. Domain0
   - b. Thing
   - c. Undefined
   - d. Undefined

12. A _____ is a three-dimensional solid object bounded by six square faces, facets, or sides, with three meeting at each vertex.
   - a. Thing
   - b. Cube0
   - c. Undefined
   - d. Undefined

13. A _____ of a number is a number a such that $a^3 = x$.
   - a. Cube root0
   - b. Thing
   - c. Undefined
   - d. Undefined

14. In mathematics, a _____ of a complex-valued function f is a member x of the domain of f such that f(x) vanishes at x, that is, x : f (x) = 0.
   - a. Thing
   - b. Root0
   - c. Undefined
   - d. Undefined

15. A _____ is a symbolic representation denoting a quantity or expression. It often represents an "unknown" quantity that has the potential to change.
   - a. Thing
   - b. Variable0
   - c. Undefined
   - d. Undefined

16. In mathematics, the _____ of a function is the set of all "output" values produced by that function. Given a function $f : A \to B$, the _____ of f, is defined to be the set $\{x \in B : x = f(a)$ for some $a \in A\}$.
   - a. Thing
   - b. Range0
   - c. Undefined
   - d. Undefined

17. In mathematics, an _____ is any of the arguments, i.e. "inputs", to a function. Thus if we have a function f(x), then x is a _____.
   - a. Thing
   - b. Independent variable0
   - c. Undefined
   - d. Undefined

18. In elementary algebra, an _____ is a set that contains every real number between two indicated numbers and may contain the two numbers themselves.
   - a. Thing
   - b. Interval0
   - c. Undefined
   - d. Undefined

19. The easiest _____ prime numbers resides in the use of the Sieve of Eratosthenes, an algorithm that discovers all prime numbers to a specified integer.
   - a. Method for finding0
   - b. Thing
   - c. Undefined
   - d. Undefined

Chapter 7. EXPONENTIAL, LOGARITHMIC, AND INVERSE TRIGONOMETRIC FUNCTIONS 123

20. In mathematics, the idea of _____ generalises the concepts of negation, in relation to addition, and reciprocal, in relation to multiplication.
   a. Inverse element0 b. Thing
   c. Undefined d. Undefined

21. In astronomy, geography, geometry and related sciences and contexts, a plane is said to be _____ at a given point if it is locally perpendicular to the gradient of the gravity field, i.e., with the direction of the gravitational force at that point.
   a. Thing b. Horizontal0
   c. Undefined d. Undefined

22. _____ is a test used to determine if a function is injective, surjective or bijective.
   a. Horizontal line test0 b. Thing
   c. Undefined d. Undefined

23. Acid _____ ratio measures the ability of a company to use its near cash or quick assets to immediately extinguish its current liabilities.
   a. Thing b. Test0
   c. Undefined d. Undefined

24. In mathematics, a _____ is a statement that can be proved on the basis of explicitly stated or previously agreed assumptions.
   a. Theorem0 b. Thing
   c. Undefined d. Undefined

25. A _____ is a set of numbers that designate location in a given reference system, such as x,y in a planar _____ system or an x,y,z in a three-dimensional _____ system.
   a. Thing b. Coordinate0
   c. Undefined d. Undefined

26. _____ are the basic objects of study in graph theory. Informally speaking, a graph is a set of objects called points, nodes, or vertices connected by links called lines or edges.
   a. Graphs0 b. Thing
   c. Undefined d. Undefined

27. In common philosophical language, a proposition or _____, is the content of an assertion, that is, it is true-or-false and defined by the meaning of a particular piece of language.
   a. Statement0 b. Concept
   c. Undefined d. Undefined

28. Equivalence is the condition of being _____ or essentially equal.
   a. Equivalent0 b. Thing
   c. Undefined d. Undefined

29. The _____, the average in everyday English, which is also called the arithmetic _____ (and is distinguished from the geometric _____ or harmonic _____). The average is also called the sample _____. The expected value of a random variable, which is also called the population _____.

Chapter 7. EXPONENTIAL, LOGARITHMIC, AND INVERSE TRIGONOMETRIC FUNCTIONS

a. Mean0
b. Thing
c. Undefined
d. Undefined

30. In mathematics, a _____ (also spelled reflexion) is a map that transforms an object into its mirror image.
    a. Reflection0
    b. Concept
    c. Undefined
    d. Undefined

31. Generally, a _____ is a splitting of something into parts.
    a. Partition0
    b. Thing
    c. Undefined
    d. Undefined

32. _____ is to give an equation $R(x,y) = S(x,y)$ that at least in part has the same graph as $y = f(x)$.
    a. Implicit differentiation0
    b. Thing
    c. Undefined
    d. Undefined

33. The _____ is a measurement of how a function changes when the values of its inputs change.
    a. Thing
    b. Derivative0
    c. Undefined
    d. Undefined

34. _____, a field in mathematics, is the study of how functions change when their inputs change. The primary object of study in _____ is the derivative.
    a. Differential calculus0
    b. Thing
    c. Undefined
    d. Undefined

35. _____ statistics are statistics that estimate population parameters.
    a. Parametric0
    b. Thing
    c. Undefined
    d. Undefined

36. In mathematics, _____ bear slight similarity to functions: they allow one to use arbitrary values, called parameters, in place of independent variables in equations, which in turn provide values for dependent variables. A simple kinematical example is when one uses a time parameter to determine the position, velocity, and other information about a body in motion.
    a. Parametric equations0
    b. Thing
    c. Undefined
    d. Undefined

37. A _____ is a negotiable instrument instructing a financial institution to pay a specific amount of a specific currency from a specific demand account held in the maker/depositor's name with that institution. Both the maker and payee may be natural persons or legal entities.
    a. Check0
    b. Thing
    c. Undefined
    d. Undefined

38. _____ the expected value of a random variable displays the average or central value of the variable. It is a summary value of the distribution of the variable.
    a. Determining0
    b. Thing
    c. Undefined
    d. Undefined

Chapter 7. EXPONENTIAL, LOGARITHMIC, AND INVERSE TRIGONOMETRIC FUNCTIONS

39. In mathematics, the _____ f is the collection of all ordered pairs . In particular, graph means the graphical representation of this collection, in the form of a curve or surface, together with axes, etc. Graphing on a Cartesian plane is sometimes referred to as curve sketching.
    a. Thing
    b. Graph of a function0
    c. Undefined
    d. Undefined

40. In geometry, _____ angles are angles that have a common ray coming out of the vertex going between two other rays.
    a. Concept
    b. Adjacent0
    c. Undefined
    d. Undefined

41. The metre (or _____, see spelling differences) is a measure of length. It is the basic unit of length in the metric system and in the International System of Units (SI), used around the world for general and scientific purposes.
    a. Concept
    b. Meter0
    c. Undefined
    d. Undefined

42. A _____ is a unit of length, usually used to measure distance, in a number of different systems, including Imperial units, United States customary units and Norwegian/Swedish mil. Its size can vary from system to system, but in each is between 1 and 10 kilometers. In contemporary English contexts _____ refers to either:
    a. Thing
    b. Mile0
    c. Undefined
    d. Undefined

43. In mathematics, a _____ of a number x is the exponent y of the power by such that $x = b^y$. The value used for the base b must be neither 0 nor 1, nor a root of 1 in the case of the extension to complex numbers, and is typically 10, e, or 2.
    a. Thing
    b. Logarithm0
    c. Undefined
    d. Undefined

44. In business, particularly accounting, a _____ is the time intervals that the accounts, statement, payments, or other calculations cover.
    a. Thing
    b. Period0
    c. Undefined
    d. Undefined

45. _____ has many meanings, most of which simply .
    a. Power0
    b. Thing
    c. Undefined
    d. Undefined

46. A _____ is a deliberate process for transforming one or more inputs into one or more results.
    a. Thing
    b. Calculation0
    c. Undefined
    d. Undefined

47. In mathematics, an _____ number is any real number that is not a rational number- that is, it is a number which cannot be expressed as a fraction m/n, where m and n are integers.
    a. Thing
    b. Irrational0
    c. Undefined
    d. Undefined

Chapter 7. EXPONENTIAL, LOGARITHMIC, AND INVERSE TRIGONOMETRIC FUNCTIONS

48. In mathematics, a _____ number is a number which can be expressed as a ratio of two integers. Non-integer _____ numbers (commonly called fractions) are usually written as the vulgar fraction a / b, where b is not zero.
   a. Rational0
   b. Thing
   c. Undefined
   d. Undefined

49. _____ are external two-dimensional outlines, with the appearance or configuration of some thing - in contrast to the matter or content or substance of which it is composed.
   a. Shapes0
   b. Thing
   c. Undefined
   d. Undefined

50. A _____ function is a function for which, intuitively, small changes in the input result in small changes in the output.
   a. Event
   b. Continuous0
   c. Undefined
   d. Undefined

51. _____ is one of the most important functions in mathematics. A function commonly used to study growth and decay
   a. Thing
   b. Exponential function0
   c. Undefined
   d. Undefined

52. _____ is the fee paid on borrowed money.
   a. Thing
   b. Interest0
   c. Undefined
   d. Undefined

53. In mathematics and the mathematical sciences, a _____ is a fixed, but possibly unspecified, value. This is in contrast to a variable, which is not fixed.
   a. Thing
   b. Constant0
   c. Undefined
   d. Undefined

54. _____ is a set of numbers, in the broadest sense of the word, together with one or more operations, such as addition or multiplication.
   a. Thing
   b. Number system0
   c. Undefined
   d. Undefined

55. _____ is the logarithm to the base e, where e is an irrational constant approximately equal to 2.718281828459.
   a. Natural logarithm0
   b. Thing
   c. Undefined
   d. Undefined

56. A _____ of a number is the product of that number with any integer.
   a. Multiple0
   b. Thing
   c. Undefined
   d. Undefined

57. In mathematics, a _____ may be described informally as a number that can be given by an infinite decimal representation.

Chapter 7. EXPONENTIAL, LOGARITHMIC, AND INVERSE TRIGONOMETRIC FUNCTIONS 127

    a. Real number0
    b. Thing
    c. Undefined
    d. Undefined

58. A _____ is the result of the addition of a set of numbers. The numbers may be natural numbers, complex numbers, matrices, or still more complicated objects. An infinite _____ is a subtle procedure known as a series.
    a. Thing
    b. Sum0
    c. Undefined
    d. Undefined

59. _____ is the ability to hold, receive or absorb, or a measure thereof, similar to the concept of volume.
    a. Concept
    b. Capacity0
    c. Undefined
    d. Undefined

60. In mathematics, a _____ is a polynomial equation of the second degree. The general form is $ax^2 + bx + c = 0$.
    a. Thing
    b. Quadratic equation0
    c. Undefined
    d. Undefined

61. A quadratic equation with real solutions, called roots, which may be real or complex, is given by the _____: $x = \frac{-b \pm \sqrt{b^2 - 4ac}}{2a}$.
    a. Thing
    b. Quadratic formula0
    c. Undefined
    d. Undefined

62. In mathematics, the _____ is the logarithm with base 10.
    a. Thing
    b. Common logarithm0
    c. Undefined
    d. Undefined

63. The _____ of measurement are a globally standardized and modernized form of the metric system.
    a. Units0
    b. Thing
    c. Undefined
    d. Undefined

64. _____ is the design, analysis, and/or construction of works for practical purposes.
    a. Thing
    b. Engineering0
    c. Undefined
    d. Undefined

65. A frame of _____ is a particular perspective from which the universe is observed.
    a. Thing
    b. Reference0
    c. Undefined
    d. Undefined

66. The _____ relative to a specified or implied reference level.
    a. Thing
    b. Decibel0
    c. Undefined
    d. Undefined

67. An _____ is a combination of numbers, operators, grouping symbols and/or free variables and bound variables arranged in a meaningful way which can be evaluated..
    a. Expression0
    b. Thing
    c. Undefined
    d. Undefined

Chapter 7. EXPONENTIAL, LOGARITHMIC, AND INVERSE TRIGONOMETRIC FUNCTIONS

68. The _____ is the process of converting elements in one basis to another when both describe the same elements of the finite field $GF(p^m)$.
    a. Change of base0
    b. Thing
    c. Undefined
    d. Undefined

69. The _____ is the process of converting elements in one basis to another when both describe the same elements of the finite field $GF(p^m)$.
    a. Thing
    b. Change of bases0
    c. Undefined
    d. Undefined

70. In mathematics, the _____ of two sets A and B is the set that contains all elements of A that also belong to B (or equivalently, all elements of B that also belong to A), but no other elements.
    a. Thing
    b. Intersection0
    c. Undefined
    d. Undefined

71. In mathematics and its applications, a _____ is a system for assigning an n-tuple of numbers or scalars to each point in an n-dimensional space.
    a. Coordinate system0
    b. Concept
    c. Undefined
    d. Undefined

72. In mathematics, a _____ is a mathematical statement which appears likely to be true, but has not been formally proven to be true under the rules of mathematical logic.
    a. Concept
    b. Conjecture0
    c. Undefined
    d. Undefined

73. Initial objects are also called _____, and terminal objects are also called final.
    a. Coterminal0
    b. Thing
    c. Undefined
    d. Undefined

74. _____ is the process in which an unstable atomic nucleus loses energy by emitting radiation in the form of particles or electromagnetic waves.
    a. Radioactive decay0
    b. Thing
    c. Undefined
    d. Undefined

75. _____ is the property of a physical object that quantifies the amount of matter and energy it is equivalent to.
    a. Mass0
    b. Thing
    c. Undefined
    d. Undefined

76. A _____ is a quantity that denotes the proportional amount or magnitude of one quantity relative to another.
    a. Ratio0
    b. Thing
    c. Undefined
    d. Undefined

77. _____ is the SI unit of energy.
    a. Joule0
    b. Thing
    c. Undefined
    d. Undefined

Chapter 7. EXPONENTIAL, LOGARITHMIC, AND INVERSE TRIGONOMETRIC FUNCTIONS

78. The _____ of a mathematical object is its size: a property by which it can be larger or smaller than other objects of the same kind; in technical terms, an ordering of the class of objects to which it belongs.
    a. Thing
    b. Magnitude0
    c. Undefined
    d. Undefined

79. In Euclidean geometry, a uniform _____ is a linear transformation that enlargers or diminishes objects, and whose _____ factor is the same in all directions. This is also called homothethy.
    a. Scale0
    b. Thing
    c. Undefined
    d. Undefined

80. An _____ is the result from the sudden release of stored energy in the Earth's crust that creates seismic waves.
    a. Thing
    b. Earthquake0
    c. Undefined
    d. Undefined

81. In mathematics, an _____, mean, or central tendency of a data set refers to a measure of the "middle" or "expected" value of the data set.
    a. Concept
    b. Average0
    c. Undefined
    d. Undefined

82. The _____ of a solid object is the three-dimensional concept of how much space it occupies, often quantified numerically.
    a. Thing
    b. Volume0
    c. Undefined
    d. Undefined

83. _____ is a mathematical subject that includes the study of limits, derivatives, integrals, and power series and constitutes a major part of modern university curriculum.
    a. Thing
    b. Calculus0
    c. Undefined
    d. Undefined

84. _____ is often used to describe the measurement of the steepness, incline, gradient, or grade of a straight line. The _____ is defined as the ratio of the "rise" divided by the "run" between two points on a line, or in other words, the ratio of the altitude change to the horizontal distance between any two points on the line.
    a. Slope0
    b. Thing
    c. Undefined
    d. Undefined

85. In trigonometry, the _____ is a function defined as $\tan x = \sin x / \cos x$. The function is so-named because it can be defined as the length of a certain segment of a _____ (in the geometric sense) to the unit circle. In plane geometry, a line is _____ to a curve, at some point, if both line and curve pass through the point with the same direction.
    a. Thing
    b. Tangent0
    c. Undefined
    d. Undefined

86. _____ has two distinct but etymologically-related meanings: one in geometry and one in trigonometry.
    a. Thing
    b. Tangent line0
    c. Undefined
    d. Undefined

87. In mathematics, a _____ is the result of multiplying, or an expression that identifies factors to be multiplied.

Chapter 7. EXPONENTIAL, LOGARITHMIC, AND INVERSE TRIGONOMETRIC FUNCTIONS

a. Product0
b. Thing
c. Undefined
d. Undefined

88. In mathematics, a _____ is the end result of a division problem. It can also be expressed as the number of times the divisor divides into the dividend.
    a. Quotient0
    b. Thing
    c. Undefined
    d. Undefined

89. _____ is a mathematical operation, written a^n, involving two numbers, the base a and the exponent n.
    a. Thing
    b. Exponentiating0
    c. Undefined
    d. Undefined

90. _____ is a mathematical operation, written a^n, involving two numbers, the base a and the exponent n.
    a. Exponentiation0
    b. Thing
    c. Undefined
    d. Undefined

91. The _____ of a function is an extension of the concept of a sum, and are identified or found through the use of integration.
    a. Thing
    b. Integral0
    c. Undefined
    d. Undefined

92. In statistics, a _____ measure is one which is measuring what is supposed to measure.
    a. Valid0
    b. Thing
    c. Undefined
    d. Undefined

93. _____ is a process of combining or accumulating. It may also refer to:
    a. Integration0
    b. Thing
    c. Undefined
    d. Undefined

94. An _____ of a function f is a function F whose derivative is equal to f, i.e., F' = f.
    a. Antiderivative0
    b. Thing
    c. Undefined
    d. Undefined

95. In number theory, the _____ of arithmetic (or unique factorization theorem) states that every natural number greater than 1 can be written as a unique product of prime numbers.
    a. Fundamental theorem0
    b. Concept
    c. Undefined
    d. Undefined

96. _____ of calculus is the statement that the two central operations of calculus, differentiation and integration, are inverse operations: if a continuous function is first integrated and then differentiated, the original function is retrieved.
    a. Thing
    b. Fundamental Theorem of Calculus0
    c. Undefined
    d. Undefined

97. _____ is a trigonemtric function that is important when studying triangles and modeling periodic phenomena, among other applications.

Chapter 7. EXPONENTIAL, LOGARITHMIC, AND INVERSE TRIGONOMETRIC FUNCTIONS   131

    a. Sine0
    c. Undefined
    b. Thing
    d. Undefined

98. _____ is a function that extends the concept of an ordinary sum
    a. Integrand0
    b. Thing
    c. Undefined
    d. Undefined

99. _____ is an extension of the concept of a sum.
    a. Thing
    b. Definite integral0
    c. Undefined
    d. Undefined

100. In mathematics, the concept of a _____ tries to capture the intuitive idea of a geometrical one-dimensional and continuous object. A simple example is the circle.
    a. Curve0
    b. Thing
    c. Undefined
    d. Undefined

101. In mathematics, _____ are the intuitive idea of a geometrical one-dimensional and continuous object.
    a. Thing
    b. Curves0
    c. Undefined
    d. Undefined

102. _____ is a straight line or curve A to which another curve B the one being studied approaches closer and closer as one moves along it.
    a. Thing
    b. Vertical asymptote0
    c. Undefined
    d. Undefined

103. An _____ is a straight line or curve A to which another curve B approaches closer and closer as one moves along it. As one moves along B, the space between it and the _____ A becomes smaller and smaller, and can in fact be made as small as one could wish by going far enough along. A curve may or may not touch or cross its _____. In fact, the curve may intersect the _____ an infinite number of times.
    a. Asymptote0
    b. Thing
    c. Undefined
    d. Undefined

104. _____ is a method of describing limiting behavior.
    a. Asymptotic0
    b. Thing
    c. Undefined
    d. Undefined

105. in mathematics, maxima and minima, known collectively as _____, are the largest value maximum or smallest value minimum, that a function takes in a point either within a given neighborhood or on the function domain in its entirety global extremum.
    a. Extrema0
    b. Thing
    c. Undefined
    d. Undefined

106. In geographic information systems, a _____ comprises an entity with a geographic location, typically determined by points, arcs, or polygons. Carriageways and cadastres exemplify _____ data.

132   Chapter 7. EXPONENTIAL, LOGARITHMIC, AND INVERSE TRIGONOMETRIC FUNCTIONS

a. Thing
b. Feature0
c. Undefined
d. Undefined

107. _____ is a a point on a curve at which the tangent crosses the curve itself.
a. Thing
b. Inflection point0
c. Undefined
d. Undefined

108. The _____ is the highest point in a certain portion of a graph.
a. Thing
b. Relative maximum0
c. Undefined
d. Undefined

109. _____ is a set, with some particular properties and usually some additional structure, such as the operations of addition or multiplication, for instance.
a. Thing
b. Space0
c. Undefined
d. Undefined

110. In sociology and biology a _____ is the collection of people or organisms of a particular species living in a given geographic area or space, usually measured by a census.
a. Population0
b. Thing
c. Undefined
d. Undefined

111. _____ Any process by which a specified characteristic usually amplitude of the output of a device is prevented from exceeding a predetermined value.
a. Limiting0
b. Thing
c. Undefined
d. Undefined

112. _____ is change in population over time, and can be quantified as the change in the number of individuals in a population per unit time.
a. Population growth0
b. Thing
c. Undefined
d. Undefined

113. In mathematics, the _____ of a coordinate system is the point where the axes of the system intersect.
a. Thing
b. Origin0
c. Undefined
d. Undefined

114. In mathematics, the additive inverse, or _____ of a number n is the number that, when added to n, yields zero. The additive inverse of n is denoted −n. For example, 7 is −7, because 7 + (−7) = 0, and the additive inverse of −0.3 is 0.3, because −0.3 + 0.3 = 0.
a. Thing
b. Opposite0
c. Undefined
d. Undefined

115. In mathematics, the _____ of a number n is the number that, when added to n, yields zero. The _____ of n is denoted −n. For example, 7 is −7, because 7 + (−7) = 0, and the _____ of −0.3 is 0.3, because −0.3 + 0.3 = 0.
a. Additive inverse0
b. Thing
c. Undefined
d. Undefined

Chapter 7. EXPONENTIAL, LOGARITHMIC, AND INVERSE TRIGONOMETRIC FUNCTIONS

116. A _____ is a special kind of ratio, indicating a relationship between two measurements with different units, such as miles to gallons or cents to pounds.
  a. Rate0
  b. Thing
  c. Undefined
  d. Undefined

117. In economics, economic _____ is simply a state of the world where economic forces are balanced and in the absence of external influences the values of economic variables will not change.
  a. Thing
  b. Equilibrium0
  c. Undefined
  d. Undefined

118. _____ is a physical property of a system that underlies the common notions of hot and cold; something that is hotter has the greater _____.
  a. Temperature0
  b. Thing
  c. Undefined
  d. Undefined

119. In plane geometry, a _____ is a polygon with four equal sides, four right angles, and parallel opposite sides. In algebra, the _____ of a number is that number multiplied by itself.
  a. Square0
  b. Thing
  c. Undefined
  d. Undefined

120. _____ of an object is its speed in a particular direction.
  a. Thing
  b. Velocity0
  c. Undefined
  d. Undefined

121. Sir Isaac _____, was an English physicist, mathematician, astronomer, natural philosopher, and alchemist, regarded by many as the greatest figure in the history of science
  a. Newton0
  b. Person
  c. Undefined
  d. Undefined

122. In mathematics, an _____ is a statement about the relative size or order of two objects.
  a. Thing
  b. Inequality0
  c. Undefined
  d. Undefined

123. In mathematics, _____ geometry was the traditional name for the geometry of three-dimensional Euclidean space — for practical purposes the kind of space we live in.
  a. Thing
  b. Solid0
  c. Undefined
  d. Undefined

124. In Euclidean geometry, an _____ is a closed segment of a differentiable curve in the two-dimensional plane; for example, a circular _____ is a segment of a circle.
  a. Arc0
  b. Concept
  c. Undefined
  d. Undefined

125. _____ also called rectification of a curve—was historically difficult.

Chapter 7. EXPONENTIAL, LOGARITHMIC, AND INVERSE TRIGONOMETRIC FUNCTIONS

a. Thing
b. Arc length0
c. Undefined
d. Undefined

126. A _____ is the quantity that defines certain relatively constant characteristics of systems or functions..
a. Thing
b. Parameter0
c. Undefined
d. Undefined

127. _____ is the symbold used to indicate the nth root of a number
a. Thing
b. Radical0
c. Undefined
d. Undefined

128. An _____ is a straight line around which a geometric figure can be rotated.
a. Axis0
b. Thing
c. Undefined
d. Undefined

129. _____ is the middle point of a line segment.
a. Thing
b. Midpoint0
c. Undefined
d. Undefined

130. In mathematics, a _____ is a demonstration that, assuming certain axioms, some statement is necessarily true.
a. Proof0
b. Thing
c. Undefined
d. Undefined

131. A _____ is a mathematical statement which follows easily from a previously proven statement, typically a mathematical theorem.
a. Corollary0
b. Thing
c. Undefined
d. Undefined

132. _____ is the chance that something is likely to happen or be the case.
a. Thing
b. Probability0
c. Undefined
d. Undefined

133. Mathematical _____ is used to represent ideas.
a. Notation0
b. Thing
c. Undefined
d. Undefined

134. _____ is a mathematical science pertaining to the collection, analysis, interpretation or explanation, and presentation of data. It is applicable to a wide variety of academic disciplines, from the physical and social sciences to the humanities.
a. Statistics0
b. Thing
c. Undefined
d. Undefined

135. In mathematics, the _____ also called the Gauss _____ is a non-elementary function which occurs in probability, statistics and partial differential equations.

Chapter 7. EXPONENTIAL, LOGARITHMIC, AND INVERSE TRIGONOMETRIC FUNCTIONS

a. Thing
c. Undefined
b. Error function0
d. Undefined

136. The _____ of an angle is the ratio of the length of the adjacent side to the length of the hypotenuse.
a. Concept
c. Undefined
b. Cosine0
d. Undefined

137. _____ is a kind of property which exists as magnitude or multitude. It is among the basic classes of things along with quality, substance, change, and relation.
a. Amount0
c. Undefined
b. Thing
d. Undefined

138. In calculus, the _____ is a formula for the derivative of the composite of two functions.
a. Concept
c. Undefined
b. Chain rule0
d. Undefined

139. When _____ symmetry one can determine whether or not an object is symmetric with respect to a given mathematical operation, if, when applied to the object, this operation does not change the object or its appearance.
a. Investigating0
c. Undefined
b. Thing
d. Undefined

140. Sir _____ was an English physicist, mathematician, astronomer, natural philosopher, and alchemist, regarded by many as the greatest figure in the history of science.
a. Person
c. Undefined
b. Isaac Newton0
d. Undefined

141. A _____ defined function $f(x)$ of a real variable x is a function whose definition is given differently on disjoint subsets of its domain.
a. Thing
c. Undefined
b. Piecewise0
d. Undefined

142. Deductive _____ is the kind of _____ in which the conclusion is necessitated by, or reached from, previously known facts (the premises).
a. Reasoning0
c. Undefined
b. Thing
d. Undefined

143. In mathematics, science including computer science, linguistics and engineering, an _____ is, generally speaking, an independent variable or input to a function.
a. Argument0
c. Undefined
b. Thing
d. Undefined

144. In mathematics, the multiplicative inverse of a number x, denoted $1/x$ or x^{-1}, is the number which, when multiplied by x, yields 1. The multiplicative inverse of x is also called the _____ of x.
a. Reciprocal0
c. Undefined
b. Thing
d. Undefined

Chapter 7. EXPONENTIAL, LOGARITHMIC, AND INVERSE TRIGONOMETRIC FUNCTIONS

145. _____ is a trigonometric function that is the reciprocal of cosine.
   a. Thing
   b. Secant0
   c. Undefined
   d. Undefined

146. _____ is a branch of mathematics which deals with triangles, particularly triangles in a plane where one angle of the triangle is 90 degrees, and a variety of other topological relations such as spheres, in other branches, such as spherical _____.
   a. Thing
   b. Trigonometry0
   c. Undefined
   d. Undefined

147. In mathematics and logic, a _____ proof is a way of showing the truth or falsehood of a given statement by a straightforward combination of established facts, usually existing lemmas and theorems, without making any further assumptions.
   a. Thing
   b. Direct0
   c. Undefined
   d. Undefined

148. An _____ is an equality that remains true regardless of the values of any variables that appear within it, to distinguish it from an equality which is true under more particular conditions.
   a. Identity0
   b. Thing
   c. Undefined
   d. Undefined

149. The _____ is a unit of plane angle. It is represented by the symbol "rad" or, more rarely, by the superscript c (for "circular measure"). For example, an angle of 1.2 radians would be written "1.2 rad" or "1.2c" (second symbol can produce confusion with centigrads).
   a. Thing
   b. Radian0
   c. Undefined
   d. Undefined

150. _____ is a unit of plane angle, equal to 180/ð degrees, or about 57.2958 degrees
   a. Radian measure0
   b. Thing
   c. Undefined
   d. Undefined

151. A _____ is a function that assigns a number to subsets of a given set.
   a. Thing
   b. Measure0
   c. Undefined
   d. Undefined

152. _____ is a term in Trigonometry used to describe the secant of the complement of a cirlce.
   a. Thing
   b. Cosecant0
   c. Undefined
   d. Undefined

153. _____ is the ratio of the adjacent to the opposite side of a right-angeled triangle
   a. Cotangent0
   b. Thing
   c. Undefined
   d. Undefined

154. In mathematics, there are several meanings of _____ depending on the subject.

Chapter 7. EXPONENTIAL, LOGARITHMIC, AND INVERSE TRIGONOMETRIC FUNCTIONS 137

a. Degree0
b. Thing
c. Undefined
d. Undefined

155. In classical geometry, a _____ of a circle or sphere is any line segment from its center to its boundary. By extension, the _____ of a circle or sphere is the length of any such segment. The _____ is half the diameter. In science and engineering the term _____ of curvature is commonly used as a synonym for _____.
    a. Radius0
    b. Thing
    c. Undefined
    d. Undefined

156. _____ is a professional society that focuses on undergraduate mathematics education.
    a. Person
    b. Mathematical Association of America0
    c. Undefined
    d. Undefined

157. _____ is the path a moving object follows through space.
    a. Projectile motion0
    b. Thing
    c. Undefined
    d. Undefined

158. In mathematics, the _____ is a conic section generated by the intersection of a right circular conical surface and a plane parallel to a generating straight line of that surface. It can also be defined as locus of points in a plane which are equidistant from a given point.
    a. Thing
    b. Parabola0
    c. Undefined
    d. Undefined

159. _____ is defined as the rate of change or derivative with respect to time of velocity.
    a. Thing
    b. Acceleration0
    c. Undefined
    d. Undefined

160. A _____ is one of the basic shapes of geometry: a polygon with three vertices and three sides which are straight line segments.
    a. Triangle0
    b. Thing
    c. Undefined
    d. Undefined

161. _____, usually denoted symbolically by the Greek letter phi, Î¦, gives the location of a place on Earth north or south of the equator. _____ is an angular measurement in degrees (marked with Â°) ranging from 0Â° at the Equator (low _____) to 90Â° at the poles (90Â° N for the North Pole or 90Â° S for the South Pole; high _____). The complementary angle of a _____ is called the colatitude.
    a. Thing
    b. Latitude0
    c. Undefined
    d. Undefined

162. The _____ is a statement about a general triangle which relates the lengths of its sides to the cosine of one of its angles.
    a. Law of cosines0
    b. Thing
    c. Undefined
    d. Undefined

163. A _____ consists of one quarter of the coordinate plane.

Chapter 7. EXPONENTIAL, LOGARITHMIC, AND INVERSE TRIGONOMETRIC FUNCTIONS

    a. Thing
    b. Quadrant0
    c. Undefined
    d. Undefined

164. In mathematical analysis and related areas of mathematics, a set is called _____, if it is, in a certain sense, of finite size.
    a. Bounded0
    b. Thing
    c. Undefined
    d. Undefined

165. _____ is a method for approximating the values of integrals.
    a. Riemann sum0
    b. Thing
    c. Undefined
    d. Undefined

166. A _____ is 360° or 2δ radians.
    a. Turn0
    b. Thing
    c. Undefined
    d. Undefined

167. In mathematics, a set is called _____ if there is a bijection between the set and some set of the form {1, 2, ..., n} where n is a natural number.
    a. Thing
    b. Finite0
    c. Undefined
    d. Undefined

168. In calculus and other branches of mathematical analysis, an _____ is an algebraic expression obtained in the context of limits.
    a. Indeterminate form0
    b. Thing
    c. Undefined
    d. Undefined

169. A _____ is a numeral used to indicate a count. The most common use of the word today is to name the part of a fraction that tells the number or count of equal parts.
    a. Numerator0
    b. Thing
    c. Undefined
    d. Undefined

170. In mathematics, _____ is the decomposition of an object into a product of other objects, or factors, which when multiplied together give the original.
    a. Thing
    b. Factoring0
    c. Undefined
    d. Undefined

171. A _____ is the part of a fraction that tells how many equal parts make up a whole, and which is used in the name of the fraction: "halves", "thirds", "fourths" or "quarters", "fifths" and so on.
    a. Denominator0
    b. Concept
    c. Undefined
    d. Undefined

172. In a mathematical proof or a syllogism, a _____ is a statement that is the logical consequence of preceding statements.
    a. Conclusion0
    b. Concept
    c. Undefined
    d. Undefined

Chapter 7. EXPONENTIAL, LOGARITHMIC, AND INVERSE TRIGONOMETRIC FUNCTIONS 139

173. In physics, _____ is an influence that may cause an object to accelerate. It may be experienced as a lift, a push, or a pull. The actual acceleration of the body is determined by the vector sum of all forces acting on it, known as net _____ or resultant _____.
   a. Force0
   b. Thing
   c. Undefined
   d. Undefined

174. The _____ are the only integral domain whose positive elements are well-ordered, and in which order is preserved by addition. Like the natural numbers, the _____ form a countably infinite set. The set of all _____ is usually denoted in mathematics by a boldface Z .
   a. Integers0
   b. Thing
   c. Undefined
   d. Undefined

175. _____ is the difference of electrical potential between two points of an electrical or electronic circuit, expressed in volts
   a. Thing
   b. Voltage0
   c. Undefined
   d. Undefined

176. _____ is a term used to characterize electrical devices, such as voltaic cells, thermoelectric devices, electrical generators and transformers, and even resistors.
   a. Thing
   b. Electromotive force0
   c. Undefined
   d. Undefined

177. The ratio of the magnetic flux to the current is called the _____, or more accurately self-_____ of the circuit.
   a. Thing
   b. Inductance0
   c. Undefined
   d. Undefined

178. A _____ is a simplified and structured visual representation of concepts, ideas, constructions, relations, statistical data, anatomy etc used in all aspects of human activities to visualize and clarify the topic.
   a. Thing
   b. Diagram0
   c. Undefined
   d. Undefined

179. In mathematics, a _____ of a number x is a number r such that $r^2 = x$, or in words, a number r whose square (the result of multiplying the number by itself) is x.
   a. Thing
   b. Square root0
   c. Undefined
   d. Undefined

180. A _____ is an analog of an ordinary trigonometric, or circular, function.
   a. Thing
   b. Hyperbolic function0
   c. Undefined
   d. Undefined

181. Mathematical _____ are demonstrations that, assuming certain axioms, some statement is necessarily true.
   a. Thing
   b. Proofs0
   c. Undefined
   d. Undefined

Chapter 7. EXPONENTIAL, LOGARITHMIC, AND INVERSE TRIGONOMETRIC FUNCTIONS

182. The Jefferson National Expansion Memorial or _____ is located in St. Louis, Missouri near the start of the Lewis and Clark Expedition. It was designated as a National Memorial by Executive Order 7523, on December 21, 1935, and is maintained by the National Park Service ..
   a. Gateway Arch0   b. Place
   c. Undefined   d. Undefined

183. In mathematics, the _____ (or modulus) of a real number is its numerical value without regard to its sign.
   a. Thing   b. Absolute value0
   c. Undefined   d. Undefined

184. _____ is the shape of a hanging flexible chain or cable when supported at its ends and acted upon by a uniform gravitational force. The chain is steepest near the points of suspension because this part of the chain has the most weight pulling down on it. Toward the bottom, the slope of the chain decreases because the chain is supporting less weight.
   a. Catenary0   b. Thing
   c. Undefined   d. Undefined

185. _____ is a branch of mathematics concerning the study of structure, relation and quantity.
   a. Concept   b. Algebra0
   c. Undefined   d. Undefined

186. The _____ integers are all the integers from zero on upwards.
   a. Thing   b. Nonnegative0
   c. Undefined   d. Undefined

187. _____ variables are variables other than the independent variable that may bear any effect on the behavior of the subject being studied.
   a. Extraneous0   b. Thing
   c. Undefined   d. Undefined

188. The plus and _____ signs are mathematical symbols used to represent the notions of positive and negative as well as the operations of addition and subtraction.
   a. Thing   b. Minus0
   c. Undefined   d. Undefined

189. In mathematics, a _____ is an expression that is constructed from one or more variables and constants, using only the operations of addition, subtraction, multiplication, and constant positive whole number exponents. is a _____. Note in particular that division by an expression containing a variable is not in general allowed in polynomials. [1]
   a. Thing   b. Polynomial0
   c. Undefined   d. Undefined

190. _____ are functions which satisfy particular symmetry relations, with respect to taking additive inverses.
   a. Thing   b. Even function0
   c. Undefined   d. Undefined

191. Angles smaller than a right angle are called _____ angles (less than 90 degrees).

Chapter 7. EXPONENTIAL, LOGARITHMIC, AND INVERSE TRIGONOMETRIC FUNCTIONS

a. Acute0
b. Concept
c. Undefined
d. Undefined

192. The _____ rule, also known as a slipstick, is a mechanical analog computer, consisting of at least two finely divided scales, most often a fixed outer pair and a movable inner one, with a sliding window called the cursor.
a. Thing
b. Slide0
c. Undefined
d. Undefined

193. _____ is the force that opposes the relative motion or tendency toward such motion of two surfaces in contact.
a. Thing
b. Friction0
c. Undefined
d. Undefined

194. A pair of angles is _____ if their respective measures sum to 180 degrees.
a. Supplementary0
b. Concept
c. Undefined
d. Undefined

195. The term _____ refers to the largest and the smallest element of a set.
a. Thing
b. Extreme value0
c. Undefined
d. Undefined

196. In geometry, an _____ is a point at which a line segment or ray terminates.
a. Endpoint0
b. Thing
c. Undefined
d. Undefined

Chapter 8. PRINCIPLES OF INTEGRAL EVALUATION

1. _____ is a process of combining or accumulating. It may also refer to:
   a. Integration0
   b. Thing
   c. Undefined
   d. Undefined

2. The _____ of a function is an extension of the concept of a sum, and are identified or found through the use of integration.
   a. Integral0
   b. Thing
   c. Undefined
   d. Undefined

3. _____ is a function that extends the concept of an ordinary sum
   a. Integrand0
   b. Thing
   c. Undefined
   d. Undefined

4. The mathematical concept of a _____ expresses the intuitive idea of deterministic dependence between two quantities, one of which is viewed as primary and the other as secondary. A _____ then is a way to associate a unique output for each input of a specified type, for example, a real number or an element of a given set.
   a. Thing
   b. Function0
   c. Undefined
   d. Undefined

5. In mathematics, a _____ is a countable collection of open covers of a topological space that satisfies certain separation axioms.
   a. Development0
   b. Thing
   c. Undefined
   d. Undefined

6. In mathematics, a _____ in elementary terms is any of a variety of different functions from geometry, such as rotations, reflections and translations.
   a. Thing
   b. Transformation0
   c. Undefined
   d. Undefined

7. _____ is the fee paid on borrowed money.
   a. Interest0
   b. Thing
   c. Undefined
   d. Undefined

8. An _____ of a function f is a function F whose derivative is equal to f, i.e., F' = f.
   a. Thing
   b. Antiderivative0
   c. Undefined
   d. Undefined

9. In mathematics, a _____ is the result of multiplying, or an expression that identifies factors to be multiplied.
   a. Thing
   b. Product0
   c. Undefined
   d. Undefined

10. The _____ governs the differentiation of products of differentiable functions.
    a. Product rule0
    b. Thing
    c. Undefined
    d. Undefined

11. In a mathematical proof or a syllogism, a _____ is a statement that is the logical consequence of preceding statements.

Chapter 8. PRINCIPLES OF INTEGRAL EVALUATION

    a. Concept   b. Conclusion0
    c. Undefined   d. Undefined

12. The _____ is a measurement of how a function changes when the values of its inputs change.
    a. Thing   b. Derivative0
    c. Undefined   d. Undefined

13. In mathematics and the mathematical sciences, a _____ is a fixed, but possibly unspecified, value. This is in contrast to a variable, which is not fixed.
    a. Constant0   b. Thing
    c. Undefined   d. Undefined

14. In calculus, the indefinite integral of a given function i.e. the set of all antiderivatives of the function is always written with a constant, the _____.
    a. Constant of integration0   b. Thing
    c. Undefined   d. Undefined

15. A _____ signifies a point or points of probability on a subject e.g., the _____ of creativity, which allows for the formation of rule or norm or law by interpretation of the phenomena events that can be created.
    a. Thing   b. Principle0
    c. Undefined   d. Undefined

16. In mathematics, a _____ is an expression that is constructed from one or more variables and constants, using only the operations of addition, subtraction, multiplication, and constant positive whole number exponents. is a _____. Note in particular that division by an expression containing a variable is not in general allowed in polynomials. [1]
    a. Polynomial0   b. Thing
    c. Undefined   d. Undefined

17. _____, a field in mathematics, is the study of how functions change when their inputs change. The primary object of study in _____ is the derivative.
    a. Thing   b. Differential calculus0
    c. Undefined   d. Undefined

18. In mathematics, a matrix can be thought of as each row or _____ being a vector. Hence, a space formed by row vectors or _____ vectors are said to be a row space or a _____ space.
    a. Concept   b. Column0
    c. Undefined   d. Undefined

19. In mathematics, the additive inverse, or _____ of a number n is the number that, when added to n, yields zero. The additive inverse of n is denoted −n. For example, 7 is −7, because 7 + (−7) = 0, and the additive inverse of −0.3 is 0.3, because −0.3 + 0.3 = 0.
    a. Opposite0   b. Thing
    c. Undefined   d. Undefined

20. In mathematics, the _____ of a number n is the number that, when added to n, yields zero. The _____ of n is denoted −n. For example, 7 is −7, because 7 + (−7) = 0, and the _____ of −0.3 is 0.3, because −0.3 + 0.3 = 0.

Chapter 8. PRINCIPLES OF INTEGRAL EVALUATION

    a. Thing
    b. Additive inverse0
    c. Undefined
    d. Undefined

21. A _____ is the result of the addition of a set of numbers. The numbers may be natural numbers, complex numbers, matrices, or still more complicated objects. An infinite _____ is a subtle procedure known as a series.
    a. Sum0
    b. Thing
    c. Undefined
    d. Undefined

22. A _____ can refer to a line joining two nonadjacent vertices of a polygon or polyhedron, or in some contexts any upward or downward sloping line. .
    a. Diagonal0
    b. Thing
    c. Undefined
    d. Undefined

23. A _____ is a symbolic representation denoting a quantity or expression. It often represents an "unknown" quantity that has the potential to change.
    a. Variable0
    b. Thing
    c. Undefined
    d. Undefined

24. _____ is an extension of the concept of a sum.
    a. Definite integral0
    b. Thing
    c. Undefined
    d. Undefined

25. In mathematics, science including computer science, linguistics and engineering, an _____ is, generally speaking, an independent variable or input to a function.
    a. Argument0
    b. Thing
    c. Undefined
    d. Undefined

26. In mathematics, _____ refers to the rewriting of an expression into a simpler form.
    a. Reduction0
    b. Thing
    c. Undefined
    d. Undefined

27. _____ is a trigonemtric function that is important when studying triangles and modeling periodic phenomena, among other applications.
    a. Thing
    b. Sine0
    c. Undefined
    d. Undefined

28. The _____ of an angle is the ratio of the length of the adjacent side to the length of the hypotenuse.
    a. Concept
    b. Cosine0
    c. Undefined
    d. Undefined

29. The _____ of a solid object is the three-dimensional concept of how much space it occupies, often quantified numerically.
    a. Thing
    b. Volume0
    c. Undefined
    d. Undefined

Chapter 8. PRINCIPLES OF INTEGRAL EVALUATION

30. In mathematics, _____ geometry was the traditional name for the geometry of three-dimensional Euclidean space — for practical purposes the kind of space we live in.
    a. Solid0
    b. Thing
    c. Undefined
    d. Undefined

31. _____ of an object is its speed in a particular direction.
    a. Velocity0
    b. Thing
    c. Undefined
    d. Undefined

32. _____ is the design, analysis, and/or construction of works for practical purposes.
    a. Thing
    b. Engineering0
    c. Undefined
    d. Undefined

33. A _____ function is a function for which, intuitively, small changes in the input result in small changes in the output.
    a. Event
    b. Continuous0
    c. Undefined
    d. Undefined

34. In mathematics, a _____ is a statement that can be proved on the basis of explicitly stated or previously agreed assumptions.
    a. Theorem0
    b. Thing
    c. Undefined
    d. Undefined

35. _____ element of an element x with respect to a binary operation * with identity element e is an element y such that x * y = y * x = e. In particular,
    a. Inverse0
    b. Thing
    c. Undefined
    d. Undefined

36. An _____ is a function which does the reverse of a given function.
    a. Thing
    b. Inverse function0
    c. Undefined
    d. Undefined

37. In mathematics, the _____ functions are functions of an angle; they are important when studying triangles and modeling periodic phenomena, among many other applications.
    a. Trigonometric0
    b. Thing
    c. Undefined
    d. Undefined

38. An _____ is an equality that remains true regardless of the values of any variables that appear within it, to distinguish it from an equality which is true under more particular conditions.
    a. Identity0
    b. Thing
    c. Undefined
    d. Undefined

39. In mathematics, the concept of a _____ tries to capture the intuitive idea of a geometrical one-dimensional and continuous object. A simple example is the circle.

Chapter 8. PRINCIPLES OF INTEGRAL EVALUATION

    a. Curve0
    c. Undefined
    b. Thing
    d. Undefined

40. In elementary algebra, an _____ is a set that contains every real number between two indicated numbers and may contain the two numbers themselves.
    a. Thing
    c. Undefined
    b. Interval0
    d. Undefined

41. _____ has many meanings, most of which simply .
    a. Power0
    c. Undefined
    b. Thing
    d. Undefined

42. In trigonometry, the _____ is a function defined as $\tan x = \sin x / \cos x$. The function is so-named because it can be defined as the length of a certain segment of a _____ (in the geometric sense) to the unit circle. In plane geometry, a line is _____ to a curve, at some point, if both line and curve pass through the point with the same direction.
    a. Tangent0
    c. Undefined
    b. Thing
    d. Undefined

43. _____ is a trigonometric function that is the reciprocal of cosine.
    a. Secant0
    c. Undefined
    b. Thing
    d. Undefined

44. In mathematics, a _____ is any one of several different types of functions, mappings, operations, or transformations.
    a. Projection0
    c. Undefined
    b. Thing
    d. Undefined

45. The _____ is an imaginary line on the Earth's surface equidistant from the North Pole and South Pole.
    a. Thing
    c. Undefined
    b. Equator0
    d. Undefined

46. _____, usually denoted symbolically by the Greek letter phi, Î¦, gives the location of a place on Earth north or south of the equator. _____ is an angular measurement in degrees (marked with Â°) ranging from 0Â° at the Equator (low _____) to 90Â° at the poles (90Â° N for the North Pole or 90Â° S for the South Pole; high _____). The complementary angle of a _____ is called the colatitude.
    a. Latitude0
    c. Undefined
    b. Thing
    d. Undefined

47. The _____ is a cylindrical map projection presented by the Flemish geographer and cartographer Gerardus Mercator, in 1569.
    a. Thing
    c. Undefined
    b. Mercator projection0
    d. Undefined

48. The _____ integers are all the integers from zero on upwards.

Chapter 8. PRINCIPLES OF INTEGRAL EVALUATION 147

    a. Thing
    b. Nonnegative0
    c. Undefined
    d. Undefined

49. In mathematical analysis and related areas of mathematics, a set is called _____, if it is, in a certain sense, of finite size.
    a. Bounded0
    b. Thing
    c. Undefined
    d. Undefined

50. John Brehaut _____ was born in Ashford, Kent, the third of five children.
    a. Wallis0
    b. Person
    c. Undefined
    d. Undefined

51. _____ is the symbold used to indicate the nth root of a number
    a. Radical0
    b. Thing
    c. Undefined
    d. Undefined

52. In mathematics, an _____ .
    a. Thing
    b. Ellipse0
    c. Undefined
    d. Undefined

53. A _____ consists of one quarter of the coordinate plane.
    a. Thing
    b. Quadrant0
    c. Undefined
    d. Undefined

54. In plane geometry, a _____ is a polygon with four equal sides, four right angles, and parallel opposite sides. In algebra, the _____ of a number is that number multiplied by itself.
    a. Thing
    b. Square0
    c. Undefined
    d. Undefined

55. In mathematics, a _____ of a number x is a number r such that $r^2 = x$, or in words, a number r whose square (the result of multiplying the number by itself) is x.
    a. Thing
    b. Square root0
    c. Undefined
    d. Undefined

56. An _____ is when two lines intersect somewhere on a plane creating a right angle at intersection
    a. Axes0
    b. Thing
    c. Undefined
    d. Undefined

57. In mathematics, a _____ of a complex-valued function f is a member x of the domain of f such that f(x) vanishes at x, that is, x : f (x) = 0.
    a. Root0
    b. Thing
    c. Undefined
    d. Undefined

58. In Euclidean geometry, a _____ is the set of all points in a plane at a fixed distance, called the radius, from a given point, the center.

Chapter 8. PRINCIPLES OF INTEGRAL EVALUATION

    a. Circle0
    c. Undefined
    b. Thing
    d. Undefined

59. In classical geometry, a _____ of a circle or sphere is any line segment from its center to its boundary. By extension, the _____ of a circle or sphere is the length of any such segment. The _____ is half the diameter. In science and engineering the term _____ of curvature is commonly used as a synonym for _____.
    a. Thing
    c. Undefined
    b. Radius0
    d. Undefined

60. In Euclidean geometry, an _____ is a closed segment of a differentiable curve in the two-dimensional plane; for example, a circular _____ is a segment of a circle.
    a. Arc0
    c. Undefined
    b. Concept
    d. Undefined

61. _____ also called rectification of a curve—was historically difficult.
    a. Thing
    c. Undefined
    b. Arc length0
    d. Undefined

62. _____ is a technique used in algebra to solve quadratic equations, in analytic geometry for determining the shapes of graphs, and in calculus for computing integrals, including, but hardly limited to, the integrals that define Laplace transforms. The essential objective is to reduce a quadratic polynomial in a variable in an equation or expression to a squared polynomial of linear order. This can reduce an equation or integral to one that is more easily solved or evaluated.
    a. Completing the square0
    c. Undefined
    b. Thing
    d. Undefined

63. In mathematics, _____ is the substitution of trigonometric functions for other expressions.
    a. Trigonometric substitution0
    c. Undefined
    b. Thing
    d. Undefined

64. Equivalence is the condition of being _____ or essentially equal.
    a. Equivalent0
    c. Undefined
    b. Thing
    d. Undefined

65. A _____ is a numeral used to indicate a count. The most common use of the word today is to name the part of a fraction that tells the number or count of equal parts.
    a. Thing
    c. Undefined
    b. Numerator0
    d. Undefined

66. A _____ is a quantity that denotes the proportional amount or magnitude of one quantity relative to another.
    a. Ratio0
    c. Undefined
    b. Thing
    d. Undefined

67. In mathematics, a _____ number is a number which can be expressed as a ratio of two integers. Non-integer _____ numbers (commonly called fractions) are usually written as the vulgar fraction a / b, where b is not zero.

Chapter 8. PRINCIPLES OF INTEGRAL EVALUATION

a. Thing
b. Rational0
c. Undefined
d. Undefined

68. In mathematics, a _____ is any function which can be written as the ratio of two polynomial functions.
a. Rational function0
b. Thing
c. Undefined
d. Undefined

69. In algebra, the _____ decomposition or _____ expansion is used to reduce the degree of either the numerator or the denominator of a rational function.
a. Partial fraction0
b. Thing
c. Undefined
d. Undefined

70. _____ is a branch of mathematics concerning the study of structure, relation and quantity.
a. Concept
b. Algebra0
c. Undefined
d. Undefined

71. A _____ is the part of a fraction that tells how many equal parts make up a whole, and which is used in the name of the fraction: "halves", "thirds", "fourths" or "quarters", "fifths" and so on.
a. Denominator0
b. Concept
c. Undefined
d. Undefined

72. In mathematics, factorization (British English: factorisation) or factoring is the decomposition of an object (for example, a number, a polynomial, or a matrix) into a product of other objects, or _____, which when multiplied together give the original.
a. Thing
b. Factors0
c. Undefined
d. Undefined

73. In mathematics, a _____ is a constant multiplicative factor of a certain object. The object can be such things as a variable, a vector, a function, etc. For example, the _____ of $9x^2$ is 9.
a. Coefficient0
b. Thing
c. Undefined
d. Undefined

74. A _____ fraction is a fraction in which the absolute value of the numerator is less than the denominator--hence, the absolute value of the fraction is less than 1.
a. Thing
b. Proper0
c. Undefined
d. Undefined

75. _____ refers to the reduction of the body of a formerly living organism into simpler forms of matter.
a. Thing
b. Decomposing0
c. Undefined
d. Undefined

76. _____ the expected value of a random variable displays the average or central value of the variable. It is a summary value of the distribution of the variable.
a. Determining0
b. Thing
c. Undefined
d. Undefined

Chapter 8. PRINCIPLES OF INTEGRAL EVALUATION

77. The word _____ comes from the Latin word linearis, which means created by lines.
   a. Thing
   b. Linear0
   c. Undefined
   d. Undefined

78. The easiest _____ prime numbers resides in the use of the Sieve of Eratosthenes, an algorithm that discovers all prime numbers to a specified integer.
   a. Method for finding0
   b. Thing
   c. Undefined
   d. Undefined

79. _____ traditionally refers to the statistical process of determining comparable scores on different forms of an exam
   a. Thing
   b. Equating0
   c. Undefined
   d. Undefined

80. In abstract algebra, _____ consists of sets with binary operations that satisfy certain axioms.
   a. Grouping0
   b. Thing
   c. Undefined
   d. Undefined

81. In mathematics, there are several meanings of _____ depending on the subject.
   a. Thing
   b. Degree0
   c. Undefined
   d. Undefined

82. A _____ is the part of the dividend that is left over when the dividend is not evenly divisible by the divisor.
   a. Thing
   b. Remainder0
   c. Undefined
   d. Undefined

83. In mathematics, a _____ of an integer n, also called a factor of n, is an integer which evenly divides n without leaving a remainder.
   a. Thing
   b. Divisor0
   c. Undefined
   d. Undefined

84. In arithmetic, _____ is a procedure for calculating the division of one integer, called the dividend, by another integer called the divisor, to produce a result called the quotient.
   a. Thing
   b. Long division0
   c. Undefined
   d. Undefined

85. A _____ is a negotiable instrument instructing a financial institution to pay a specific amount of a specific currency from a specific demand account held in the maker/depositor's name with that institution. Both the maker and payee may be natural persons or legal entities.
   a. Check0
   b. Thing
   c. Undefined
   d. Undefined

86. In mathematics, the multiplicative inverse of a number x, denoted $1/x$ or x^{-1}, is the number which, when multiplied by x, yields 1. The multiplicative inverse of x is also called the _____ of x.

Chapter 8. PRINCIPLES OF INTEGRAL EVALUATION

    a. Reciprocal0   b. Thing
    c. Undefined   d. Undefined

87. One of the three formats applicable to a quadratic function is the _____ which is defined as $f = ax^2 + bx + c$.
    a. General form0   b. Thing
    c. Undefined   d. Undefined

88. In statistics, a _____ measure is one which is measuring what is supposed to measure.
    a. Thing   b. Valid0
    c. Undefined   d. Undefined

89. In mathematics, the _____ (or modulus) of a real number is its numerical value without regard to its sign.
    a. Thing   b. Absolute value0
    c. Undefined   d. Undefined

90. An _____ is a combination of numbers, operators, grouping symbols and/or free variables and bound variables arranged in a meaningful way which can be evaluated..
    a. Expression0   b. Thing
    c. Undefined   d. Undefined

91. In mathematics, _____ are the intuitive idea of a geometrical one-dimensional and continuous object.
    a. Thing   b. Curves0
    c. Undefined   d. Undefined

92. A _____ is a set of numbers that designate location in a given reference system, such as x,y in a planar _____ system or an x,y,z in a three-dimensional _____ system.
    a. Thing   b. Coordinate0
    c. Undefined   d. Undefined

93. _____ constitutes a broad family of algorithms for calculating the numerical value of a definite integral, and by extension, the term is also sometimes used to describe the numerical solution of differential equations.
    a. Thing   b. Numerical integration0
    c. Undefined   d. Undefined

94. _____ is a method for approximating the values of integrals.
    a. Riemann sum0   b. Thing
    c. Undefined   d. Undefined

95. _____ is a mathematical subject that includes the study of limits, derivatives, integrals, and power series and constitutes a major part of modern university curriculum.
    a. Thing   b. Calculus0
    c. Undefined   d. Undefined

96. In number theory, the _____ of arithmetic (or unique factorization theorem) states that every natural number greater than 1 can be written as a unique product of prime numbers.

Chapter 8. PRINCIPLES OF INTEGRAL EVALUATION

    a. Concept
    c. Undefined
    b. Fundamental theorem0
    d. Undefined

97. _____ of calculus is the statement that the two central operations of calculus, differentiation and integration, are inverse operations: if a continuous function is first integrated and then differentiated, the original function is retrieved.
    a. Fundamental Theorem of Calculus0
    c. Undefined
    b. Thing
    d. Undefined

98. In geometry, an _____ is a point at which a line segment or ray terminates.
    a. Thing
    c. Undefined
    b. Endpoint0
    d. Undefined

99. _____ is the middle point of a line segment.
    a. Thing
    c. Undefined
    b. Midpoint0
    d. Undefined

100. A _____ is a function for which, intuitively, small changes in the input result in small changes in the output.
    a. Event
    c. Undefined
    b. Continuous function0
    d. Undefined

101. A _____ is a quadrilateral, which is defined as a shape with four sides, which has a pair of parallel sides.
    a. Thing
    c. Undefined
    b. Trapezoid0
    d. Undefined

102. A _____ is one of the basic shapes of geometry: a polygon with three vertices and three sides which are straight line segments.
    a. Triangle0
    c. Undefined
    b. Thing
    d. Undefined

103. Two mathematical objects are equal if and only if they are precisely the same in every way. This defines a binary relation, _____, denoted by the sign of _____ "=" in such a way that the statement "x = y" means that x and y are equal.
    a. Equality0
    c. Undefined
    b. Thing
    d. Undefined

104. In geometry, a _____ is defined as a quadrilateral where all four of its angles are right angles.
    a. Rectangle0
    c. Undefined
    b. Thing
    d. Undefined

105. _____ has two distinct but etymologically-related meanings: one in geometry and one in trigonometry.
    a. Tangent line0
    c. Undefined
    b. Thing
    d. Undefined

106. The deductive-nomological model is a formalized view of scientific _____ in natural language.

Chapter 8. PRINCIPLES OF INTEGRAL EVALUATION

a. Explanation0
b. Thing
c. Undefined
d. Undefined

107. In geometry, two sets are called _____ if one can be transformed into the other by an isometry, i.e., a combination of translations, rotations and reflections.
    a. Congruent0
    b. Thing
    c. Undefined
    d. Undefined

108. The word _____ means curving in or hollowed inward.
    a. Concavity0
    b. Thing
    c. Undefined
    d. Undefined

109. _____ or arithmetics is the oldest and most elementary branch of mathematics, used by almost everyone, for tasks ranging from simple daily counting to advanced science and business calculations.
    a. Thing
    b. Arithmetic0
    c. Undefined
    d. Undefined

110. In Euclidean geometry, a _____ is moving every point a constant distance in a specified direction.
    a. Translation0
    b. Concept
    c. Undefined
    d. Undefined

111. _____ is a branch of mathematics which deals with triangles, particularly triangles in a plane where one angle of the triangle is 90 degrees, and a variety of other topological relations such as spheres, in other branches, such as spherical _____.
    a. Trigonometry0
    b. Thing
    c. Undefined
    d. Undefined

112. A _____ is a three-dimensional geometric shape formed by straight lines through a fixed point (vertex) to the points of a fixed curve (directrix)
    a. Cone0
    b. Concept
    c. Undefined
    d. Undefined

113. In mathematics, _____ is the term used for reducing the number of digits right of the decimal point, by discarding the least significant ones.
    a. Thing
    b. Truncation0
    c. Undefined
    d. Undefined

114. In mathematics, especially in order theory, an _____ of a subset S of some partially ordered set is an element of P which is greater than or equal to every element of S.
    a. Upper bound0
    b. Thing
    c. Undefined
    d. Undefined

115. In mathematics, an _____ is a statement about the relative size or order of two objects.
    a. Thing
    b. Inequality0
    c. Undefined
    d. Undefined

Chapter 8. PRINCIPLES OF INTEGRAL EVALUATION

116. _____ the American term is a way to approximately calculate the definite integral
    a. Thing
    b. Trapezoidal Rule0
    c. Undefined
    d. Undefined

117. In mathematics, an inequality is a statement about the relative size or order of two objects. For example 14 > 10, or 14 is _____ 10.
    a. Greater than0
    b. Thing
    c. Undefined
    d. Undefined

118. In mathematics, the hypothesis is _____ by the use of scientific method.
    a. Experimentally determined0
    b. Thing
    c. Undefined
    d. Undefined

119. Acid _____ ratio measures the ability of a company to use its near cash or quick assets to immediately extinguish its current liabilities.
    a. Thing
    b. Test0
    c. Undefined
    d. Undefined

120. _____ is defined as the rate of change or derivative with respect to time of velocity.
    a. Thing
    b. Acceleration0
    c. Undefined
    d. Undefined

121. A _____ is a unit of length, usually used to measure distance, in a number of different systems, including Imperial units, United States customary units and Norwegian/Swedish mil. Its size can vary from system to system, but in each is between 1 and 10 kilometers. In contemporary English contexts _____ refers to either:
    a. Mile0
    b. Thing
    c. Undefined
    d. Undefined

122. _____ is the transport of people on a trip/journey or the process or time involved in a person or object moving from one location to another.
    a. Thing
    b. Travel0
    c. Undefined
    d. Undefined

123. Compass and straightedge or ruler-and-compass _____ is the _____ of lengths or angles using only an idealized ruler and compass.
    a. Thing
    b. Construction0
    c. Undefined
    d. Undefined

124. An _____ is the limit of a definite integral, as an endpoint of the interval of integration approaches either a specified real number or ‡ or − ‡ or, in some cases, as both endpoints approach limits.
    a. Improper integral0
    b. Thing
    c. Undefined
    d. Undefined

125. In mathematics, a set is called _____ if there is a bijection between the set and some set of the form {1, 2, ..., n} where n is a natural number.

Chapter 8. PRINCIPLES OF INTEGRAL EVALUATION

a. Thing
c. Undefined

b. Finite0
d. Undefined

126. _____ is the state of being greater than any finite real or natural number, however large.
a. Thing
c. Undefined

b. Infinite0
d. Undefined

127. In calculus and other branches of mathematical analysis, an _____ is an algebraic expression obtained in the context of limits.
a. Thing
c. Undefined

b. Indeterminate form0
d. Undefined

128. In mathematics, a _____ may be described informally as a number that can be given by an infinite decimal representation.
a. Thing
c. Undefined

b. Real number0
d. Undefined

129. Continuous functions are of utmost importance in mathematics and applications. However, not all functions are continuous. If a function is not continuous at a point in its domain, one says that it has a _____ there. The set of all points of _____ of a function may be a discrete set, a dense set, or even the entire domain of the function.
a. Thing
c. Undefined

b. Discontinuity0
d. Undefined

130. The _____ is the distance around a closed curve. _____ is a kind of perimeter.
a. Circumference0
c. Undefined

b. Thing
d. Undefined

131. In mathematics, an _____, mean, or central tendency of a data set refers to a measure of the "middle" or "expected" value of the data set.
a. Average0
c. Undefined

b. Concept
d. Undefined

132. _____ is a physical property of a system that underlies the common notions of hot and cold; something that is hotter has the greater _____.
a. Thing
c. Undefined

b. Temperature0
d. Undefined

133. In mathematics, a _____ is a mathematical statement which appears likely to be true, but has not been formally proven to be true under the rules of mathematical logic.
a. Conjecture0
c. Undefined

b. Concept
d. Undefined

134. A _____ is an object that is attached to a pivot point so that it can swing freely.
a. Pendulum0
c. Undefined

b. Thing
d. Undefined

Chapter 8. PRINCIPLES OF INTEGRAL EVALUATION

135. In business, particularly accounting, a _____ is the time intervals that the accounts, statement, payments, or other calculations cover.
  a. Thing
  b. Period0
  c. Undefined
  d. Undefined

136. _____ is the force that opposes the relative motion or tendency toward such motion of two surfaces in contact.
  a. Friction0
  b. Thing
  c. Undefined
  d. Undefined

137. In mathematics, in the field of group theory, a _____ of a group is a quasisimple subnormal subgroup.
  a. Component0
  b. Concept
  c. Undefined
  d. Undefined

138. The metre (or _____, see spelling differences) is a measure of length. It is the basic unit of length in the metric system and in the International System of Units (SI), used around the world for general and scientific purposes.
  a. Concept
  b. Meter0
  c. Undefined
  d. Undefined

Chapter 9. MATHEMATICAL MODELING WITH DIFFERENTIAL EQUATIONS

1. A _____ signifies a point or points of probability on a subject e.g., the _____ of creativity, which allows for the formation of rule or norm or law by interpretation of the phenomena events that can be created.
   a. Thing
   b. Principle0
   c. Undefined
   d. Undefined

2. A _____ is a special kind of ratio, indicating a relationship between two measurements with different units, such as miles to gallons or cents to pounds.
   a. Rate0
   b. Thing
   c. Undefined
   d. Undefined

3. The _____ is a measurement of how a function changes when the values of its inputs change.
   a. Thing
   b. Derivative0
   c. Undefined
   d. Undefined

4. A _____ is traditionally an infinitesimally small change in a variable.
   a. Differential0
   b. Thing
   c. Undefined
   d. Undefined

5. A _____ is a mathematical equation for an unknown function of one or several variables which relates the values of the function itself and of its derivatives of various orders.
   a. Differential equation0
   b. Thing
   c. Undefined
   d. Undefined

6. _____ is the study of terms and their use — of words and compound words that are used in specific contexts.
   a. Terminology0
   b. Thing
   c. Undefined
   d. Undefined

7. The mathematical concept of a _____ expresses the intuitive idea of deterministic dependence between two quantities, one of which is viewed as primary and the other as secondary. A _____ then is a way to associate a unique output for each input of a specified type, for example, a real number or an element of a given set.
   a. Thing
   b. Function0
   c. Undefined
   d. Undefined

8. In elementary algebra, an _____ is a set that contains every real number between two indicated numbers and may contain the two numbers themselves.
   a. Interval0
   b. Thing
   c. Undefined
   d. Undefined

9. _____ is a process of combining or accumulating. It may also refer to:
   a. Thing
   b. Integration0
   c. Undefined
   d. Undefined

10. In mathematics and the mathematical sciences, a _____ is a fixed, but possibly unspecified, value. This is in contrast to a variable, which is not fixed.
    a. Constant0
    b. Thing
    c. Undefined
    d. Undefined

Chapter 9. MATHEMATICAL MODELING WITH DIFFERENTIAL EQUATIONS

11. Initial objects are also called _____, and terminal objects are also called final.
    a. Coterminal0
    b. Thing
    c. Undefined
    d. Undefined

12. In mathematics, the concept of a _____ tries to capture the intuitive idea of a geometrical one-dimensional and continuous object. A simple example is the circle.
    a. Thing
    b. Curve0
    c. Undefined
    d. Undefined

13. In mathematics, _____ are the intuitive idea of a geometrical one-dimensional and continuous object.
    a. Thing
    b. Curves0
    c. Undefined
    d. Undefined

14. In mathematics, in the field of differential equations, an initial value problem is a differential equation together with specified value, called the _____, of the unknown function at a given point in the domain of the solution.
    a. Initial condition0
    b. Thing
    c. Undefined
    d. Undefined

15. The _____ of a function is an extension of the concept of a sum, and are identified or found through the use of integration.
    a. Thing
    b. Integral0
    c. Undefined
    d. Undefined

16. The word _____ comes from the Latin word linearis, which means created by lines.
    a. Thing
    b. Linear0
    c. Undefined
    d. Undefined

17. A _____ is an equation in which each term is either a constant or the product of a constant times the first power of a variable.
    a. Linear equation0
    b. Thing
    c. Undefined
    d. Undefined

18. In mathematics, factorization (British English: factorisation) or factoring is the decomposition of an object (for example, a number, a polynomial, or a matrix) into a product of other objects, or _____, which when multiplied together give the original.
    a. Factors0
    b. Thing
    c. Undefined
    d. Undefined

19. _____ is a function that is chosen to facilitate the solving of a given ordinary differential equation. Consider an ordinary differential equation of the form
    a. Thing
    b. Integrating factor0
    c. Undefined
    d. Undefined

20. A _____ is a symbolic representation denoting a quantity or expression. It often represents an "unknown" quantity that has the potential to change.

Chapter 9. MATHEMATICAL MODELING WITH DIFFERENTIAL EQUATIONS

    a. Thing
    c. Undefined
    b. Variable0
    d. Undefined

21. An _____ of a function f is a function F whose derivative is equal to f, i.e., F' = f.
    a. Antiderivative0
    c. Undefined
    b. Thing
    d. Undefined

22. _____ is often used to describe the measurement of the steepness, incline, gradient, or grade of a straight line. The _____ is defined as the ratio of the "rise" divided by the "run" between two points on a line, or in other words, the ratio of the altitude change to the horizontal distance between any two points on the line.
    a. Slope0
    c. Undefined
    b. Thing
    d. Undefined

23. In trigonometry, the _____ is a function defined as $\tan x = \sin x / \cos x$. The function is so-named because it can be defined as the length of a certain segment of a _____ (in the geometric sense) to the unit circle. In plane geometry, a line is _____ to a curve, at some point, if both line and curve pass through the point with the same direction.
    a. Thing
    c. Undefined
    b. Tangent0
    d. Undefined

24. _____ has two distinct but etymologically-related meanings: one in geometry and one in trigonometry.
    a. Thing
    c. Undefined
    b. Tangent line0
    d. Undefined

25. _____ is a kind of property which exists as magnitude or multitude. It is among the basic classes of things along with quality, substance, change, and relation.
    a. Amount0
    c. Undefined
    b. Thing
    d. Undefined

26. _____ are a measure of time.
    a. Thing
    c. Undefined
    b. Minutes0
    d. Undefined

27. In mathematics, science including computer science, linguistics and engineering, an _____ is, generally speaking, an independent variable or input to a function.
    a. Thing
    c. Undefined
    b. Argument0
    d. Undefined

28. An _____ is a straight line around which a geometric figure can be rotated.
    a. Axis0
    c. Undefined
    b. Thing
    d. Undefined

29. In physics, _____ is an influence that may cause an object to accelerate. It may be experienced as a lift, a push, or a pull. The actual acceleration of the body is determined by the vector sum of all forces acting on it, known as net _____ or resultant _____.

160 *Chapter 9. MATHEMATICAL MODELING WITH DIFFERENTIAL EQUATIONS*

    a. Force0
    c. Undefined
    b. Thing
    d. Undefined

30. In mathematics, the additive inverse, or _____ of a number n is the number that, when added to n, yields zero. The additive inverse of n is denoted −n. For example, 7 is −7, because 7 + (−7) = 0, and the additive inverse of −0.3 is 0.3, because −0.3 + 0.3 = 0.
    a. Opposite0
    c. Undefined
    b. Thing
    d. Undefined

31. In mathematics, the _____ of a number n is the number that, when added to n, yields zero. The _____ of n is denoted −n. For example, 7 is −7, because 7 + (−7) = 0, and the _____ of −0.3 is 0.3, because −0.3 + 0.3 = 0.
    a. Additive inverse0
    c. Undefined
    b. Thing
    d. Undefined

32. In mathematics, two quantities are called _____ if they vary in such a way that one of the quantities is a constant multiple of the other, or equivalently if they have a constant ratio.
    a. Thing
    c. Undefined
    b. Proportional0
    d. Undefined

33. _____ of an object is its speed in a particular direction.
    a. Thing
    c. Undefined
    b. Velocity0
    d. Undefined

34. _____ is to give an equation R(x,y) = S(x,y) that at least in part has the same graph as y = f(x).
    a. Thing
    c. Undefined
    b. Implicit differentiation0
    d. Undefined

35. _____, a field in mathematics, is the study of how functions change when their inputs change. The primary object of study in _____ is the derivative.
    a. Differential calculus0
    c. Undefined
    b. Thing
    d. Undefined

36. In mathematics, a _____ may be described informally as a number that can be given by an infinite decimal representation.
    a. Real number0
    c. Undefined
    b. Thing
    d. Undefined

37. An _____ is a collection of two not necessarily distinct objects, one of which is distinguished as the first coordinate and the other as the second coordinate.
    a. Ordered pair0
    c. Undefined
    b. Thing
    d. Undefined

38. In mathematics, the conjugate _____ or adjoint matrix of an m-by-n matrix A with complex entries is the n-by-m matrix A* obtained from A by taking the transpose and then taking the complex conjugate of each entry.

Chapter 9. MATHEMATICAL MODELING WITH DIFFERENTIAL EQUATIONS 161

    a. Thing
    b. Pairs0
    c. Undefined
    d. Undefined

39. In geometry, two lines or planes if one falls on the other in such a way as to create congruent adjacent angles. The term may be used as a noun or adjective. Thus, referring to Figure 1, the line AB is the _____ to CD through the point B.
    a. Thing
    b. Perpendicular0
    c. Undefined
    d. Undefined

40. _____ is the ability to hold, receive or absorb, or a measure thereof, similar to the concept of volume.
    a. Capacity0
    b. Concept
    c. Undefined
    d. Undefined

41. In geometry, a _____ (Greek words diairo = divide and metro = measure) of a circle is any straight line segment that passes through the centre and whose endpoints are on the circular boundary, or, in more modern usage, the length of such a line segment. When using the word in the more modern sense, one speaks of the _____ rather than a _____, because all diameters of a circle have the same length. This length is twice the radius. The _____ of a circle is also the longest chord that the circle has.
    a. Thing
    b. Diameter0
    c. Undefined
    d. Undefined

42. A _____ is a vehicle, missile or aircraft which obtains thrust by the reaction to the ejection of fast moving fluid from within a _____ engine.
    a. Thing
    b. Rocket0
    c. Undefined
    d. Undefined

43. _____ is defined as the rate of change or derivative with respect to time of velocity.
    a. Acceleration0
    b. Thing
    c. Undefined
    d. Undefined

44. _____ is the property of a physical object that quantifies the amount of matter and energy it is equivalent to.
    a. Mass0
    b. Thing
    c. Undefined
    d. Undefined

45. _____, Greek for "knowledge of nature," is the branch of science concerned with the discovery and characterization of universal laws which govern matter, energy, space, and time.
    a. Thing
    b. Physics0
    c. Undefined
    d. Undefined

46. In plane geometry, a _____ is a polygon with four equal sides, four right angles, and parallel opposite sides. In algebra, the _____ of a number is that number multiplied by itself.
    a. Thing
    b. Square0
    c. Undefined
    d. Undefined

47. In geometry, a line _____ is a part of a line that is bounded by two end points, and contains every point on the line between its end points.

Chapter 9. MATHEMATICAL MODELING WITH DIFFERENTIAL EQUATIONS

   a. Concept
   c. Undefined
   b. Segment0
   d. Undefined

48. A _____ is a graphical tool to qualitatively visualize, or aid in numerical approximation of, solutions to differential equations.
   a. Slope field0
   c. Undefined
   b. Thing
   d. Undefined

49. Leonhard _____ was a pioneering Swiss mathematician and physicist, who spent most of his life in Russia and Germany.
   a. Person
   c. Undefined
   b. Euler0
   d. Undefined

50. A _____ is a part of a line that is bounded by two end points, and contains every point on the line between its end points.
   a. Thing
   c. Undefined
   b. Line segment0
   d. Undefined

51. In mathematics, a _____ is a mathematical statement which appears likely to be true, but has not been formally proven to be true under the rules of mathematical logic.
   a. Conjecture0
   c. Undefined
   b. Concept
   d. Undefined

52. A _____ is a negotiable instrument instructing a financial institution to pay a specific amount of a specific currency from a specific demand account held in the maker/depositor's name with that institution. Both the maker and payee may be natural persons or legal entities.
   a. Check0
   c. Undefined
   b. Thing
   d. Undefined

53. Deductive _____ is the kind of _____ in which the conclusion is necessitated by, or reached from, previously known facts (the premises).
   a. Thing
   c. Undefined
   b. Reasoning0
   d. Undefined

54. In sociology and biology a _____ is the collection of people or organisms of a particular species living in a given geographic area or space, usually measured by a census.
   a. Thing
   c. Undefined
   b. Population0
   d. Undefined

55. _____ is change in population over time, and can be quantified as the change in the number of individuals in a population per unit time.
   a. Thing
   c. Undefined
   b. Population growth0
   d. Undefined

Chapter 9. MATHEMATICAL MODELING WITH DIFFERENTIAL EQUATIONS 163

56. _____, or Drosophila Melanoaster is a two-winged insect that belongs to the Diptera, the order of the flies. The species is commonly known as the fruit fly, and is one of the most commonly used model organisms in biology, including studies in genetics, physiology and life history evolution.
- a. Thing
- b. Fruit flies0
- c. Undefined
- d. Undefined

57. _____ is a special mathematical relationship between two quantities. Two quantities are called proportional if they vary in such a way that one of the quantities is a constant multiple of the other, or equivalently if they have a constant ratio.
- a. Thing
- b. Proportionality0
- c. Undefined
- d. Undefined

58. Mathematical _____ really refers to two distinct areas of research: the first is the application of the techniques of formal _____ to mathematics and mathematical reasoning, and the second, in the other direction, the application of mathematical techniques to the representation and analysis of formal _____.
- a. Thing
- b. Logic0
- c. Undefined
- d. Undefined

59. A _____ is an abstract model that uses mathematical language to describe the behavior of a system. Eykhoff defined a _____ as 'a representation of the essential aspects of an existing system which presents knowledge of that system in usable form'.
- a. Mathematical model0
- b. Thing
- c. Undefined
- d. Undefined

60. _____ usually refers to the biological _____ of a population level that can be supported for an organism, given the quantity of food, habitat, water and other life infrastructure present.
- a. Thing
- b. Carrying capacity0
- c. Undefined
- d. Undefined

61. In mathematics, a _____ is a condition that a solution to an optimization problem must satisfy in order to be acceptable.
- a. Constraint0
- b. Thing
- c. Undefined
- d. Undefined

62. Pierre François _____ was a mathematician and a doctor in number theory from the University of Ghent in 1825.
- a. Verhulst0
- b. Person
- c. Undefined
- d. Undefined

63. _____ is a synonym for information.
- a. Thing
- b. Data0
- c. Undefined
- d. Undefined

64. Acid _____ ratio measures the ability of a company to use its near cash or quick assets to immediately extinguish its current liabilities.

Chapter 9. MATHEMATICAL MODELING WITH DIFFERENTIAL EQUATIONS

a. Test0
b. Thing
c. Undefined
d. Undefined

65. In mathematics, _____ growth occurs when the growth rate of a function is always proportional to the function's current size.
a. Thing
b. Exponential0
c. Undefined
d. Undefined

66. The _____ is the total number of human beings alive on the planet Earth at a given time.
a. World population0
b. Thing
c. Undefined
d. Undefined

67. _____ is essentially exponential growth based on a constant rate of compound interest.
a. Exponential growth model0
b. Thing
c. Undefined
d. Undefined

68. _____ is a decrease that follows an exponential function.
a. Thing
b. Exponential decay0
c. Undefined
d. Undefined

69. The _____ is the period of time required for a quantity to double in size or value.
a. Doubling time0
b. Thing
c. Undefined
d. Undefined

70. A _____ is 360° or 2δ radians.
a. Thing
b. Turn0
c. Undefined
d. Undefined

71. The _____ of measurement are a globally standardized and modernized form of the metric system.
a. Units0
b. Thing
c. Undefined
d. Undefined

72. An _____ or member of a set is an object that when collected together make up the set.
a. Element0
b. Thing
c. Undefined
d. Undefined

73. _____ is a radiometric dating method that uses the naturally occurring isotope carbon-14 to determine the age of carbonaceous materials up to about 60,000 years.
a. Thing
b. Radiocarbon dating0
c. Undefined
d. Undefined

74. _____ is the logarithm to the base e, where e is an irrational constant approximately equal to 2.718281828459.
a. Natural logarithm0
b. Thing
c. Undefined
d. Undefined

75. In mathematics, the _____ of a coordinate system is the point where the axes of the system intersect.

Chapter 9. MATHEMATICAL MODELING WITH DIFFERENTIAL EQUATIONS

a. Thing
b. Origin0
c. Undefined
d. Undefined

76. In mathematics, a _____ of a number x is the exponent y of the power by such that $x = b^y$. The value used for the base b must be neither 0 nor 1, nor a root of 1 in the case of the extension to complex numbers, and is typically 10, e, or 2.
a. Thing
b. Logarithm0
c. Undefined
d. Undefined

77. The _____, the average in everyday English, which is also called the arithmetic _____ (and is distinguished from the geometric _____ or harmonic _____). The average is also called the sample _____. The expected value of a random variable, which is also called the population _____.
a. Mean0
b. Thing
c. Undefined
d. Undefined

78. _____ are external two-dimensional outlines, with the appearance or configuration of some thing - in contrast to the matter or content or substance of which it is composed.
a. Thing
b. Shapes0
c. Undefined
d. Undefined

79. In algebra, the _____ decomposition or _____ expansion is used to reduce the degree of either the numerator or the denominator of a rational function.
a. Thing
b. Partial fraction0
c. Undefined
d. Undefined

80. A _____ function is a function for which, intuitively, small changes in the input result in small changes in the output.
a. Event
b. Continuous0
c. Undefined
d. Undefined

81. _____ are the basic objects of study in graph theory. Informally speaking, a graph is a set of objects called points, nodes, or vertices connected by links called lines or edges.
a. Thing
b. Graphs0
c. Undefined
d. Undefined

82. A _____ is any object propelled through space by the applicationp of a force.
a. Projectile0
b. Thing
c. Undefined
d. Undefined

83. In business, particularly accounting, a _____ is the time intervals that the accounts, statement, payments, or other calculations cover.
a. Period0
b. Thing
c. Undefined
d. Undefined

84. Sir Isaac _____, was an English physicist, mathematician, astronomer, natural philosopher, and alchemist, regarded by many as the greatest figure in the history of science

a. Newton0
b. Person
c. Undefined
d. Undefined

85. _____ is a physical property of a system that underlies the common notions of hot and cold; something that is hotter has the greater _____.
   a. Temperature0
   b. Thing
   c. Undefined
   d. Undefined

86. _____ is a mathematical subject that includes the study of limits, derivatives, integrals, and power series and constitutes a major part of modern university curriculum.
   a. Calculus0
   b. Thing
   c. Undefined
   d. Undefined

87. In geometry, an _____ of a triangle is a straight line through a vertex and perpendicular to (i.e. forming a right angle with) the opposite side or an extension of the opposite side.
   a. Concept
   b. Altitude0
   c. Undefined
   d. Undefined

88. Mathematical _____ is used to represent ideas.
   a. Thing
   b. Notation0
   c. Undefined
   d. Undefined

89. In mathematics, a _____ is a constant multiplicative factor of a certain object. The object can be such things as a variable, a vector, a function, etc. For example, the _____ of $9x^2$ is 9.
   a. Thing
   b. Coefficient0
   c. Undefined
   d. Undefined

90. A _____ of a number is the product of that number with any integer.
   a. Multiple0
   b. Thing
   c. Undefined
   d. Undefined

91. In mathematics, a _____ is a statement that can be proved on the basis of explicitly stated or previously agreed assumptions.
   a. Thing
   b. Theorem0
   c. Undefined
   d. Undefined

92. _____ is a function whose values do not vary and thus are constant.
   a. Constant function0
   b. Thing
   c. Undefined
   d. Undefined

93. A quadratic equation with real solutions, called roots, which may be real or complex, is given by the _____: $x = \frac{-b \pm \sqrt{b^2 - 4ac}}{2a}$.
   a. Quadratic formula0
   b. Thing
   c. Undefined
   d. Undefined

Chapter 9. MATHEMATICAL MODELING WITH DIFFERENTIAL EQUATIONS

94. In mathematics, _____ is the decomposition of an object into a product of other objects, or factors, which when multiplied together give the original.
    a. Thing
    b. Factoring0
    c. Undefined
    d. Undefined

95. In mathematics, a _____ of a complex-valued function f is a member x of the domain of f such that f(x) vanishes at x, that is, $x : f(x) = 0$.
    a. Root0
    b. Thing
    c. Undefined
    d. Undefined

96. In mathematics, a _____ is a polynomial equation of the second degree. The general form is $ax^2 + bx + c = 0$.
    a. Thing
    b. Quadratic equation0
    c. Undefined
    d. Undefined

97. In mathematics, a _____ is an expression that is constructed from one or more variables and constants, using only the operations of addition, subtraction, multiplication, and constant positive whole number exponents. is a _____. Note in particular that division by an expression containing a variable is not in general allowed in polynomials. [1]
    a. Polynomial0
    b. Thing
    c. Undefined
    d. Undefined

98. In algebra, a _____ is a binomial formed by taking the opposite of the second term of a binomial.
    a. Conjugate0
    b. Thing
    c. Undefined
    d. Undefined

99. A _____ is a set of numbers that designate location in a given reference system, such as x,y in a planar _____ system or an x,y,z in a three-dimensional _____ system.
    a. Thing
    b. Coordinate0
    c. Undefined
    d. Undefined

100. In economics, economic _____ is simply a state of the world where economic forces are balanced and in the absence of external influences the values of economic variables will not change.
    a. Thing
    b. Equilibrium0
    c. Undefined
    d. Undefined

101. _____ is the weakest of the four fundamental forces of bature, as described by Issac Newton
    a. Gravitational force0
    b. Thing
    c. Undefined
    d. Undefined

102. The _____ of a mathematical object is its size: a property by which it can be larger or smaller than other objects of the same kind; in technical terms, an ordering of the class of objects to which it belongs.
    a. Magnitude0
    b. Thing
    c. Undefined
    d. Undefined

103. The _____ is a nonnegative scalar measure of a wave's magnitude of oscillation, that is, the magnitude of the maximum disturbance in the medium during one wave cycle.

Chapter 9. MATHEMATICAL MODELING WITH DIFFERENTIAL EQUATIONS

a. Amplitude0
b. Thing
c. Undefined
d. Undefined

104. In statistics the _____ of an event i is the number n_i of times the event occurred in the experiment or the study. These frequencies are often graphically represented in histograms.
    a. Concept
    b. Frequency0
    c. Undefined
    d. Undefined

105. A _____ is a quantity that denotes the proportional amount or magnitude of one quantity relative to another.
    a. Thing
    b. Ratio0
    c. Undefined
    d. Undefined

106. In mathematics and its applications, a _____ is a system for assigning an n-tuple of numbers or scalars to each point in an n-dimensional space.
    a. Coordinate system0
    b. Concept
    c. Undefined
    d. Undefined

107. In classical geometry, a _____ of a circle or sphere is any line segment from its center to its boundary. By extension, the _____ of a circle or sphere is the length of any such segment. The _____ is half the diameter. In science and engineering the term _____ of curvature is commonly used as a synonym for _____.
    a. Thing
    b. Radius0
    c. Undefined
    d. Undefined

108. U.S. liquid _____ is legally defined as 231 cubic inches, and is equal to 3.785411784 litres or abotu 0.13368 cubic feet. This is the most common definition of a _____. The U.S. fluid ounce is defined as 1/128 of a U.S. _____.
    a. Thing
    b. Gallon0
    c. Undefined
    d. Undefined

109. In chemistry, a _____ is substance made by combining two or more different materials in such a way that no chemical reaction occurs.
    a. Thing
    b. Mixture0
    c. Undefined
    d. Undefined

110. A pair of angles is _____ if their respective measures sum to 180 degrees.
    a. Concept
    b. Supplementary0
    c. Undefined
    d. Undefined

111. _____ generally derives from name. A _____ quantity e.g., length, diameter, volume, voltage, value is generally the quantity according to which some item has been named or is generally referred to.
    a. Thing
    b. Nominal0
    c. Undefined
    d. Undefined

112. _____ is the fee paid on borrowed money.

a. Thing
b. Interest0
c. Undefined
d. Undefined

113. _____ interest refers to the fact that whenever interest is calculated, it is based not only on the original principal, but also on any unpaid interest that has been added to the principal.
   a. Thing
   b. Compound0
   c. Undefined
   d. Undefined

114. _____ refers to the fact that whenever interest is calculated, it is based not only on the original principal, but also on any unpaid interest that has been added to the principal. The more frequently interest is compounded, the faster the balance grows.
   a. Concept
   b. Compound interest0
   c. Undefined
   d. Undefined

Chapter 10. INFINITE SERIES

1. A measure of variability, the _____ is the distance from the lowest to the highest score.
   a. Range1
   b. 15 theorem
   c. Undefined
   d. Undefined

2. The Greek letter _____ indicates summation.
   a. 15 theorem
   b. Sigma1
   c. Undefined
   d. Undefined

3. _____ is the process by which sample data are used to indicate the value of an unknown quantity in a population.
   a. ACTRAN
   b. Estimation1
   c. Undefined
   d. Undefined

4. _____ is used synonymously for variable.
   a. 15 theorem
   b. Factor1
   c. Undefined
   d. Undefined

5. A number that does not change in value in a given situation is a _____.
   a. 15 theorem
   b. Constant1
   c. Undefined
   d. Undefined

6. The probability of correctly rejecting a false Ho is referred to as _____.
   a. Power1
   b. 15 theorem
   c. Undefined
   d. Undefined

7. The most important measure of central tendency, and one of the basic building blocks of all statistical analysis, is the arithmetic _____. It is simply the sum of all the set of values divided by the number of values involved. As a measure of central tendency, it is affected by extreme scores, and it assumes a ratio scale of measurement.
   a. Mean1
   b. 15 theorem
   c. Undefined
   d. Undefined

8. A _____ is a scheme for the numerical representation of the values of a variable. The interpretation we place upon the numbers of the scale, rather than the numbers themselves, makes the _____ useful. The most common scales are nominal, ordinal, interval
   a. Scale1
   b. 15 theorem
   c. Undefined
   d. Undefined

9. The _____ is often confused with the median. The Median is a statistic for the distribution whereas the _____ provides a statistic for an interval; it is the center of the interval; the arithmetic average of the upper and lower limits.
   a. 15 theorem
   b. Midpoint1
   c. Undefined
   d. Undefined

10. An _____ is an indication of the value of an unknown quantity based on observed data. More formally, an _____ is the particular value of an estimator that is obtained from a particular sample of data and used to indicate the value of a parameter.
    a. ACTRAN
    b. Estimate1
    c. Undefined
    d. Undefined

Chapter 10. INFINITE SERIES 171

11. At times we must contend with variables that assume a large number of values. In this case it is typical to create _____ of values of the variable and then make a frequency tally of the number of observations falling within each interval. As is the case with any data reduction technique, detail is lost.
   a. ACTRAN
   b. Intervals1
   c. Undefined
   d. Undefined

12. _____ is a measure of how close an estimator is expected to be to the true value of a parameter.
   a. 15 theorem
   b. Precision1
   c. Undefined
   d. Undefined

13. Another word for independent variables in the analysis of variance is _____.
   a. 15 theorem
   b. Factors1
   c. Undefined
   d. Undefined

14. The number of times a particular score or event occurs with respect to the total number of events or scores is called its _____.
   a. Proportion1
   b. 15 theorem
   c. Undefined
   d. Undefined

15. A population, also referred to as a universe, is any well-defined collection of things. By well-defined we mean that the members of the _____ are spelled out, or an unequivocal statement is made as to which things belong in it and which do not.
   a. 15 theorem
   b. Population1
   c. Undefined
   d. Undefined

16. There are properties of objects that do assume one and only value, and we refer to these characteristics as constants. _____, then, are the invariables that differentiate one class of objects from another.
   a. 15 theorem
   b. Constants1
   c. Undefined
   d. Undefined

17. The very fact that we are measuring objects with respect to some characteristic implies that the objects differ in that characteristic; or stated in another way, that the characteristic can take on a number of different values. These properties or characteristics of an object that can assume two or more different values are referred to as a _____.
   a. 15 theorem
   b. Variable1
   c. Undefined
   d. Undefined

Chapter 11. ANALYTIC GEOMETRY IN CALCULUS

1. _____ refer to any data source, whether individuals, physical or biological things, geographic locations, time periods, or events; that is, anything upon which observations can be made.
   a. Objects1
   b. ACTRAN
   c. Undefined
   d. Undefined

2. One major objective of statistical analysis is the identification of associations or _____ that exist between and among sets of observations. In other words, does knowledge about about one set of data allow us to infer or predict characteristics about another set or sets of data.
   a. Relationships1
   b. 15 theorem
   c. Undefined
   d. Undefined

3. _____ are characteristics or properties of an object that can take on one or more different values.
   a. 15 theorem
   b. Variables1
   c. Undefined
   d. Undefined

4. The most important measure of central tendency, and one of the basic building blocks of all statistical analysis, is the arithmetic _____. It is simply the sum of all the set of values divided by the number of values involved. As a measure of central tendency, it is affected by extreme scores, and it assumes a ratio scale of measurement.
   a. Mean1
   b. 15 theorem
   c. Undefined
   d. Undefined

5. _____ is implied when data values are distributed in the same way above and below the middle of the sample.
   a. Symmetry1
   b. 15 theorem
   c. Undefined
   d. Undefined

6. A number that does not change in value in a given situation is a _____.
   a. 15 theorem
   b. Constant1
   c. Undefined
   d. Undefined

7. At times we must contend with variables that assume a large number of values. In this case it is typical to create _____ of values of the variable and then make a frequency tally of the number of observations falling within each interval. As is the case with any data reduction technique, detail is lost.
   a. Intervals1
   b. ACTRAN
   c. Undefined
   d. Undefined

8. There are properties of objects that do assume one and only value, and we refer to these characteristics as constants. _____, then, are the invariables that differentiate one class of objects from another.
   a. Constants1
   b. 15 theorem
   c. Undefined
   d. Undefined

9. A _____ is a value used to represent a certain population characteristic. Because of the impracticality of measuring an entire population to determine this value, parameters are usually estimated.
   a. Parameter1
   b. 15 theorem
   c. Undefined
   d. Undefined

10. The _____ refers to the amount of change in Y for a 1 unit change in X; or in-other-words, the rate of change in the predicted value as a function of a change in the predictor variable.

Chapter 11. ANALYTIC GEOMETRY IN CALCULUS

a. 15 theorem
b. Slope1
c. Undefined
d. Undefined

11. A measure of variability, the _____ is the distance from the lowest to the highest score.
    a. 15 theorem
    b. Range1
    c. Undefined
    d. Undefined

12. The _____ is often confused with the median. The Median is a statistic for the distribution whereas the _____ provides a statistic for an interval; it is the center of the interval; the arithmetic average of the upper and lower limits.
    a. Midpoint1
    b. 15 theorem
    c. Undefined
    d. Undefined

13. _____ is used synonymously for variable.
    a. Factor1
    b. 15 theorem
    c. Undefined
    d. Undefined

14. By _____ we mean the cumulative frequency, counting in from the nearer end.
    a. 15 theorem
    b. Depth1
    c. Undefined
    d. Undefined

15. By _____ we mean collecting observations made upon our environment -- observations, which are the results of measurements using clocks, balances, measuring rods, counting operations, or other objectively defined measuring instruments or procedures. _____ may mean simply counting the number of times a particular property occurs.
    a. 15 theorem
    b. Data1
    c. Undefined
    d. Undefined

16. A _____ is a scheme for the numerical representation of the values of a variable. The interpretation we place upon the numbers of the scale, rather than the numbers themselves, makes the _____ useful. The most common scales are nominal, ordinal, interval
    a. 15 theorem
    b. Scale1
    c. Undefined
    d. Undefined

17. A _____ provides a quantitative description of the likely occurrence of a particular event. _____ is conventionally expressed on a scale from 0 to 1; a rare event has a _____ close to 0, a very common event has a _____ close to 1.
    a. Probability1
    b. 15 theorem
    c. Undefined
    d. Undefined

18. The defining characteristics of populations are called _____. Observations must be made on every single member of the population in question in order to precisely state the value of _____.
    a. Parameters1
    b. 15 theorem
    c. Undefined
    d. Undefined

Chapter 12. THREE-DIMENSIONAL SPACE; VECTORS

1. _____ refer to any data source, whether individuals, physical or biological things, geographic locations, time periods, or events; that is, anything upon which observations can be made.
   a. Objects1
   b. ACTRAN
   c. Undefined
   d. Undefined

2. _____ are characteristics or properties of an object that can take on one or more different values.
   a. 15 theorem
   b. Variables1
   c. Undefined
   d. Undefined

3. The very fact that we are measuring objects with respect to some characteristic implies that the objects differ in that characteristic; or stated in another way, that the characteristic can take on a number of different values. These properties or characteristics of an object that can assume two or more different values are referred to as a _____.
   a. Variable1
   b. 15 theorem
   c. Undefined
   d. Undefined

4. The _____ is often confused with the median. The Median is a statistic for the distribution whereas the _____ provides a statistic for an interval; it is the center of the interval; the arithmetic average of the upper and lower limits.
   a. Midpoint1
   b. 15 theorem
   c. Undefined
   d. Undefined

5. One major objective of statistical analysis is the identification of associations or _____ that exist between and among sets of observations. In other words, does knowledge about about one set of data allow us to infer or predict characteristics about another set or sets of data.
   a. 15 theorem
   b. Relationships1
   c. Undefined
   d. Undefined

6. A common requirement for parametric tests is that the population of scores from which the sample observations came should be normally distributed. While many variables are close enough to a normal distribution and many of the tests that we will encounter are quite robust to moderate departures, occasionally there is a need to transform a variable so that the requirement of normality is better met; called _____. Essentially this means transforming the distribution such that the symmetry of the distribution is made to resemble a normal distribution more closely.
   a. 15 theorem
   b. Normalizing1
   c. Undefined
   d. Undefined

7. _____ is implied when data values are distributed in the same way above and below the middle of the sample.
   a. 15 theorem
   b. Symmetry1
   c. Undefined
   d. Undefined

8. A number that does not change in value in a given situation is a _____.
   a. Constant1
   b. 15 theorem
   c. Undefined
   d. Undefined

9. Another word for independent variables in the analysis of variance is _____.
   a. 15 theorem
   b. Factors1
   c. Undefined
   d. Undefined

Chapter 12. THREE-DIMENSIONAL SPACE; VECTORS

10. The same statistical principles apply to the evaluation of observed _____ between sets of data. The field of statistics provides the necessary techniques for making statements of our certainty that there are real as opposed to chance differences.
    a. Differences1
    b. 15 theorem
    c. Undefined
    d. Undefined

11. The most important measure of central tendency, and one of the basic building blocks of all statistical analysis, is the arithmetic _____. It is simply the sum of all the set of values divided by the number of values involved. As a measure of central tendency, it is affected by extreme scores, and it assumes a ratio scale of measurement.
    a. 15 theorem
    b. Mean1
    c. Undefined
    d. Undefined

12. _____ refers to those points that cut off the bottom and top quarter of a distribution
    a. Hinges1
    b. 15 theorem
    c. Undefined
    d. Undefined

13. The defining characteristics of populations are called _____. Observations must be made on every single member of the population in question in order to precisely state the value of _____.
    a. Parameters1
    b. 15 theorem
    c. Undefined
    d. Undefined

14. A _____ is a value used to represent a certain population characteristic. Because of the impracticality of measuring an entire population to determine this value, parameters are usually estimated.
    a. 15 theorem
    b. Parameter1
    c. Undefined
    d. Undefined

15. There are properties of objects that do assume one and only value, and we refer to these characteristics as constants. _____, then, are the invariables that differentiate one class of objects from another.
    a. Constants1
    b. 15 theorem
    c. Undefined
    d. Undefined

16. By _____ we mean collecting observations made upon our environment -- observations, which are the results of measurements using clocks, balances, measuring rods, counting operations, or other objectively defined measuring instruments or procedures. _____ may mean simply counting the number of times a particular property occurs.
    a. 15 theorem
    b. Data1
    c. Undefined
    d. Undefined

Chapter 13. VECTOR-VALUED FUNCTIONS

1. A _____ is a value used to represent a certain population characteristic. Because of the impracticality of measuring an entire population to determine this value, parameters are usually estimated.
   a. 15 theorem
   b. Parameter1
   c. Undefined
   d. Undefined

2. There are properties of objects that do assume one and only value, and we refer to these characteristics as constants. _____, then, are the invariables that differentiate one class of objects from another.
   a. 15 theorem
   b. Constants1
   c. Undefined
   d. Undefined

3. _____ are characteristics or properties of an object that can take on one or more different values.
   a. 15 theorem
   b. Variables1
   c. Undefined
   d. Undefined

4. The very fact that we are measuring objects with respect to some characteristic implies that the objects differ in that characteristic; or stated in another way, that the characteristic can take on a number of different values. These properties or characteristics of an object that can assume two or more different values are referred to as a _____.
   a. Variable1
   b. 15 theorem
   c. Undefined
   d. Undefined

5. The _____ refers to the amount of change in Y for a 1 unit change in X; or in-other-words, the rate of change in the predicted value as a function of a change in the predictor variable.
   a. 15 theorem
   b. Slope1
   c. Undefined
   d. Undefined

6. A number that does not change in value in a given situation is a _____.
   a. 15 theorem
   b. Constant1
   c. Undefined
   d. Undefined

7. Another word for independent variables in the analysis of variance is _____.
   a. Factors1
   b. 15 theorem
   c. Undefined
   d. Undefined

8. A measure of variability, the _____ is the distance from the lowest to the highest score.
   a. Range1
   b. 15 theorem
   c. Undefined
   d. Undefined

9. The defining characteristics of populations are called _____. Observations must be made on every single member of the population in question in order to precisely state the value of _____.
   a. 15 theorem
   b. Parameters1
   c. Undefined
   d. Undefined

10. A common requirement for parametric tests is that the population of scores from which the sample observations came should be normally distributed. While many variables are close enough to a normal distribution and many of the tests that we will encounter are quite robust to moderate departures, occasionally there is a need to transform a variable so that the requirement of normality is better met; called _____. Essentially this means transforming the distribution such that the symmetry of the distribution is made to resemble a normal distribution more closely.

Chapter 13. VECTOR-VALUED FUNCTIONS 177

a. 15 theorem
b. Normalizing1
c. Undefined
d. Undefined

11. One major objective of statistical analysis is the identification of associations or _____ that exist between and among sets of observations. In other words, does knowledge about about one set of data allow us to infer or predict characteristics about another set or sets of data.
    a. Relationships1
    b. 15 theorem
    c. Undefined
    d. Undefined

12. At times we must contend with variables that assume a large number of values. In this case it is typical to create _____ of values of the variable and then make a frequency tally of the number of observations falling within each interval. As is the case with any data reduction technique, detail is lost.
    a. ACTRAN
    b. Intervals1
    c. Undefined
    d. Undefined

13. An _____ is an indication of the value of an unknown quantity based on observed data. More formally, an _____ is the particular value of an estimator that is obtained from a particular sample of data and used to indicate the value of a parameter.
    a. Estimate1
    b. ACTRAN
    c. Undefined
    d. Undefined

14. _____ refer to any data source, whether individuals, physical or biological things, geographic locations, time periods, or events; that is, anything upon which observations can be made.
    a. Objects1
    b. ACTRAN
    c. Undefined
    d. Undefined

15. Horizontal axis of display containing the trailing digits is called _____.
    a. 15 theorem
    b. Leaves1
    c. Undefined
    d. Undefined

16. _____ are observations made upon the environment.
    a. ACTRAN
    b. Empirical data1
    c. Undefined
    d. Undefined

17. By _____ we mean collecting observations made upon our environment -- observations, which are the results of measurements using clocks, balances, measuring rods, counting operations, or other objectively defined measuring instruments or procedures. _____ may mean simply counting the number of times a particular property occurs.
    a. 15 theorem
    b. Data1
    c. Undefined
    d. Undefined

18. A special case of the dichtomous variable is the _____ which is created by converting a level of a qualitative variable into a binary variable.
    a. Dummy variable1
    b. 15 theorem
    c. Undefined
    d. Undefined

Chapter 14. PARTIAL DERIVATIVES

1. _____ are characteristics or properties of an object that can take on one or more different values.
   a. Variables1
   b. 15 theorem
   c. Undefined
   d. Undefined

2. The very fact that we are measuring objects with respect to some characteristic implies that the objects differ in that characteristic; or stated in another way, that the characteristic can take on a number of different values. These properties or characteristics of an object that can assume two or more different values are referred to as a _____.
   a. 15 theorem
   b. Variable1
   c. Undefined
   d. Undefined

3. The _____ in inferential statistics is the variable whose values depend on the relative grouping or categories of the independent variable. A dependent variable, for example, can be scores on a test and the independent variable might have been students with groups male and female.
   a. Dependent variable1
   b. 15 theorem
   c. Undefined
   d. Undefined

4. _____ are those factors controlled by the experimenter.
   a. ACTRAN
   b. Independent variables1
   c. Undefined
   d. Undefined

5. An _____ is an indication of the value of an unknown quantity based on observed data. More formally, an _____ is the particular value of an estimator that is obtained from a particular sample of data and used to indicate the value of a parameter.
   a. ACTRAN
   b. Estimate1
   c. Undefined
   d. Undefined

6. A measure of variability, the _____ is the distance from the lowest to the highest score.
   a. Range1
   b. 15 theorem
   c. Undefined
   d. Undefined

7. A number that does not change in value in a given situation is a _____.
   a. Constant1
   b. 15 theorem
   c. Undefined
   d. Undefined

8. The _____ refers to the amount of change in Y for a 1 unit change in X; or in-other-words, the rate of change in the predicted value as a function of a change in the predictor variable.
   a. Slope1
   b. 15 theorem
   c. Undefined
   d. Undefined

9. Another word for independent variables in the analysis of variance is _____.
   a. 15 theorem
   b. Factors1
   c. Undefined
   d. Undefined

10. The most important measure of central tendency, and one of the basic building blocks of all statistical analysis, is the arithmetic _____. It is simply the sum of all the set of values divided by the number of values involved. As a measure of central tendency, it is affected by extreme scores, and it assumes a ratio scale of measurement.

Chapter 14. PARTIAL DERIVATIVES

a. 15 theorem
b. Mean1
c. Undefined
d. Undefined

11. One major objective of statistical analysis is the identification of associations or _____ that exist between and among sets of observations. In other words, does knowledge about about one set of data allow us to infer or predict characteristics about another set or sets of data.
a. 15 theorem
b. Relationships1
c. Undefined
d. Undefined

12. Horizontal axis of display containing the trailing digits is called _____.
a. Leaves1
b. 15 theorem
c. Undefined
d. Undefined

13. There are properties of objects that do assume one and only value, and we refer to these characteristics as constants. _____, then, are the invariables that differentiate one class of objects from another.
a. 15 theorem
b. Constants1
c. Undefined
d. Undefined

14. _____ is the result of assigning numbers to objects to abstractly represent the objects or characteristics of the objects.
a. 15 theorem
b. Measurement1
c. Undefined
d. Undefined

15. A _____ is a value used to represent a certain population characteristic. Because of the impracticality of measuring an entire population to determine this value, parameters are usually estimated.
a. 15 theorem
b. Parameter1
c. Undefined
d. Undefined

16. The defining characteristics of populations are called _____. Observations must be made on every single member of the population in question in order to precisely state the value of _____.
a. Parameters1
b. 15 theorem
c. Undefined
d. Undefined

17. A _____ is a scheme for the numerical representation of the values of a variable. The interpretation we place upon the numbers of the scale, rather than the numbers themselves, makes the _____ useful. The most common scales are nominal, ordinal, interval
a. 15 theorem
b. Scale1
c. Undefined
d. Undefined

18. _____, the height of the curve for a given value of X; closely related to the probability of an observation in an interval around X.
a. 15 theorem
b. Density1
c. Undefined
d. Undefined

Chapter 14. PARTIAL DERIVATIVES

19. At times we must contend with variables that assume a large number of values. In this case it is typical to create _____ of values of the variable and then make a frequency tally of the number of observations falling within each interval. As is the case with any data reduction technique, detail is lost.
   a. Intervals1
   b. ACTRAN
   c. Undefined
   d. Undefined

20. By _____ we mean collecting observations made upon our environment -- observations, which are the results of measurements using clocks, balances, measuring rods, counting operations, or other objectively defined measuring instruments or procedures. _____ may mean simply counting the number of times a particular property occurs.
   a. 15 theorem
   b. Data1
   c. Undefined
   d. Undefined

21. The method of _____ is a criterion for fitting a specified model to observed data.
   a. Least Squares1
   b. 15 theorem
   c. Undefined
   d. Undefined

22. The 'line of best fit' that represents a straight line drawn through the data points is the _____. .
   a. Regression line1
   b. 15 theorem
   c. Undefined
   d. Undefined

23. An _____ is any process or study, which results in the collection of data, the outcome of which is unknown. In statistics, the term is usually restricted to situations in which the researcher has control over some of the conditions under which the _____ takes place.
   a. Experiment1
   b. ACTRAN
   c. Undefined
   d. Undefined

24. _____ refers to those points that cut off the bottom and top quarter of a distribution
   a. 15 theorem
   b. Hinges1
   c. Undefined
   d. Undefined

25. _____ is used synonymously for variable.
   a. Factor1
   b. 15 theorem
   c. Undefined
   d. Undefined

Chapter 15. MULTIPLE INTEGRALS

1. _____ are characteristics or properties of an object that can take on one or more different values.
   a. 15 theorem
   b. Variables1
   c. Undefined
   d. Undefined

2. The very fact that we are measuring objects with respect to some characteristic implies that the objects differ in that characteristic; or stated in another way, that the characteristic can take on a number of different values. These properties or characteristics of an object that can assume two or more different values are referred to as a _____.
   a. Variable1
   b. 15 theorem
   c. Undefined
   d. Undefined

3. Horizontal axis of display containing the trailing digits is called _____.
   a. 15 theorem
   b. Leaves1
   c. Undefined
   d. Undefined

4. A number that does not change in value in a given situation is a _____.
   a. 15 theorem
   b. Constant1
   c. Undefined
   d. Undefined

5. The most important measure of central tendency, and one of the basic building blocks of all statistical analysis, is the arithmetic _____. It is simply the sum of all the set of values divided by the number of values involved. As a measure of central tendency, it is affected by extreme scores, and it assumes a ratio scale of measurement.
   a. Mean1
   b. 15 theorem
   c. Undefined
   d. Undefined

6. An _____ is an indication of the value of an unknown quantity based on observed data. More formally, an _____ is the particular value of an estimator that is obtained from a particular sample of data and used to indicate the value of a parameter.
   a. Estimate1
   b. ACTRAN
   c. Undefined
   d. Undefined

7. A _____ provides a quantitative description of the likely occurrence of a particular event. _____ is conventionally expressed on a scale from 0 to 1; a rare event has a _____ close to 0, a very common event has a _____ close to 1.
   a. Probability1
   b. 15 theorem
   c. Undefined
   d. Undefined

8. By _____ we mean the cumulative frequency, counting in from the nearer end.
   a. 15 theorem
   b. Depth1
   c. Undefined
   d. Undefined

9. A _____ is a value used to represent a certain population characteristic. Because of the impracticality of measuring an entire population to determine this value, parameters are usually estimated.
   a. Parameter1
   b. 15 theorem
   c. Undefined
   d. Undefined

10. The defining characteristics of populations are called _____. Observations must be made on every single member of the population in question in order to precisely state the value of _____.

a. Parameters1
b. 15 theorem
c. Undefined
d. Undefined

11. There are properties of objects that do assume one and only value, and we refer to these characteristics as constants. _____, then, are the invariables that differentiate one class of objects from another.
    a. 15 theorem
    b. Constants1
    c. Undefined
    d. Undefined

12. At times we must contend with variables that assume a large number of values. In this case it is typical to create _____ of values of the variable and then make a frequency tally of the number of observations falling within each interval. As is the case with any data reduction technique, detail is lost.
    a. Intervals1
    b. ACTRAN
    c. Undefined
    d. Undefined

13. _____, the height of the curve for a given value of X; closely related to the probability of an observation in an interval around X.
    a. 15 theorem
    b. Density1
    c. Undefined
    d. Undefined

14. _____ is used synonymously for variable.
    a. 15 theorem
    b. Factor1
    c. Undefined
    d. Undefined

15. _____ is implied when data values are distributed in the same way above and below the middle of the sample.
    a. 15 theorem
    b. Symmetry1
    c. Undefined
    d. Undefined

Chapter 16. TOPICS IN VECTOR CALCULUS

1. A measure of variability, the _____ is the distance from the lowest to the highest score.
   a. 15 theorem
   b. Range1
   c. Undefined
   d. Undefined

2. By _____ we mean the cumulative frequency, counting in from the nearer end.
   a. 15 theorem
   b. Depth1
   c. Undefined
   d. Undefined

3. _____ refer to any data source, whether individuals, physical or biological things, geographic locations, time periods, or events; that is, anything upon which observations can be made.
   a. Objects1
   b. ACTRAN
   c. Undefined
   d. Undefined

4. A number that does not change in value in a given situation is a _____.
   a. Constant1
   b. 15 theorem
   c. Undefined
   d. Undefined

5. _____ are characteristics or properties of an object that can take on one or more different values.
   a. 15 theorem
   b. Variables1
   c. Undefined
   d. Undefined

6. The most important measure of central tendency, and one of the basic building blocks of all statistical analysis, is the arithmetic _____. It is simply the sum of all the set of values divided by the number of values involved. As a measure of central tendency, it is affected by extreme scores, and it assumes a ratio scale of measurement.
   a. 15 theorem
   b. Mean1
   c. Undefined
   d. Undefined

7. A _____ is a scheme for the numerical representation of the values of a variable. The interpretation we place upon the numbers of the scale, rather than the numbers themselves, makes the _____ useful. The most common scales are nominal, ordinal, interval
   a. 15 theorem
   b. Scale1
   c. Undefined
   d. Undefined

8. The number of times a particular score or event occurs with respect to the total number of events or scores is called its _____.
   a. Proportion1
   b. 15 theorem
   c. Undefined
   d. Undefined

9. A _____ provides a quantitative description of the likely occurrence of a particular event. _____ is conventionally expressed on a scale from 0 to 1; a rare event has a _____ close to 0, a very common event has a _____ close to 1.
   a. 15 theorem
   b. Probability1
   c. Undefined
   d. Undefined

10. The very fact that we are measuring objects with respect to some characteristic implies that the objects differ in that characteristic; or stated in another way, that the characteristic can take on a number of different values. These properties or characteristics of an object that can assume two or more different values are referred to as a _____.

Chapter 16. TOPICS IN VECTOR CALCULUS

a. 15 theorem
c. Undefined
b. Variable1
d. Undefined

11. At times we must contend with variables that assume a large number of values. In this case it is typical to create _____ of values of the variable and then make a frequency tally of the number of observations falling within each interval. As is the case with any data reduction technique, detail is lost.
   a. ACTRAN
   b. Intervals1
   c. Undefined
   d. Undefined

12. A _____ is a value used to represent a certain population characteristic. Because of the impracticality of measuring an entire population to determine this value, parameters are usually estimated.
   a. Parameter1
   b. 15 theorem
   c. Undefined
   d. Undefined

13. _____, the height of the curve for a given value of X; closely related to the probability of an observation in an interval around X.
   a. 15 theorem
   b. Density1
   c. Undefined
   d. Undefined

14. Horizontal axis of display containing the trailing digits is called _____.
   a. 15 theorem
   b. Leaves1
   c. Undefined
   d. Undefined

15. The _____ in inferential statistics is the variable whose values depend on the relative grouping or categories of the independent variable. A dependent variable, for example, can be scores on a test and the independent variable might have been students with groups male and female.
   a. Dependent variable1
   b. 15 theorem
   c. Undefined
   d. Undefined

16. The goal of most inferential statistical analyses is to be able to generalize or apply the findings to the entire population and not just to the sample. The concept of _____ requires that the researcher determine some level of probability that the findings were due to chance or that they actually describe the population. The value of the probability that the findings were due to chance is usually reported when the findings of an analysis is reported.
   a. 15 theorem
   b. Generalization1
   c. Undefined
   d. Undefined

17. In statistics an arrangement of values of a variable showing their observed or theoretical frequency of occurrence is called a _____.
   a. 15 theorem
   b. Distribution1
   c. Undefined
   d. Undefined

18. The defining characteristics of populations are called _____. Observations must be made on every single member of the population in question in order to precisely state the value of _____.
   a. 15 theorem
   b. Parameters1
   c. Undefined
   d. Undefined

Chapter 16. TOPICS IN VECTOR CALCULUS

19. _____ are those factors controlled by the experimenter.
    a. ACTRAN
    b. Independent variables1
    c. Undefined
    d. Undefined

20. _____ is a measure of how close an estimator is expected to be to the true value of a parameter.
    a. 15 theorem
    b. Precision1
    c. Undefined
    d. Undefined

21. One major objective of statistical analysis is the identification of associations or _____ that exist between and among sets of observations. In other words, does knowledge about about one set of data allow us to infer or predict characteristics about another set or sets of data.
    a. 15 theorem
    b. Relationships1
    c. Undefined
    d. Undefined

22. A population, also referred to as a universe, is any well-defined collection of things. By well-defined we mean that the members of the _____ are spelled out, or an unequivocal statement is made as to which things belong in it and which do not.
    a. 15 theorem
    b. Population1
    c. Undefined
    d. Undefined

23. By _____ we mean collecting observations made upon our environment -- observations, which are the results of measurements using clocks, balances, measuring rods, counting operations, or other objectively defined measuring instruments or procedures. _____ may mean simply counting the number of times a particular property occurs.
    a. 15 theorem
    b. Data1
    c. Undefined
    d. Undefined

24. There are properties of objects that do assume one and only value, and we refer to these characteristics as constants. _____, then, are the invariables that differentiate one class of objects from another.
    a. Constants1
    b. 15 theorem
    c. Undefined
    d. Undefined

25. An _____ is an indication of the value of an unknown quantity based on observed data. More formally, an _____ is the particular value of an estimator that is obtained from a particular sample of data and used to indicate the value of a parameter.
    a. ACTRAN
    b. Estimate1
    c. Undefined
    d. Undefined

26. _____ is implied when data values are distributed in the same way above and below the middle of the sample.
    a. 15 theorem
    b. Symmetry1
    c. Undefined
    d. Undefined

Chapter 1

1. b	2. a	3. b	4. a	5. a	6. b	7. a	8. a	9. b	10. a
11. b	12. b	13. a	14. a	15. b	16. b	17. a	18. a	19. b	20. a
21. b	22. a	23. b	24. b	25. b	26. a	27. b	28. a	29. b	30. b
31. b	32. b	33. b	34. a	35. a	36. b	37. b	38. b	39. a	40. a
41. a	42. a	43. a	44. a	45. b	46. a	47. a	48. a	49. a	50. b
51. a	52. a	53. b	54. b	55. b	56. b	57. b	58. a	59. b	60. a
61. b	62. a	63. b	64. a	65. b	66. a	67. a	68. a	69. a	70. b
71. b	72. a	73. b	74. a	75. b	76. b	77. a	78. b	79. a	80. a
81. b	82. b	83. a	84. b	85. b	86. a	87. b	88. b	89. b	90. a
91. a	92. b	93. a	94. a	95. a	96. b	97. b	98. a	99. b	100. a
101. a	102. a	103. b	104. b	105. b	106. a	107. b	108. a	109. a	110. b
111. b	112. a	113. a	114. b	115. b	116. b	117. a	118. b	119. b	120. b
121. b	122. a	123. b	124. b	125. b	126. a	127. a	128. b	129. a	130. b
131. b	132. b	133. a	134. b	135. a	136. b	137. a	138. b	139. b	140. b
141. a	142. a	143. a	144. b	145. a	146. b	147. b	148. b	149. a	150. b
151. b	152. b	153. b	154. b	155. a	156. b	157. a	158. a	159. a	160. a
161. a	162. b	163. b	164. b	165. a	166. b	167. a	168. b	169. a	170. b
171. a	172. a	173. a	174. a	175. a	176. a	177. b	178. a	179. a	180. b
181. b	182. a	183. b	184. b	185. b	186. b	187. b	188. a	189. a	190. b
191. a	192. b	193. b	194. b	195. a	196. a	197. a	198. b	199. a	200. b
201. b	202. b	203. a	204. b	205. a	206. a	207. b	208. b	209. b	210. b
211. b	212. a	213. a	214. a	215. b	216. a	217. a	218. b	219. b	220. a
221. a	222. b	223. b	224. b	225. b	226. a	227. a	228. b	229. a	230. a
231. b	232. a	233. b	234. a	235. b	236. a	237. a	238. a	239. b	240. b
241. b	242. b	243. b	244. a	245. a	246. a	247. a	248. b	249. a	250. b
251. b	252. b	253. b	254. b	255. b	256. a	257. a	258. b	259. b	260. a
261. a	262. b	263. b	264. a	265. a	266. b	267. b	268. b	269. a	270. a
271. a	272. b	273. a	274. a						

Chapter 2

1. a	2. a	3. b	4. a	5. b	6. a	7. b	8. a	9. b	10. b
11. a	12. b	13. a	14. b	15. a	16. b	17. a	18. b	19. a	20. b
21. b	22. a	23. b	24. a	25. b	26. a	27. a	28. b	29. b	30. b
31. b	32. b	33. b	34. b	35. a	36. b	37. a	38. a	39. a	40. b
41. a	42. a	43. b	44. b	45. a	46. a	47. b	48. b	49. a	50. a
51. b	52. b	53. b	54. b	55. a	56. a	57. b	58. a	59. a	60. a
61. a	62. b	63. a	64. a	65. a	66. a	67. a	68. b	69. a	70. a
71. b	72. a	73. a	74. b	75. b	76. b	77. a	78. a	79. b	80. b
81. b	82. a	83. a	84. b	85. b	86. a	87. b	88. b	89. a	90. b
91. a	92. a	93. a	94. a	95. b	96. b	97. a	98. a	99. b	100. b
101. a	102. a	103. b	104. a	105. a	106. b	107. a	108. b	109. b	110. a
111. b	112. a	113. b	114. b	115. a	116. b	117. b	118. b	119. a	120. b
121. a	122. b	123. a	124. a	125. a	126. a	127. a	128. a		

ANSWER KEY

Chapter 3

1. a	2. a	3. b	4. a	5. b	6. a	7. a	8. a	9. a	10. a
11. b	12. a	13. a	14. b	15. a	16. a	17. b	18. a	19. b	20. b
21. b	22. b	23. b	24. a	25. b	26. a	27. b	28. a	29. a	30. a
31. a	32. a	33. b	34. a	35. b	36. b	37. a	38. b	39. b	40. a
41. b	42. a	43. b	44. b	45. a	46. a	47. b	48. b	49. a	50. a
51. a	52. b	53. a	54. a	55. b	56. b	57. b	58. a	59. a	60. a
61. a	62. a	63. a	64. b	65. a	66. b	67. b	68. a	69. a	70. a
71. b	72. b	73. b	74. a	75. b	76. b	77. b	78. b	79. b	80. a
81. a	82. b	83. b	84. a	85. a	86. b	87. a	88. a	89. b	90. b
91. b	92. a	93. a	94. a	95. a	96. a	97. a	98. b	99. a	100. b
101. b	102. b	103. a	104. a	105. b	106. b	107. a	108. a	109. a	110. a
111. b	112. a	113. a	114. a	115. b	116. a	117. b	118. a	119. a	120. a
121. a	122. b	123. b	124. a	125. b	126. b	127. b	128. a	129. a	130. b
131. b	132. b	133. b	134. a	135. b	136. a	137. a	138. a	139. b	140. b
141. b	142. b	143. a	144. a	145. a	146. b	147. b	148. b	149. a	150. b
151. b	152. a	153. a	154. b	155. b	156. b	157. b	158. a	159. a	160. a
161. a	162. b	163. a	164. b	165. a	166. b	167. b	168. b	169. a	170. b
171. a	172. b	173. b	174. a	175. a	176. a	177. b	178. a		

Chapter 4

1. a	2. b	3. b	4. a	5. b	6. b	7. a	8. b	9. a	10. b
11. a	12. b	13. b	14. a	15. b	16. b	17. b	18. a	19. a	20. a
21. b	22. a	23. a	24. a	25. b	26. b	27. b	28. a	29. a	30. a
31. a	32. b	33. b	34. a	35. b	36. b	37. a	38. b	39. b	40. a
41. a	42. b	43. b	44. a	45. b	46. a	47. a	48. b	49. b	50. a
51. a	52. b	53. b	54. a	55. b	56. a	57. b	58. b	59. a	60. a
61. b	62. b	63. b	64. b	65. b	66. a	67. b	68. a	69. b	70. b
71. b	72. a	73. a	74. a	75. a	76. b	77. b	78. a	79. b	80. a
81. a	82. b	83. a	84. a	85. a	86. b	87. b	88. b	89. a	90. b
91. a	92. b	93. a	94. b	95. a	96. a	97. a	98. a	99. a	100. b
101. b	102. a	103. a	104. a	105. b	106. b	107. b	108. a	109. b	110. a
111. b	112. b	113. b	114. b	115. b	116. a	117. b	118. b	119. a	120. a
121. a	122. a	123. a	124. a	125. a	126. b	127. b	128. b	129. a	130. b
131. a	132. b	133. b	134. b	135. a	136. a	137. a	138. b	139. b	140. a
141. a	142. a	143. a	144. a	145. b	146. b	147. a	148. a	149. b	150. a
151. a	152. a	153. a	154. b	155. b	156. b	157. a	158. a	159. a	160. a
161. b	162. a	163. b	164. b	165. b	166. a	167. b	168. b	169. a	170. b
171. a	172. a	173. b	174. a	175. a	176. a	177. a	178. a	179. b	180. b
181. a	182. a	183. b	184. b	185. b	186. a	187. a	188. b	189. a	190. a
191. b	192. a	193. b	194. b	195. a	196. a	197. b	198. a	199. b	200. a
201. b	202. b	203. b	204. a	205. b	206. a	207. a	208. b	209. b	210. b
211. a	212. b	213. b	214. b	215. a	216. b	217. b	218. b	219. a	220. b
221. b	222. b								

Chapter 5

1. b	2. a	3. b	4. a	5. b	6. a	7. b	8. b	9. b	10. a
11. a	12. b	13. b	14. a	15. a	16. a	17. a	18. b	19. a	20. a
21. a	22. a	23. b	24. b	25. a	26. a	27. a	28. a	29. a	30. a
31. a	32. b	33. a	34. a	35. a	36. b	37. b	38. a	39. b	40. b
41. b	42. a	43. a	44. b	45. a	46. a	47. b	48. b	49. b	50. a
51. b	52. a	53. a	54. b	55. b	56. a	57. b	58. a	59. a	60. a
61. b	62. a	63. b	64. b	65. b	66. a	67. b	68. a	69. a	70. b
71. a	72. a	73. a	74. a	75. b	76. b	77. a	78. a	79. b	80. b
81. b	82. a	83. b	84. a	85. a	86. b	87. a	88. b	89. b	90. a
91. a	92. a	93. b	94. b	95. a	96. b	97. a	98. a	99. b	100. b
101. b	102. a	103. a	104. a	105. a	106. a	107. a	108. b	109. a	110. b
111. b	112. b	113. a	114. a	115. b	116. b	117. b	118. b	119. a	120. a
121. a	122. b	123. a	124. b	125. b	126. b	127. b	128. b	129. b	130. b
131. a	132. a	133. a	134. b	135. a	136. b	137. b	138. a	139. a	140. a
141. b	142. b	143. a	144. a	145. a	146. a	147. b	148. b	149. a	150. a
151. b	152. a	153. a	154. a	155. b	156. a	157. b	158. b	159. a	160. b
161. b	162. a	163. b	164. a	165. b	166. a	167. a	168. b	169. a	170. b
171. a	172. a	173. a	174. b	175. b	176. b	177. b	178. a	179. a	

Chapter 6

1. b	2. b	3. a	4. a	5. a	6. b	7. b	8. a	9. b	10. b
11. b	12. b	13. a	14. a	15. b	16. b	17. b	18. b	19. b	20. b
21. b	22. b	23. a	24. b	25. a	26. b	27. a	28. b	29. b	30. a
31. b	32. b	33. a	34. b	35. b	36. a	37. a	38. a	39. a	40. b
41. a	42. b	43. b	44. b	45. a	46. b	47. b	48. a	49. a	50. a
51. b	52. b	53. b	54. a	55. a	56. b	57. a	58. a	59. a	60. b
61. a	62. b	63. a	64. a	65. a	66. b	67. a	68. a	69. b	70. b
71. b	72. a	73. a	74. a	75. b	76. a	77. b	78. a	79. a	80. b
81. a	82. a	83. b	84. a	85. a	86. b	87. a	88. a	89. b	90. b
91. b	92. a	93. b	94. a	95. b	96. b	97. b	98. a	99. a	100. b
101. a	102. a	103. a	104. a	105. b	106. b	107. b	108. a	109. a	110. a
111. b	112. a	113. b	114. a	115. b	116. b				

ANSWER KEY

Chapter 7

1. b	2. b	3. a	4. b	5. a	6. a	7. b	8. b	9. b	10. a
11. a	12. b	13. a	14. b	15. b	16. b	17. b	18. b	19. a	20. a
21. b	22. a	23. b	24. a	25. b	26. a	27. a	28. a	29. a	30. a
31. a	32. a	33. b	34. a	35. a	36. a	37. a	38. a	39. b	40. b
41. b	42. b	43. b	44. b	45. a	46. b	47. b	48. a	49. a	50. b
51. b	52. b	53. b	54. b	55. a	56. a	57. a	58. b	59. b	60. b
61. b	62. b	63. a	64. b	65. b	66. b	67. a	68. a	69. b	70. b
71. a	72. b	73. a	74. a	75. a	76. a	77. a	78. b	79. a	80. b
81. b	82. b	83. b	84. a	85. b	86. b	87. a	88. a	89. b	90. a
91. b	92. a	93. a	94. a	95. a	96. b	97. a	98. a	99. b	100. a
101. b	102. b	103. a	104. a	105. a	106. b	107. b	108. b	109. b	110. a
111. a	112. a	113. b	114. b	115. a	116. a	117. b	118. a	119. a	120. b
121. a	122. b	123. b	124. a	125. b	126. b	127. b	128. a	129. b	130. a
131. a	132. b	133. a	134. a	135. b	136. b	137. a	138. b	139. a	140. b
141. b	142. a	143. a	144. a	145. b	146. b	147. b	148. a	149. b	150. a
151. b	152. b	153. a	154. a	155. a	156. b	157. a	158. b	159. b	160. a
161. b	162. a	163. b	164. a	165. a	166. a	167. b	168. a	169. a	170. b
171. a	172. a	173. a	174. a	175. b	176. b	177. b	178. b	179. b	180. b
181. b	182. a	183. b	184. a	185. b	186. b	187. a	188. b	189. b	190. b
191. a	192. b	193. b	194. a	195. b	196. a				

Chapter 8

1. a	2. a	3. a	4. b	5. a	6. b	7. a	8. b	9. b	10. a
11. b	12. b	13. a	14. a	15. b	16. a	17. b	18. b	19. a	20. b
21. a	22. a	23. a	24. a	25. a	26. a	27. b	28. b	29. b	30. a
31. a	32. b	33. b	34. a	35. a	36. b	37. a	38. a	39. a	40. b
41. a	42. a	43. a	44. a	45. b	46. a	47. b	48. b	49. a	50. a
51. a	52. b	53. b	54. b	55. b	56. a	57. a	58. a	59. b	60. a
61. b	62. a	63. a	64. a	65. b	66. a	67. b	68. a	69. a	70. b
71. a	72. b	73. a	74. b	75. b	76. a	77. b	78. a	79. b	80. a
81. b	82. b	83. b	84. b	85. a	86. a	87. a	88. b	89. b	90. a
91. b	92. b	93. b	94. a	95. b	96. b	97. a	98. b	99. b	100. b
101. b	102. a	103. a	104. a	105. a	106. a	107. a	108. a	109. b	110. a
111. a	112. a	113. b	114. a	115. b	116. b	117. a	118. a	119. b	120. b
121. a	122. b	123. b	124. a	125. b	126. b	127. b	128. b	129. b	130. a
131. a	132. b	133. a	134. a	135. b	136. a	137. a	138. b		

Chapter 9

1. b	2. a	3. b	4. a	5. a	6. a	7. b	8. a	9. b	10. a
11. a	12. b	13. b	14. a	15. b	16. b	17. a	18. a	19. b	20. b
21. a	22. a	23. b	24. b	25. a	26. b	27. b	28. a	29. a	30. a
31. a	32. b	33. b	34. b	35. a	36. a	37. a	38. b	39. b	40. a
41. b	42. b	43. a	44. a	45. b	46. b	47. b	48. a	49. b	50. b
51. a	52. a	53. b	54. b	55. b	56. b	57. b	58. b	59. a	60. b
61. a	62. a	63. b	64. a	65. b	66. a	67. a	68. b	69. a	70. b
71. a	72. a	73. b	74. a	75. b	76. b	77. a	78. b	79. b	80. b
81. b	82. a	83. a	84. a	85. a	86. a	87. b	88. b	89. b	90. a
91. b	92. a	93. a	94. b	95. a	96. b	97. a	98. a	99. b	100. b
101. a	102. a	103. a	104. b	105. b	106. a	107. b	108. b	109. b	110. b
111. b	112. b	113. b	114. b						

Chapter 10

| 1. a | 2. b | 3. b | 4. b | 5. b | 6. a | 7. a | 8. a | 9. b | 10. b |
| 11. b | 12. b | 13. b | 14. a | 15. b | 16. b | 17. b | | | |

Chapter 11

| 1. a | 2. a | 3. b | 4. a | 5. a | 6. b | 7. a | 8. a | 9. a | 10. b |
| 11. b | 12. a | 13. a | 14. b | 15. b | 16. b | 17. a | 18. a | | |

Chapter 12

| 1. a | 2. b | 3. a | 4. a | 5. b | 6. b | 7. b | 8. a | 9. b | 10. a |
| 11. b | 12. a | 13. a | 14. b | 15. a | 16. b | | | | |

Chapter 13

| 1. b | 2. b | 3. b | 4. a | 5. b | 6. b | 7. a | 8. a | 9. b | 10. b |
| 11. a | 12. b | 13. a | 14. a | 15. b | 16. b | 17. b | 18. a | | |

Chapter 14

1. a	2. b	3. a	4. b	5. b	6. a	7. a	8. a	9. b	10. b
11. b	12. a	13. b	14. b	15. b	16. a	17. b	18. b	19. a	20. b
21. a	22. a	23. a	24. b	25. a					

Chapter 15

| 1. b | 2. a | 3. b | 4. b | 5. a | 6. a | 7. a | 8. b | 9. a | 10. a |
| 11. b | 12. a | 13. b | 14. b | 15. b | | | | | |

Chapter 16

1. b	2. b	3. a	4. a	5. b	6. b	7. b	8. a	9. b	10. b
11. b	12. a	13. b	14. b	15. a	16. b	17. b	18. b	19. b	20. b
21. b	22. b	23. b	24. a	25. b	26. b				